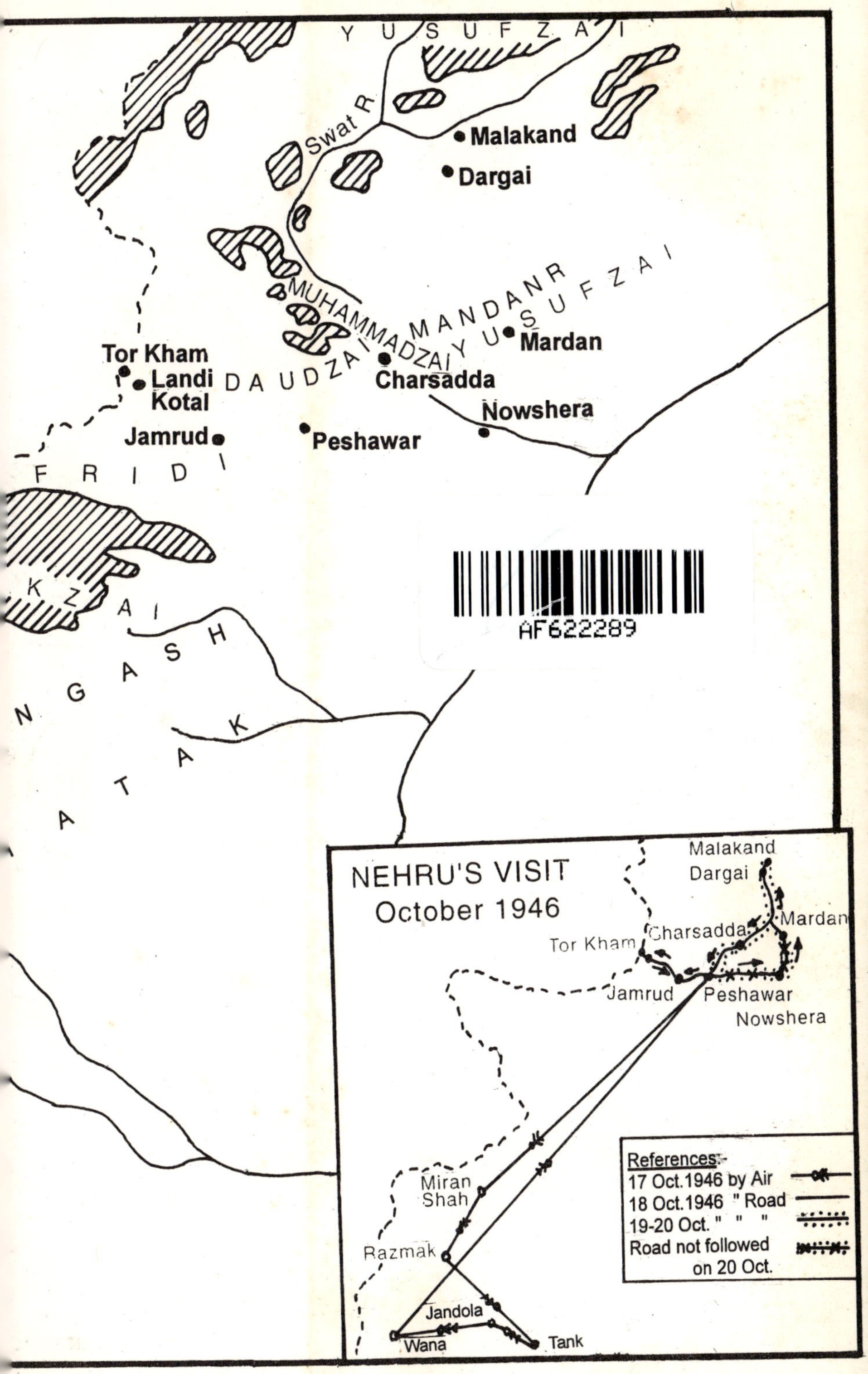
Y U S U F Z A I
Swat R.
Malakand
Dargai
MUHAMMADZAI
MANDANR
Y U S U F Z A I
Mardan
Tor Kham
Landi Kotal
D A U D Z A I
Charsadda
Nowshera
Jamrud
Peshawar
F R I D I
K Z A I
N G A S H
A T A K
NEHRU'S VISIT
October 1946
Malakand
Dargai
Mardan
Charsadda
Tor Kham
Jamrud
Peshawar
Nowshera
Miran Shah
Razmak
Jandola
Wana
Tank
References:-
17 Oct.1946 by Air
18 Oct.1946 " Road
19-20 Oct. " " "
Road not followed on 20 Oct.

THE NORTH-WEST FRONTIER DRAMA
1945–1947
A RE-ASSESSMENT

UNIVERSITY OF ST. ANDREWS

A. N. MITCHELL, O.B.E., M.A.
Secretary & Registrar
TELEPHONE No. 1211

3 North Street
~~College Gate~~
St Andrews

HL/O/1.

23rd September, 1968.

Sir Olaf Caroe, K.C.S.I., K.C.I.E., D.Litt.,
Newham House,
STEYNING,
Sussex.
BN4 3GF.

Dear Sir Olaf,

I am extremely grateful to you for your letter of 21st September, 1968, and for the enormous amount of trouble which you have taken in writing notes on my book. I appreciate this very much, and will pay the closest attention to all that you have said. Meanwhile I hope you will forgive me for dictating my answer. It is the only way in which I can handle the matter by return of post; and incidentally, the lady who is taking the dictation has had a big hand in the production of the manuscript.

I am particularly concerned to give you an answer on the point which you make about your own tenure of office. The first point I would make is that, in writing a Memoir within strict limitations, I have tried to avoid as far as possible anything that might injure feelings and possibly defeat the object of the book by introducing controversial matter about individuals. I did not in fact know how badly you had been treated in 1947 until I read Sir George's diaries. I do not have them any longer, but I distinctly remember a mention of the fact that Mountbatten's conduct in this respect was unpardonable. In all the circumstances, however, I thought it better to say nothing at all. At the same time I fully appreciate the point which you make, namely that silence might be interpreted as some sort of adverse criticism of yourself. I shall, therefore, now put the whole of that period under the microscope again and try to make it quite clear (and I am most sincere in this) with what fortitude and distinction you bore the burden of those almost intolerable years.

Your detailed criticisms will of course be of extreme value; and I am very pleased that in general you have found the book enjoyable and faithful.

Yours sincerely,

Norval

Norval Mitchell to Sir Olaf Caroe.

The North-West Frontier Drama 1945–1947 A Re-Assessment

PARSHOTAM MEHRA

MANOHAR
1998

First published 1998

ISBN 81-7304-097-4

Published by
Ajay Kumar Jain for
Manohar Publishers & Distributors
2/6 Ansari Road, Daryaganj
New Delhi 110002

Lasertypeset by
A J Software Publishing Co. Pvt. Ltd.
305, Durga Chambers,
1333, D.B. Gupta Road,
Karol Bagh, New Delhi 110005

Printed at
Rajkamal Electric Press
B 35/9 G T Karnal Road Indl Area
Delhi 110033

To the memory of
Sir Olaf Kirkpatrick Caroe

Contents

List of Illustrations and Maps

FACSIMILES

CARTOONS

MAPS

Abbreviations

CM: Caroe Manuscript
GCD: George Cunningham Diary
HMG: His (Her) Majesty's Government
HMSO: His (Her) Majesty's Stationery Office
IOL & R: India Office Library & Records
NAI: Natioanl Archives of India (New Delhi)
NMML: Nehru Memorial Museum & Library (New Delhi)

Preface

LONG BEFORE this thin volume was thought of, its author developed a great fascination for the Frontier. As a young student, he visited Peshawar (1939) and took the then regular half-weekly train to Landi Kotal. Later he was to teach at a college in D I Khan (1944-5) where he came to know the deputy commissioner, J O S Donald as well as the province's premier, Dr Khan Sahib while on a visit to the campus. This brief stint offered him a very welcome opportunity to travel, by road, to the provincial capital and be part of the hockey squad invited to the annual Jashn, 'Roz-i-Istiqlal', celebrations at Kabul. Part of the contingent in which he was lucky to be included, returned home via Ghazni and Kandahar. All in all, a memorable experience and, in retrospect, a valuable exposure to the life and times with which this study deals at some length.

The first attempt to tackle the subject took the shape of a short paper with a long title, 'A Frontier Governor and his conflict with Authority: A case-study of the North-West Frontier Province of India, 1946-7', for presentation at a conference in Mexico.[1] The response was not unencouraging and years later led to a larger, and heavily annotated, version: 'Pathans and the Birth of Pakistan: Transfer of Power in the North-West Frontier Province, 1945-47', published in the *Indo-British Review.*[2] A few years later a seminar on Khan Abdul Ghaffar Khan at the Nehru Memorial Museum & Library (1992) invited the author to present a paper on 'Olaf Caroe, the Khan brothers and the transfer of power in the North-West Frontier Province, 1945-1947: an interpretation'.[3] A distinct advantage was that among the participants at the New Delhi seminar was Khan Abdul Wali Khan (son of Badshah Khan) and some friends from Pakistan apart from a number of distinguished academics from home and abroad. The interaction proved rewarding and a valuable input for the slender volume now before the reader.

Over the many years that this study took shape and form, a host of friends and institutions lent a helping hand. And nothing is pleasanter than to acknowledge the author's deep indebtedness to one and all.

To start with, it is a pleasure to record my debt to the late Sir Olaf Caroe whom the writer came to know in the course of one of his long sojourns in London (1968-9) while researching on a study of the North-east Frontier and the McMahon Line.[4] Sir Olaf was generous with his time and patient with the numerous queries relating to his long and not undistinguished innings in the Indian Civil Service (1919-47) culminating in a stormy tenure at the Government House in Peshawar. He was kind enough to loan his papers including private letters. Sadly, this study had to wait many a long summer or else Sir Olaf's reactions to some of the conclusions drawn here would have been illuminating. As a small return for a large debt this study is dedicated to him.

A long meeting with Lord Mountbatten resulted in his gracious permission to afford access to his Broadlands Archives apart from a free-wheeling discussion on men and events in the Frontier drama. Here too his sad and tragic demise came in the way of inviting his views on the broad outlines of this essay and by no means an unimportant role in the events with which it deals.

Nearer home a three-hour meeting with Khan Abdul Wali Khan was invaluable. His own personality apart, his father, Badshah Khan, and uncle, Dr Khan Sahib—and Sir Olaf Caroe—came out alive in the course of a long and meandering *tete-a-tete*. Apart from the two-day seminar discussions, the author thus had the privilege of interacting with him at some length.

The writer never met Sir Fraser Noble but came to know of him through an article in an historical journal[5] resulting in a very valuable and rewarding friendship. Sir Fraser not only mailed me a copy of the relevant chapters of his unpublished memoirs but was also good enough to scrutinise an earlier draft of the typescript and make detailed comments and observations. These, as the reader would discover, have been no small help in constructing the narrative. An eye-witness to all that was happening in the Frontier in those momentous, if troubled, times, he was patient in answering the author's innumerable queries. And in working out a rough draft of the sketch map of Peshawar (1945-7) which appears on the outside endpaper. This study owes a lot to him.

Dr Amit Kumar Gupta offered useful comments on my essay which appeared in the *Indo-British Review* and lent a hand in acquiring a copy of his book. Needless to add, both the comments and the book were a great help.

Dr G T Verghese, a great scholar and a good friend on a visit to London (1994) was of no small assistance in obtaining photostat copies of Sir George Cunningham's Diary and his papers. So also a friend, Dr R J Bingle of the Oriental and India Office Collections of the British Library for obtaining photocopies of parts of the memoirs of Norval Mitchell.

Last but by no means the least my old friend, Dr S R Bakshi of the Indian Council of Historical Research has been a source of no small encouragement. Tying a number of loose ends without even a whisper of protest. It is not possible to thank him adequately.

Among institutions, pride of place goes to Nehru Memorial Museum & Library. Its director, Professor Ravinder Kumar, has always been encouraging and well-disposed; its librarian, Ms Kanwal Verma, rarely refusing a request for help. Her colleague, Mr S K Bhatnagar was good enough to acquire almost the first available copy of the *Jinnah Papers*. At Teen Murti House, another friend, Mr S K Sharma was helpful in a variety of ways; so also Mr A K Avasthy and his colleague Mr B N Mandal, of the reprographic section, in meeting my numerous demands, some not always reasonable.

At the National Archives of India, the microfilms of Sir George Cunningham's Diary helped fill in some gaps. The Director, Dr S Sarkar was able to arrange, after considerable effort, the full text of Norval Mitchell's memoirs. His library staff and those manning the research room were invariably helpful and cooperative.

The Panjab University library in Chandigarh has been a source of no small help in ways too numerous to catalogue. The new librarian, Mr A R Sethi; and his colleague Mr Vinod Grover in the reference section have provided valuable inputs as also the Gandhi Bhavan library headed by Ms Moninder Bhatia. Mr Jagan Nath also of the Panjab University and a dedicated cartographer helped me with the sketch maps; he was patient, and understanding, with the many changes the maps underwent.

At a pretty late stage when the TS had almost been finalised, the *Tribune* in Chandigarh came into the picture. It was a pleasure to work there, my task made easier and pleasanter by the personal interest Mr S D Bhambri, the general manager, took in my work. What a pleasure for me to record my indebtedness to the *Tribune* in general and Mr Bhambri in particular.

My publishers have been quite understanding and met nearly all my requests without much hesitation. In the event, Mr Ramesh Jain and his son Ajay as well as the editor, Mr B N Varma, whom I have known for many years, have made valuable contribution for which I am deeply beholden.

Not for the first time my wife did not comment on my conference/ seminar papers or the successive versions of the TS. She did not read, much less lend a hand in correcting the page proofs. All the same, she was a useful, and perceptive, sounding board and in a number of ways helped me to undertake, and complete, this labour of love. My debt of gratitude to her is difficult to convey in mere words!

NOTES

1. The Thirtieth International Congress of Human Sciences in Asia and Africa, 3-8 August 1976, Mexico. A summary of the paper was published in the proceedings of the Congress.
2. The *Indo-British Review* (Madras), XVII, 1-2, September and December 1989, pp. 71-106.
3. Nehru Memorial Museum & Library, *Khan Abdul Ghaffar Khan: A Centennial Tribute*, New Delhi, 1995, pp. 129-57.
4. *The McMahon Line & After: A Study of the Triangular Contest on India's North-eastern Frontier between Britain, China and Tibet, 1904-47,* Macmillan, 1974.
5. Sir Fraser Noble, 'Recollections of Civil Disobedience Movement; NWFP 1947', *Indo-British Review*, X1X, 2, pp. 41-50.

Introduction

THE STORY OF THE transfer of power from the British Raj to India and Pakistan, in 1945-7, has all the makings of high drama. Events on the North-West Frontier during those two years form a vital and exciting act in that grand play of forces which resulted, to start with, in the creation of the two Dominions.

In its long and chequered annals, India's north-west frontier has known little if any peace; nor has the story been different under the Raj or the fifty odd years since the birth of Pakistan. This is especially true of the last decade which has been a witness to the remorseless spill-over into the Frontier of a seemingly interminable civil war in Afghanistan.

Nor was the situation any less explosive on the eve of the transfer of power and the birth of Pakistan. Early in 1947, there was an official Kabul claim that the Frontier which allegedly had nothing to do with India, should be given every opportunity to establish its independence and, if it so chose, to join Afghanistan. Nehru had in fact written to Abdul Ghaffar Khan about Kabul's loud campaign in the media for the 'separation' of the North-West Frontier Province from India 'with a view no doubt about its incorporation' into Afghanistan. He had warned that Badshah Khan's views had been 'partly supported and partly distorted' so that the Afghan case could be put forward. For its part, New Delhi stoutly repudiated Kabul's claims as tantamount to interference in India's domestic affairs.

Two years earlier, in March 1945, there was the installation of a Congress (read Khudai Khidmatgar) ministry in Peshawar headed by the older of the two Khan brothers, the redoubtable Dr Khan Sahib. Way back in 1939, he had been thrown into the political wilderness by the inept policies of the Congress Party and its central leadership to whom the twosome swore political allegiance. In 1939, as now in 1945, Khan Sahib had an excellent personal rapport with the provincial Governor, Sir George Cunningham.

During the 1945-6 general elections all over British India, and in the face of a virulent, no-holds-barred campaign by his political rivals in the Muslim League, Khan Sahib's popular mandate had been overwhelmingly renewed. Literally though on its morrow, the Khan's troubles began. In March 1946, a new governor in the person of Sir Olaf Caroe took over at Peshawar. A member of the ICS with long and wide-ranging experience as Frontier administrator, Caroe was strikingly different from his predecessor. Sir George, cool and collected and at home both with men and things; Sir Olaf, sharp and intelligent, yet high-strung and edgy, singularly ill-at-ease with all those he had to deal with. To no one's surprise then, in the months ahead the new governor found himself on a collision course with his premier.*

In the final days of the Raj, the pace of political developments in the country became hectic, almost breathless. Briefly, a few of the more relevant facts may be highlighted. The Cabinet Mission plan of May 1946 for the devolution of political power to Indian hands led to acute differences between the Congress and the Muslim League. Governor-General Wavell invited the former to cobble together an interim government at the centre (July). Determined to stay out in the cold, for the time being at any rate, the League's response to the viceroy's initiative was a call for 'Direct Action Day' (16 August) whose observance, on conservative estimates, claimed a toll of 5,000 dead on the blood-spattered streets of Calcutta alone. The gory spectacle of death, which in the following twelve months was to leave few areas of the country unscathed, was now a grim reality. It was against this grisly background that Jawaharlal Nehru was sworn into office on 2 September 1946.

As Vice-President of the Governor-General's Executive Council and Member for External Affairs and Commonwealth Relations, Nehru's portfolio *included* tribal affairs. The latter locally, and as an additional charge, were handled by the governor of the NWFP in his capacity as agent (to) the governor-general (AGG). If only Sir Olaf and those of his way of thinking had succeeded, the new Member would have been denied this charge. They did not; in the event, Nehru came into official contact with Sir Olaf Caroe. Hypercritical of governmental policy, Nehru almost from day one pulled in a diametrically opposite direction to that of his hardboiled if crusty civil servant who had long known and dealt with the tribes on the ground. Nehru's visit to the tribal areas in October 1946 in the wake of some aerial bombing there (August-September) and in the

* Under the Government of India Act 1935, the term 'Premier'/'Prime Minister' was used for the provincial chief minister.

face of Caroe's explicit advice to the contrary was to prove a disastrous start. The new member was exposed to not just hostile demonstrations but also what proved to be an almost fatal assault on his person. These Nehru, and his supporters, suspected were master-minded by the political agents at the governor's behest. In sum, Caroe and his new official boss in New Delhi were soon set on a collision course.

Not unexpectedly, this cast fearsome, if ominous shadows over provincial politics which lengthened with every passing day, worsening an already, none-too-happy relationship between the governor and his council of ministers. The final act of the drama spans the period March–July 1947 and its principal *dramatis personae* include, apart from Olaf Caroe, Dr Khan Sahib, Abdul Ghaffar Khan, Nehru, Mountbatten and the ragtag leadership of the Frontier Muslim League.

Briefly, even before the new governor-general arrived, towards the end of March 1947, Nehru had demanded the resignation of Sir Olaf Caroe. A demand strongly backed by Khan Sahib and his younger brother, Abdul Ghaffar Khan, and even the Mahatma, so powerful was the miasma of suspicion and distrust which mired Caroe's image for his alleged sins of omission and commission. But the governor had an excellent prop in Jinnah and his Muslim League who, even as Sir Olaf himself, now pleaded strongly for a dissolution of the Provincial Assembly and holding of fresh elections. This was advocated to test the political waters afresh and what was perceived to be a complete erosion of popular support for the Khan Sahib ministry.

In his fortnightly letter of 7 April 1947 to the governor-general, Caroe had enclosed a comprehensive note drawn up by his Chief Secretary Norval Mitchell on the situation in the province. His policy, Caroe wrote years later, was 'to work up to a vote—either an election or a plebiscite—to make certain whether the Pathans really wanted to follow Congress now that the chips were down'. Mitchell's note, he had hoped, would help the new viceroy grasp the necessity of this, 'As indeed, I think, it did.'

Caroe's proposed course of action did not elicit an immediate response. After an initial endorsement, Mountbatten appeared to be opposed, as was Nehru and his Congress Party, albeit for diametrically different reasons. To sort out what Ismay, Mountbatten's Chief of Staff, was to call this 'bastard situation' of fitting a predominantly Muslim, yet Congress-ruled, NWFP into the larger whole of Muslim League dominated West Panjab, Sind and Baluchistan which had, by early July, taken shape and form, it was decided to hold a referendum in the province. This had only grudging Congress support in New Delhi and outright opposition from

Khan Sahib, Badshah Khan and the entire Khudai Khidmatgar political outfit in Kabul. His *bona fides* increasingly suspect with the Congress and his own ministers, Sir Olaf Caroe was eased out of office (June 1947) and General Rob Lockhart took over as his temporary replacement, to organize the referendum.

In the July 1947 vote on the referendum, the Pathans had a Hobson's choice; between joining an existing New Delhi-based and, by definition, Hindu-dominated Constituent Assembly and another yet to be convened in the impending Pakistan's new capital, Karachi. In this patently 'No Win' situation, Khan Sahib and his political mentor, Abdul Ghaffar Khan had demanded a third choice—an independent Pathanistan. Refused, they opted for a boycott of the referendum.

Expectedly, the voters' choice went overwhelmingly in favour of Jinnah's Pakistan. Sir Olaf who had proforma proceeded on leave in the hope that Pakistan's new rulers will opt for him as their choice of the Frontier's new governor was sorely disappointed when on 4 July, and behind his back, Jinnah finally revealed his hand and asked for George Cunningham who was initially none too keen to return. The Pathans and their Badshah Khan were an unhappy lot for Congress and its central leadership had at a critical juncture abandoned them to the tender mercies of their political adversaries, the Frontier Muslim League. Khan Sahib was dismissed within a little over a week of the birth of Pakistan; in the event, on the morrow of the transfer of power by the Raj, the NWFP and its people became an integral part of the state of Pakistan.

Nearly a half century has passed since. The period is now the stuff of history. More, all the chief actors—Olaf Caroe; Khan Sahib, Nehru, Badshah Khan, Mountbatten, Jinnah, Wavell—are dead. In the event, the play can be staged with honour and without embarrassment.

CHAPTER 1

The Backdrop

THE ERSTWHILE North-West Frontier Province of the Raj had towards its west as well as the north, an international border with Afghanistan; in the east, it nestled with the Gilgit Agency in Kashmir and the Panjab; to the south, with Baluchistan. As the gateway to India, its strategic importance was immense; every empire-builder in Central Asia or the Indian subcontinent sought to control and conquer it.

Physically, the Frontier is difficult to describe, largely because no part of it is of the same nature even twenty miles on end. Here and there miles of cliff and stony slopes give way to open fans of cultivation backed by more sheer cliffs. There are also narrow river gorges opening out to fir-covered mountains which drop to swelling bush-covered hills or bare grazing grounds with patches of forest, and open plains flanked by low, bare hills cut by deep ravines. As may be evident, much in the Frontier is harsh but all is drawn in strong tones and unfolds a tremendous scenic canvass.

Today the province embraces three distinct geographical regions: the cis-Sutlej district of Hazara; the narrow strip between the Indus and hills constituting the settled trans-Indus districts of Peshawar, Kohat, Bannu, Mardan and D I Khan; and the rugged mountain region between these hills and the border of Afghanistan. Of its total area of 97,400 sq kms, a little over one-third, is covered by the settled districts; the remaining two-thirds, roughly 64,000 sq kms, by the tribal belt. For administrative purposes, the latter was divided into five political agencies: Malakand, Kurram, Khyber, North and South Waziristan.

The authority of the various empires who claimed to rule this frontier extended merely to the plains and a passage or two through the mountains. The latter was by no means easy and had often to be effected by *force majeure* and held with great difficulty against the refractory tribes who controlled the road in use at the time. This would largely explain why the tribal belt as a whole escaped subjection to any external power and why a tribal form of society persisted despite the countless invasions by Alexander, Chinghiz Khan, Tamerlane and their likes.

The tribal belt is held by four important tribes: the Afridis, around the Khyber and to the south thereof; the Mohmands, beyond the Kabul river and Swat; the Wazirs, between the rivers Kurram and Gomal; and the Mahsuds between the Tochi and Gomal rivers. Among the lesser known tribes, mention may be made of the Orakzais, Muhammadzais, Bhittanis and the Shinwaris. As for the settled districts, Peshawar has a mixed cauldron that includes the Utman Khel, Muhammadzais, Shilman and Khalil; from Bannu to Kohat is the land of the Khattaks; Bannu is inhabited by the Bannuchis and the Marwats. Both Hazara and D I Khan are predominantly non-Pathan; in the former, Panjabi Muslims dominate, in the latter, Jats.

The physical boundaries of the Frontier have changed over time. Under the Aryans, it stretched from the Indus valley to far away Central Asia; from the sixth century BC until the opening decade of the nineteenth, the area was part of the Iranian, Greek, Kushan, Gupta, Turki, Ghorian, Mughal and Durrani empires. In 1849, after about a quarter century of Sikh rule, the region known as the settled districts was taken over by the British. The modified frontier line, the Durand Line, was laid down in 1893 along the crest of the Sulaiman range of mountains and brought the tribes living in the tribal belt within the British sphere of influence.

Under British rule, the North-West Frontier was 'the frontier'—the Raj's Achilles heel; its most vulnerable part. Way back in 1808, fearing Napoleon's onslaught through Persia and Afghanistan, the John Company sent a friendly mission to the Afghan Amir who then held court at Peshawar. Four decades later, the British inherited the area after a decisive defeat inflicted on the post-Ranjit Singh Sikh state of the Panjab. And while it lasted, the Raj's principal preoccupation continued to be the security of the frontier.

To start with, the external threat emanated from Afghanistan. Later, as the nineteenth century wore on, a Russian advance through the soft underbelly of Asia became a major obsession. In the event, the worst scenario the British conjured up was of a Russian assault to which the Afghans were privy and the Pakhtuns, at best, indifferent.

From day one as it were, in the corridors of power in Calcutta and later Delhi/New Delhi, as no doubt in Whitehall itself, two major issues clamoured for solution and were the subject of well-nigh interminable, unending, debate: where to stop the Raj's expansion to the north-west and how to control the Frontier. Two schools of thought emerged. Advocates of the 'Close Border' held that India should not assume responsibility for the area it could not directly administer. They favoured the Indus as the natural boundary and were prepared to withdraw beyond it. The only problem this line of thinking posed was that it left unresolved the alignment of the no man's land between India and Afghanistan. To prevent these areas from falling into hostile Afghan/Russian hands, diplomacy was to be employed.

The opposing school was that of 'Forward Policy'. To contain the Russians, its adherents favoured extending British rule as far as possible, to the west as well as the north-west. Not a few viewed the Oxus as the natural border of India and talked of a scientific frontier along a line from Kabul, through Ghazni and Kandahar. It followed that any stretch of 'no man's land' between India and Afghanistan was deemed undesirable and was sought to be controlled.

In 1893, an agreement was knocked into shape with the Afghan Amir delineating an international border between British India and Afghanistan. Known as the Durand Line, after its British negotiator, Sir Mortimer Durand, it left a broad hilly tract in the west—which later came to be known as the Tribal Area—under a vague British suzerainty, with the Raj exercising only the most tenuous control over it. There were thus two boundaries: an internal boundary, marking the end of direct British administration; and an external boundary, the Durand Line. Between the two stretched the tribal belt or area.

The North-West Frontier Province came into being in 1901. Prior thereto, for a little over half a century, the unadministered belt as well as the districts adjoining it, were the responsibility of the neighbouring British Indian province of the Panjab. With a view to bringing the Frontier under closer imperial control, Curzon had devised a new scheme which placed the province directly under the government of India.

Compared to British India's other provinces, the Frontier was much smaller in area, with only a third thereof directly administered. The unadministered tribal area, was divided into five 'political agencies', each under a political agent; the latter's main function was to ensure that there was no large-scale unrest among the tribes placed under his charge. Relations between the tribes in the tribal area and the Raj were governed by treaties which broadly enjoined the tribes not to harbour outlaws who were fugitives from British justice, nor yet raid the adjoining settled districts. Sadly, the injunctions were observed more in their breach than compliance. A recalcitrant tribe was subjected to an economic blockade, an armed assault and, not unoften, pounding from the air. For good behaviour and maintenance of peace, on the other hand, there was no end of incentives. Tribes were paid cash subsidies: to the tribe as a whole; or, individually, to its most influential members. A loose political control was exercised in the tribal area with the aid of militia forces and levies, drawn largely from among the tribes themselves.

The Raj's blandishments notwithstanding, the tribes as a whole refused to sever fraternal ties with their kith and kin across the Durand Line, in Afghan territory. Not that the regime in Kabul obliged. On the contrary, the Afghans too—not unlike the Raj—bribed the tribes in the tribal area by way of subsidies and an occasional pat on the back. In the event, the Durand Line proved to be a porous frontier and raised no end of problems for the Raj.

Even as he carved out a separate frontier province, Curzon initiated a modified version of the 'Close Border' system. Briefly, the Raj's overt military presence in the tribal area was reduced while communication links to, and within, the area, were improved. This would enable the British to strike more effectively, and expeditiously, if and when the need arose. At the same time, tribal subsidies were raised.

Sadly for him, the much-hoped-for peace that Curzon had bargained for did not ensue. Thus, in the decades that followed large military forces were stationed at Razmak and Wana in Waziristan and military roads built linking Wana, Razmak and Miranshah. Improved communications apart, the militia and the tribal levies were overhauled and placed on a much firmer basis. Like Curzon's, the new policy was only a partial success, for the latter half of the 1930s was witness to a serious revolt under the notorious Fakir of Ipi.

The tribal area came under the direct authority of the government of India which exercised its control through the agent to the governor-general (AGG), a charge held by the provincial governor and, prior to 1932, by the chief commissioner. Nor, with the new scheme of reforms, under the Government of India Act 1935, did the authority of provincial ministers extend to the tribal area. In the settled districts, the governor acted on the advice of his council of ministers; in the tribal area, directly under the control of the central government. The arrangement enabled New Delhi to keep Indian politics, and politicians, out of the tribal area leaving the latter more or less insulated from extraneous influences. And busy with its own unending feuds.

At the time of its formation (1901), the North-West Frontier Province comprised five districts: Hazara, Peshawar, Kohat, Bannu and D I Khan. In 1937, Peshawar was split into two, Peshawar and Mardan. Except for the cis-Indus Hazara, all the districts took their names form the towns in which district headquarters were located. Hazara's was at Abbotabad which doubled as the provincial summer capital.

For reasons of security, all the key officials in the province, including the deputy commissioners and political agents, were drawn from the very exclusive, and elitist, Indian Political Service.

The NWFP was a relatively poor province. At the same time, its administrative costs were high and, for political considerations, revenue assessments low. In the event, the provincial budget was invariably a deficit made up by doles from the central government. The latter accounting for nearly two-thirds of the provincial revenue receipts.

Thanks to the Frontier Crimes Regulations, the executive authority was vested with extraordinary powers—at the expense of the judiciary. Thus, the deputy commissioner was empowered to refer civil as well as criminal cases to a council of elders called the jirga. Trial by jirga was often resorted to, especially in cases where the guilt of the accused would not stand scrutiny in an ordinary court of law. A decision by the jirga was recommendatory; the final word lay with the deputy commissioner in whose territory the crime had been committed. Whenever unhappy with the verdict, the deputy commissioner constituted a fresh jirga for a re-trial. There was no right of appeal against the jirga's decision; it was not uncommon though to petition the governor for a revision.

In cases where no individual culprit could be found, a collective punishment was imposed—on villages, tribes, clans. Authority viewed the Frontier Crimes Regulations as integral to the maintenance of law and order in the province especially for the control of its tribal areas. Detractors assailed it for its arbitrariness and the not unlikely punishment of innocent people that it entailed.

Security considerations retarded the pace of all reform: political, social and economic. In the event, both the Minto-Morley (1909) as well as the Montagu-Chelmsford reforms (1919) left the province virtually untouched. While recommending a scheme of dyarchy for other British Indian provinces, the Montford report had suggested only the establishment of a vague advisory council for the NWFP. The actual scheme of reforms failed even to endorse this recommendation! The Simon Commission Report (1930) had envisaged for the Frontier an indirectly elected council with limited powers of taxation and voting on expenditure. The report none the less was to prove still-born.

Against its own better judgement, political compulsions soon impelled the Raj to introduce a modicum of constitutional reforms in the governance of the province. In the event, in 1932 the Montford scheme of reforms was extended to the province and its chief commissioner replaced by a lieutenant-governor as head of the administration. Additionally, a Legislative Assembly of 40 members was established.

The Government of India Act 1935 treated the NWFP on a basis of complete equality with other British Indian provinces. Under the new scheme, the Provincial Legislative Assembly was to have 50 seats, of which 9 were General (viz. Hindu), 3 Sikh, 2 from special landholders' constituencies, 3 from Muslim urban and 33 Muslim rural constituencies. It followed that the Hindus and Sikhs, who accounted for a little less than 10 per cent of the provincial population, enjoyed considerable weightage; an almost 25 per cent representation in the provincial legislature. As in the rest of British India, franchise qualifications in the Frontier were based on taxation, property rights, education, and service in the armed forces. Women were not excluded but few qualified to vote.

The relatively prosperous Peshawar area supported nearly 40 per cent of the Frontier's population; Kohat produced little. Three-fourths of all Hindus and Sikhs lived in urban centres; they accounted for one-third of the Frontier's town dwellers.

The ethnic divide in the Frontier was sharp and easily established. Almost 92 per cent of the population in the settled districts was Muslim; Hindus and Sikhs together accounting for a little less than 8 per cent. For most part, the Muslims lived in the rural areas; the non-Muslims, in the towns. And the majority among them were shopkeepers, moneylenders, and traders. Because of their education, and economic clout, the Hindus and Sikhs wielded a disproportionately larger share of influence in the life of the province.

The religious divide among Muslims and non-Muslims was overshadowed by the ethnic differences between the dominant Pakhtuns and the minority non-Pakhtuns. Loosely referred to as 'Pathans' or 'Afghans', the Pakhtuns are pronouncedly ethnocentric and governed by a code called 'Pakhtunwali'. Its two outstanding features were 'badal' (or 'badla') and 'malmastia'. The former enjoins revenge for any hurt or insult including the duty to kill, for a death inflicted on a kinsman; the latter underwrites an obligation to offer protection and hospitality to a guest.

Though a dominant group, the Frontier was by no means all Pakhtuns writ large. For in Hazara, the Pakhtuns were a small minority; as also in D I Khan. But in the settled districts of Mardan, Peshawar, Kohat and Bannu as well as the tribal area, the Pakhtuns constituted an overwhelming majority. Among the non-Pakhtuns, the Awans were a large group, so were the Gujars and the Jats. They served for the most part as tenants on the estates of the Pakhtun khans. It may be of interest to note here that the political movement in the Frontier in the 1930s claimed a large following among the Pakhtuns; other ethnic groups remained either passive or even openly hostile.

The Mughal, Durrani or Sikh rulers of the North-West Frontier exercised varying degrees of control over the Pakhtuns. By and large, they confined themselves to governance through tribal leaders and farmed out revenues to influential khans or maliks who emerged as no more than collectors of revenue from their less fortunate kinsmen. In the event, instead of representing the tribe, they came to represent the state *vis-a-vis* ordinary tribesmen. In return for services rendered to their political masters, the khans and maliks were recipients of land grants such as *jagirs* and *inams*; the latter were exempt from all revenue claims preferred by the state.

Under the Raj, the landlord class gained in strength at the expense of other groups. And within the landlord class, the bigger khans lost ground to smaller khans. The British fostered closer cooperation with the leading khans largely through what were called 'political pensions' or conferment of honorary titles such as Khan Sahib, Khan Bahadur and Nawab. The extension of the Panjab Land Alienation Act (1904) to the Frontier meant the creation of a landlord class conceived more or less in the British image of landed gentry. Land was thus a source of economic security rather than profit and essentially a basis for power. Capital was invested in acquisition of land only, *not* in its improvement.

In the three decades after World War I (1914-18), and before the transfer of power, when political developments touched the Frontier for the first time, the sharp dividing line between the big, government-backed khans and the more numerous smaller khans who enjoyed few if any favours from the rulers, became clearly marked. It was the latter, the smaller khans, who were to constitute the social and economic centre of gravity in the Frontier's rural society.

Political activity in the Frontier in recent times was synonymous with the rise of Khan Abdul Ghaffar Khan, often referred to by his initials, AGK. In September 1929, the Khan formed an organisation called the

Afghan Jirga with the threefold objective of Hindu-Muslim unity, independence for India and reform of Pakhtun society. Soon the Jirga had its branches all over the Peshawar district and in some others. Not long after came the Khudai Khidmatgars (literally, 'Servants of God') who were organised on a quasi-military basis. Clad in uniforms, dyed in red brick dust, they came to be dubbed 'Red Shirts' or Surkh Posh. In August 1931, both the Afghan Jirga and the Khudai Khidmatgars became formally affiliated to the Indian National Congress. Proforma the Congress had constituted a Provincial Congress Committee in the NWFP a few years earlier but the organization attracted little support in the Pakhtun countryside until Abdul Ghaffar Khan brought his Khudai Khidmatgar outfit into the party.

The basic tenets of the Khudai Khidmatgar movement have been identified as Pakhtun nationalism, moral and social reform among the Pakhtuns, non-violence and Islam. It was far from being a narrow, much less sectarian movement; the objective was to embrace all those living in Pakhtuns society or even in the NWFP. The essence of the Khudai Khidmatgar appeal rested on the moral and spiritual—not political—plane; its broad objective was to eradicate the ills of Pakhtun society. Since the British rulers appeared to exploit these ills to serve their own selfish, imperial, ends, the Raj was the special target of the movement's attack.

Ideologically, AGK was quite close to the Mahatma with his unflinching faith in non-violence not only as a matter of principle but also as a political creed. A devout Muslim, the Khan's Islam had few of the trappings of orthodoxy; employing a traditional religious idiom, he was yet a modernist. His hold on the Pakhtun people was beyond dispute and he waged his wars against British rule consistently and without compromising his principles.

AGK's elder brother, Dr Khan Sahib, was a study in contrast. Highly anglicised, he held an English degree in medicine and was married to an English wife. In politics, he was a moderate, clearly averse to the rough and tumble of an active political life. In the event, he remained a parliamentarian and a constitutionalist, led the party in the legislature and held ministerial office. The younger Khan, always in the forefront of the revolutionary movement, had no use for the trappings of office and never aspired to a ministerial berth.

Some salient features of the Khudai Khidmatgar movement as a political outfit may be briefly enumerated. Confined to the Frontier, the political emancipation of the Pakhtuns was its primary objective; so was its opposition to the bigger khans who were rated British toadies and, therefore, politically unreliable. The rank and file of the movement comprised tenants and petty cultivators; its leaders, small time khans. Despite appropriate noises from time to time, a social and economic programme was never fully developed; emphasis remained on freedom from British rule. The Khudai Khidmatgars' political allegiance to the Indian National Congress was mutually beneficial. The former acquired an all-India character and gained sizeable financial as well as organizational support; by cohabiting with them, the Congress claim to be a secular, all-India party which enjoyed the backing of both the principal communities, was powerfully boosted.

In a society where political mobilisation takes place on the basis of faction—and the Pakhtuns are notorious for their factionalism or *parajamba*—political cleavages run across class line, *not* along them. All factions represent similar configurations of people and interests. A vital aspect of Pakhtun social organisation, and political behaviour, known as *tarburwali* signifies rivalry between close, agnatic relatives and concerns itself primarily with the inheritance of land or the leadership of a prominent family. It makes Pakhtun politics ever more divisive, factious, riddled by bickerings and enmities.

In the years immediately preceding the transfer of power, *tarburwali* became intertwined with party politics. In the event, a khan who joined a political outfit, say the Congress, would bring his faction with him into the fold. It followed that his rival would join the Muslim League or the other way round. Pakhtun factions were highly localised in character. To buttress his support base, a candidate would often make an appeal to the voters on the strength of his tribe/clan, etc. In many areas there was a strong resentment among the lower classes against the bigger khans who had become mere rent receivers with no interest in the land, much less in the welfare of those who tilled it.

The Frontier's religious leaders belonged to three overlapping, yet clearly discernible categories: the mullahs; the maulanas and the maulvis; the sayyids, pirs or sahibzadas. The Pakhtun ethos, though intensely Muslim, had little use for religious leaders except when a threat, real or imaginary, to the Pakhtuns as Muslims was envisaged. In such cases, Islam assumed overriding importance.

Three well-known religious personalities under the Raj may deserve mention. Mullah Mastun or the 'Mad Mullah', as the British called him, led uprisings among the tribes in the Malakand Agency in 1897; Mullah Powinda, among the Mahsuds, was for almost two decades (1893-1913), in the forefront of opposition against the British. And finally, the Fakir of

Ipi who played a by no means dissimilar role in North Waziristan in the 1940s.

In Pakhtun society, the mullahs as a whole were held in contempt; useful for propaganda purposes, they were rightly viewed as a marketable commodity willing to be purchased by the highest bidder. Barring a few honourable exceptions, the Raj had the entire lot on its pay role for the anti-Nazi propaganda during World War II. So did the Muslim League in the crucial months preceding the transfer of power.

With the urban component of the provincial population at almost 16 per cent, most towns in the NWFP were important trading centres, market places, administrative headquarters and army cantonments. Before 1947, there was hardly any industry worth the name in the entire province. Peshawar deserves a special mention, not only because it was the provincial headquarters, but also because with its polyglot population and large numbers of itinerants, it was a turbulent, cosmopolitan city, full of footloose, independent characters. More, its womenfolk made themselves heard, even from behind the purdah.

The two major communities—the Muslims and the Hindus—were evenly matched in towns; the rural areas were almost entirely Muslim. While Muslim businessmen had strong linkages with landed interests, their Hindu (or Sikh) counterparts, were a commercial community; their politics dominated by businessmen. Retired government servants with a strong background of administration and public affairs, constituted an important political group, which had, by and large, pronounced pro-British leanings.

In the services, Hindus were over-represented, predominant in some branches, less so in others. In the so-called 'crucial' branches, such as the police and the army, and in positions having a direct bearing at the local level, the Muslim position was strong.

Each of the various groups—landlords, religious leaders, prosperous businessmen, professionals, government employees—had an important role to play as mediators between ordinary people and the government. The politicians leaned on these groups for support with the result that their changing affiliations were decisive in the turn provincial politics took.

The tribal areas represented a belt of territory between what was British India and Afghanistan. Defined by an international boundary, the 1893 Durand Line, it was a zone or an area under the territorial control of the government of India where British Indian administrative norms, especially the systems of taxation, were not applied. New Delhi's general control over the tribes was exercised through subsidies and, ultimately, the army. Put differently, in the conception of India these territories were included, but not in British India. It followed that the boundary of British India, which was British-administered, ended where tribal territory began.

The external affairs department was something distinct from the political department which, its other functions apart, was responsible for the conduct of foreign affairs as well as the administration of tribal areas. The department was an integral part of the central government under the control of the governor-general-in-council. The political department, on the other hand, was the secretariat of the crown representative and was controlled by the political advisor to the crown representative; it was *not* under the central government.

The only constitutional link between the political department and the external affairs department was provided by the viceroy in his dual capacity as governor-general and crown representative. The Indian Political Service belonged to a joint cadre which served both the crown representative as well as the external affairs department. All its officers were normally called political officers. Drawn from the Indian Civil Service (ICS), about one-third, and the Army, about two-thirds, there was in the Indian Political Service a smattering of the Indian Police (IP) as well. While the political advisor to the crown representative was the senior officer of the service, the secretary of state for India was ultimately incharge.

A word on the Durand Line and the processes of delineating, delimiting and demarcating a boundary. Describing a boundary in written, literal terms—as in a document—is to *delineate* it; defining it by a line on a map—with or without verbal description—is to *delimit* it; transferring these definitions physically to an actual line on the ground is to *demarcate* it. For the record, the Durand Line (1893) was demarcated; the Macdonald Line (1899) was delineated—not delimited; the McMahon Line (1914) was delimited—not demarcated. It should follow that demarcation, as no doubt delimitation, of boundaries assumes the concurrence of the concerned sovereign states. In the case of the Durand Line, that of Afghanistan and the Raj.

One final word. The time span for the events that unfold in these pages is singularly short. And, for proper perspective, needs therefore to be constantly reviewed not only against the backdrop of a hundred odd years of the Raj but also the tumultuous five decades that have elapsed since. In history, as in life, there are no abrupt breaks; only a few convenient staging posts that help in a better understanding and a clearer perspective.

CHAPTER 2

The 1937 and 1946 Elections and Nehru's Visit to the Frontier, October 1946

THE FRONTIER of the 1930s was witness to a quick succession of political upheavals interspersed with some important constitutional changes. The end-result was the province's closer liaison and linkages, than hitherto, with the rest of the country. To start with, Khan Abdul Ghaffar Khan and his Khudai Khidmatgars came in contact with the Indian National Congress and later took an active part in the Mahatma's nation-wide call for a Civil Disobedience movement. The Frontier's response, loud and clear, was followed by an angry wave of British repression and worse. Not long after, the Montford scheme of political reforms was extended to the Pathans. Also known as dyarchy, it operated for about four years before the Government of India Act 1935 was introduced with the NWFP emerging as a full-blown governor's province where, as in the rest of the country, elections were to be held in the second half of 1937.

The KKs' and AGK's, close alignment with the Indian National Congress may be said to date with the party's Lahore session (December 1929–January 1930) which the Khan attended, with a large contingent of his followers. Not long after, the Mahatma gave his call for a mass Civil Disobedience movement which was to evoke an enthusiastic response in the Frontier. Not unexpectedly, AGK was arrested; this was to trigger off an angry, loud public backlash throughout the province. Mass demonstrations and arrests followed as did innumerable police firings. Among the latter, the one in Peshawar, on 23 April 1930, was to become memorable. Badshah Khan had been arrested earlier in the day and the news took Peshawar by storm. The then Deputy Commissioner, Olaf Kirkpatrick Caroe, riding his armoured car had ordered the police to open fire on an unarmed crowd in the Kissakhani bazaar. Unofficial estimates of those killed ranged between 'two to three hundred' besides 'many more' who were wounded.[1] Hence, the site became a 'Martyrs Memorial', a place of yearly pilgrimage for the Red Shirts, and Caroe synonymous with mindless repression. The blot it left on the latter's escutcheon stuck; his role neither forgiven, nor yet forgotten. AGK certainly never trusted him afterwards, even though Caroe claimed (after 1947) that they became friends![2]

The tribal disturbances which followed large-scale civil disorder in the settled districts of the province unnerved the Raj no end. In the event, marital law had to be imposed and kept in force until the following January (1931). Government conceded that it was

> unquestionable that much of the trouble was directly due to the activities of the Congress party, and the extensive influence . . . (it had) acquired over a predominantly Muslim population . . . inflammatory ideas had been widely disseminated in the rural areas. . . . (Again) the remarkable fact (that) during the course of their numerous incursions into the Settled Districts, the tribesmen . . . abstained from looting in their customary manner . . . and that the Afridis, when negotiating a settlement with the authorities put forward demands for the release of Mr Gandhi and the repeal of the special ordinances in India. . . .

Interestingly, it was not only the Mahatma but also Badshah Khan and his KKs who were to figure in the Afridi ultimatum: 'Release the Khudai Khidmatgars' the Afridis had thundered, 'and stop the atrocities and repression against the Pakhtuns. If you don't, we shall declare war on you.'[3]

Many years later, on the eve of the transfer of power, Fraser Noble would have us believe that Badshah Khan was under the impression that the Afridis would help him in his hour of need even as they had in 1931.[4] Evidently though, the ground realities were now different, and they did not!

The official version of the 1931-2 disturbances in the Frontier underlines how a delicate situation led to police firings, killings and worse. *Inter alia*, it has been suggested that as the news of AGK's arrest spread to Peshawar, troops were summoned. Arriving at the Edwardes' Gate of the city, the troops found themselves up against 'a dense, murderous mob over which the civil police had completely' lost control. This could have been expected and forestalled, 'but evidently was not'. Hence the firing which by the afternoon of 23 April is said to have restored 'complete order' in the city. Again, by the end of 1931 the perception was that had the government 'forborne from stamping out sedition for a day longer',

AGK and his cronies' efforts to subvert law and order 'would have been crowned with success'.[5]

Meantime in the wake of the Gandhi-Irwin Pact (March 1931), the Mahatma's Civil Disobedience movement was countermanded even though the resultant truce was to prove short-lived. The widespread political agitation referred to earlier, buttressed by an impressive public pressure, both within and without the province, brought the Frontier its belated dose of constitutional reforms which earlier on (1920) had been introduced in the other provinces of British India.

The demand for a full-blown democratic constitutional set-up in the Frontier was thus conceded at the Round Table Conference (1930-2) in London when a committee under Harry Haig (later Sir Harry) looked into the question, and recommended that law be handed over to a responsible minister while 'watch and ward' was to be a central subject incharge of the provincial chief commissioner or governor.[6] Thus, from 1 December 1931, the NWFP was elevated from the chief commissioner's to a lieutenant governor's province and the Montford scheme of reforms of 1919 duly, if belatedly, introduced. Contrary to a widely held official belief that the measure would go a long way to assuage the feeling of hurt occasioned by official repression in the preceding year, it had, in fact, little if any impact. As a matter of fact, the political protest symbolized by the new-born solidarity of the KKs with the Congress Party outside the province seems to have taken firm roots and aroused the Pathans no end.

In the electoral battle—to constitute the new Provincial Legislative Council—that was soon joined, Congress withdrew from the contest and, in fact, openly boycotted the poll. In its absence, and that of any other organised political party, there were only individual contestants. Franchise too was limited and narrow with only about two lakh people, a bare 8 per cent of the population, endowed with the right to vote. And of those eligible, just about 10-15 per cent exercised the right. Nor was that all. In a legislature of 40 members, only 28 members were elected, the latter included 6 representatives of religious minorities. Of the 12 nominated members, 6 were officials and 6 non-officials.

As a result of the April 1932 election, Sahibzada Sir Abdul Qayyum emerged as the recognised leader of a group of 'constitutionalists' and was soon to assume office as minister incharge of the transferred subjects under the 1919 scheme of dyarchy.

Sir Abdul Qayyum, 'AQ', for short, along with two other legendary Britishers, Harold Deane and George Roos Keppel, has been hailed as a pioneer of Pathan renaissance in the opening decades of the twentieth century. Among his major contributions were the founding of the Islamia College which later grew into the University of Peshawar. He fought for extension to the Frontier of the political reforms that had earlier been introduced in other British Indian provinces. Sadly, for the first 12 years before their induction, the province had stood on a dead centre; its only representation in the Central Legislature in Delhi being through two of its leading citizens, nominated—*not* elected. One of them was AQ; the other, Muhammad Akbar Khan of Hoti. His friends insist that thanks to his 'breadth of vision and determination'—and singular resilience—AQ extracted from the inertia of the British government two instalments of reform within a few years: in 1932 and again, in 1937.[7]

By 1934, in the Frontier, as in the rest of the country, the Mahatma's Civil Disobedience movement had become moribund and the Congress, and the Khudai Khidmatgars (who had by now formally merged into the former), reverted to constitutional activities. The lone seat from the Frontier in the Central Legislative Assembly at Delhi was fought—and successfully won—by Khan Sahib in December 1934. It was the first election held in the Frontier in which the Congress took part. Thanks to the Raj's high-handedness, Khan Sahib was not allowed to visit the province, much less engage in electioneering. Worse, the KK outfit had been declared illegal over these many years; the ban on its activities being lifted only in November 1934, a bare few weeks before the polling.[8]

To no one's surprise, between 1931 and 1937 when the 1919 reforms were in operation in the NWFP, the Provincial Legislative Council was broadly subservient to the executive authority in the province. Some individual members did, from time to time, make appropriate noises but the Frontier Council's control over governmental functioning, as in most other British Indian provinces, remained purely perfunctory, more ornamental than real.

As the scheme of dyarchy was abandoned and Government of India Act 1935 brought into force, elections to the Provincial Legislatures all over British India were scheduled for the winter of 1936-7. In contesting these in the Frontier, the Congress–Khudai Khidmatgar combine faced many an obstacle. To start with, its principal leaders, AGK and Khan Sahib, had been barred from entering the province; the ban being lifted only in November 1936. In the elections held in February 1937, Congress contested 37 seats, out of a total of 50; it won 19. At the same time a large 'no party' group of independents emerged; as many as 25 of them. AQ, a known Raj loyalist, cobbled together a group of 'constitutionalists' and was briefly, April–November 1937, premier when Khan Sahib took his place.

The four-member Congress ministry gave a good account of itself, both in the management of provincial finances as well as a significant enhancement in the allocation of scarce resources for nation building: in the domains of education, medical and public health, agriculture and industry. More important, the Khan Sahib government tried to democratize the functioning of such local government units as municipalities and district boards by freeing them from bureaucratic control. Sadly though, its election pledges notwithstanding, the Congress ministry was not able to change the system of land revenue assessment, much less place a moratorium on agricultural debts or reform the tenancy laws.

A disturbing development was an upsurge in tribal raids on the settled districts, especially in Bannu (July 1938), D I Khan (March 1939), and Kohat (July 1939). Many suspected that these were due partly to the recalcitrance of British officials and their refusal to extend support to the provincial Congress ministry.

Happily, the new Governor, Sir George Cunningham, who had replaced Sir Ralph Griffith in March 1937, soon struck an excellent rapport with his premier and even made a public reference to this fact. To start with, this was born out of the new Governor's inability to help out his close friend, and confidant, AQ remain in office for long. Initially, the latter had been sworn in, end-March, after a great deal of overt, as well as covert, official support. Thus on 22 March, Cunningham had told a bunch of extra-assistant commissioners and tehsildars gathered in Peshawar that 'any official who did not help the ministerial party (of AQ) was being disloyal' to him. He was sanguine too that a coalition party will emerge 'and then I will have to issue a fiat as to who shall be ministers and parliamentary secretaries.'[9] A week later, Cunningham had, after 7 hours' talk, got some Hindu legislators to join AQ's party on certain conditions.[10]

Sadly for AQ, the going was far from smooth. For by 19 June, Cunningham noted, he (AQ) was 'rather desperate' about the chances of his ministry and the general situation in the province.[11] By end-July, the governor discovered that his ministers were 'very pessimistic and seem to have lost hope of a majority'.[12] Towards end-August, AQ was in deep waters and beyond any hope of redemption. Finally, on 3 September, AQ's government was voted out in the legislature by a convincing margin: 22 for and 27 against.[13]

To every one's regret though, AQ did not long survive his defeat in the legislature. His death, in December 1937, as Olaf Caroe was to note, attracted the 'largest concourse ever known' in that part of the country for it was the 'sorrowing of a whole people.'[14] Cunningham recorded that AQ's departure was 'a great loss' and that the Pathans would 'find it difficult to replace him'.[15]

Meanwhile the governor had started mending his fences with the Congress Party and its leader. Thus on 31 August he had called for Khan Sahib; his first impressions strikingly favourable:

> A fine face which seems to have a peculiarly Hindu look. He was very pleasant and a little self-conscious; no trace of bitterness. . . . He laughed when I said (that) I had deliberately been trying to keep the present ministry in office.

The governor was strongly advised that Khan Sahib would be amenable to persuasion. 'I don't think', he noted in his diary, 'that he (Dr Khan Sahib) would be difficult to work with if it comes to that. . . . .'[16]

The Khan Sahib ministry was sworn in on 6 September. Three days later Cunningham recorded that his premier 'promised to be reasonable' about the budget. 'But' the governor continued, 'I am never quite certain that he takes in everything that I say.'[17] Less than a fortnight later, Cunningham had another long chat with his premier whom he found 'very friendly and on the whole amenable'.[18]

Before long the governor gathered the impression that Khan Sahib was 'very anxious for more social intercourse' but was 'still uncertain' if his Congress discipline would allow him this indulgence.[19] Later, on 28 October, the governor recorded that Khan Sahib was 'disappointed' when told by his party high command that 'ministers should not attend (official) parties'. It was equally clear that 'he (KS) dislikes being disciplined' by the party central leadership.[20] At a dinner at Government House on 19 November, Cunningham unexpectedly found his premier and Qazi Ataullah not dressed in *khaddar* and Gandhi caps. It was the first time, the governor had ever seen him without his usual headgear.[21]

Not long after he had been in office, there was a disturbing rise in tribal raids on the settled districts. This attracted a lot of adverse comment. So did Khan Sahib and his family's growing intimacy with the provincial governor. Both developments tended to weaken Khan Sahib's own, and even more so his Congress Party's position *vis-a-vis* its pronouncedly anti-imperialist stance.

The tribal raids were politically embarrassing; the more so as the provincial government were virtually powerless in preventing them. The raids were more pronounced in the border districts of Bannu and D I

Khan during February–July 1938. Both official as well as non-official enquiries pointed a finger to the 'undercurrent of hostility' towards the Khan Sahib outfit and an unholy conspiracy to discredit it. Nor did the 'politicals' (officials, mostly British, of the Political Department), who functioned under the overall control of the provincial governor in his capacity as AGG, feel unduly comfortable under the new dispensation.[22]

A word on the governance of the tribal areas. In so far as the settled districts as well as the adjoining tribal territory in the Frontier were deemed inseparable, the British politicals functioned simultaneously as district officers under the provincial government as well as political officers for the adjoining tribal territory; in the latter capacity, under the overall control of the Political Department of the Government of India. The end-result was that they enjoyed a rare immunity from the control of the provincial ministry as well as the legislature. In the event, the ministry had little power to initiate any action against an errant political who failed to perform a civilian duty.[23]

It should be apparent that the fact that the ministers had no authority in tribal territory was a serious handicap in their ability to enforce law and order in the settled districts. It certainly led to distrust between them and the politicals as well as the governor. Cunningham understood this and handled the difficulty well. His successor, Caroe, did not. Again, Cunningham would have worked towards making tribal areas the responsibility of the provincial government. This may not have been easy, for the tribes who had treaties with the Crown may have found the change unpalatable.

The lack of any effective ministerial control over their civilian officials led the local Congress leaders to accuse the former of gross negligence of duty *vis-a-vis* tribal incursions. Even Gandhi in the course of a visit to the province in October 1938, publicly voiced his concern about tribal raids and advised the Khan Sahib government to quit if it were unable to cope with the situation:

> The Congress ministers have no effective control over the police, none over the military. The Congress ministry in this province has less than the others. I therefore feel that unless Dr Khan Sahib can cope with the question of raids, it might be better for him to tender his resignation.[24]

On another critical front though, the ministry fared better. Thanks to Khan Sahib's personal rapport with the governor such strains as Cunningham's refusal to accord his assent to some provisions of the NWFP Repealing and Amending Bill and the Teri Dues Regulations Repealing Bill of 1938, both of which had been adopted by the provincial legislature, were surmounted.[25] So also accusations by Congress members that the governor and his officials were unhelpful if not obstructive in the matter of tribal raids. When Badshah Khan made a public accusation that British officials were not extending 'their whole-hearted support' to the Congress government, Khan Sahib denied the allegation on the floor of the legislature and labelled it as 'purely imaginary'.[26]

It has been suggested that the cordiality between Mrs Mary Khan Sahib, the English wife of the provincial premier, and Lady Cunningham was a subject of considerable comment in the regional press and that the governor referred to it in a communication to the viceroy.[27] There was a modicum of truth in both these reports. No wonder, the Congress rank and file viewed their premier's proximity to the Government House as a sure sign of weakness for the nationalist cause, especially its anti-imperialist rhetoric. And not unoften Khan Sahib was embarrassed and even hauled up on hot coals.[28]

Nor was the Frontier premier enthused by the crisis (February 1938) created by Congress ministries in UP and Bihar over the release of political prisoners. The two provincial premiers, both prominent Congressmen (Govind Ballabh Pant and Sri Krishna Sinha), had resigned over the issue. Later the Governor-General, Lord Linlithgow, yielded ground and their resignations withdrawn. At one stage though, the episode threatened to develop into a first-rate constitutional impasse leading to the resignations of all Congress governments in eight British Indian provinces, including the Frontier. Khan Sahib, we are told, informed the governor that he 'would resist having to resign himself up to the very end'.[29] Later, after 'an illuminating talk' with Khan Sahib, Cunningham found his premier 'very angry' about local Congress workers coming in the way of the Peshawar District Board presenting a welcome address to the viceroy.[30] For his part, Khan Sahib and his ministerial colleagues attended the viceroy's public arrival at the Peshawar railway station. 'The first time', Cunningham noted, 'that Congress ministers have ever done this in any province.'[31]

In July 1938, Khan Sahib and his wife had come to lunch at the Government House when Cunningham found his premier 'in very good form'.[32] Later, in August, Mrs Khan Sahib and her son, John Khan Sahib, had come to stay with the governor for about a week. The boy, Cunningham noted, 'would do very well' for government service but unfortunately was a little over-age.[33]

On 31 August Khan Sahib and his family had come to lunch. Cunningham recorded that Khan Sahib was 'very much down' on officials and complained against 'some deputy commissioners . . . taking too much part in politics, anti-Congress'.[34] His premier's sympathies, Cunningham noted, were personally pro-English, for 'nothing' Khan Sahib had told the governor, 'would stop' the Pathans from enlisting in the army if the war came.[35]

In March 1939, Mrs Khan Sahib attended a ball at the Government House and seemed to enjoy it. Khan Sahib, Cunningham noted, 'wanted to come very much but was afraid what his Congress supporters would say'.[36]

When the governor advised the premier that it would help if Congress functionaries at the local level got in touch with officials and told them frankly what their difficulties were, Khan Sahib was disposed to agree. He confessed though that in Hazara he had 'no supporter whom he himself could really trust'.[37]

Cunningham was away on home leave (August–December 1939) when the Khan Sahib ministry quit office under a blanket directive from the Congress Party high command.[38]

II

The respect that the governor had developed for his premier was a matter of considerable interest. George Cunningham, it may be recalled, had, after a 5-year stint as Private Secretary to Governor-General Irwin (1926-30),[39] been posted at Peshawar as member of the Provincial Executive Council under Sir Ralph Griffith and held that position for 5 years, 1932-6. This enabled him to acquire a first-hand knowledge of the internal administration of the province, adding to his already considerable experience on the lie of the land and its people, especially in the trans-border areas.[40] His duties included such varied fields as finance, police, judiciary and the revenue administration. Another exposure was to the cut and thrust of debate in the Provincial Legislative Council where Cunningham's combination of firmness and courtesy did not so much overcome the opposition as disarm it. What endeared him further in legislative debates was his singular competence in Urdu diction spoken with a remarkable purity of language and style.[41] Early in 1937, George (now Sir George) Cunningham's appointment as governor of the province was officially announced. The first ministry under the new scheme of reforms, led by AQ, was sworn in, in April 1937. It did not last; its singular contribution lay in having the 1935 Act launched in the province. The new governor had known AQ as a colleague incharge of transferred departments (under the 1919 Act) in the province's Executive Council; he came to know his successor, Khan Sahib, even better before the latter was formally inducted into office. Happily, both for the governor and his new premier, they worked 'in complete harmony'.[42] Notwithstanding the directives from the party high command, Khan Sahib socialized too, and indulged in such unheard of blasphemies as dining at the Government House along with his wife. Sometimes even in the company of his education minister.[43]

Cunningham's relations with his Congress ministry were 'one of mutual trust, respect and affection'; his own tact and frankness making a deep impact. By November 1938 the premier 'even consulted him (viz., Cunningham)' about divisions within his Congress Party.[44] Typical of this mutual confidence was the premier's confession that the governor 'had always trusted the Ministers . . . and they had never done anything really against what they knew was my (Cunningham's) wish'.[45]

Sadly for the province, the ministerial honeymoon with the governor ended somewhat abruptly when, in the wake of World War II, the Congress Party opted for non-cooperation in the British war effort. To start with, the party embarked upon the resignations of Congress ministries in the eight governor's provinces, including the Frontier, that it controlled. Much against his better judgement, it would appear, Khan Sahib followed suit and quit office.

The next four years were to prove politically barren with the legislature in a state of suspended animation, the governor's direct rule under Section 93 of the 1935 Act in place, and the popular provincial government in limbo. During this interregnum, however, Khan Sahib's personal relations with Cunningham did not come under a cloud. They met not infrequently and exchanged views on men and things. Cunningham who had been away on leave (9 August–2 December 1939) caught up with developments no sooner than he resumed charge. One of his informants told him that Khan Sahib and Bhanju Ram 'were less perturbed than the other two Ministers' by the Congress high command's fiat to relinquish office 'mainly because they implicitly' obeyed the central leadership.[46] A week later Khan Sahib, with his wife and daughter, was at the Government House when the former premier told the governor that 'in a way he had benefited' by quitting office. And mainly because there was now a good deal of support from all those who had been criticising him for not fulfilling his election promises. He added that he was quite certain that there was no risk of non-cooperation, at any rate in the Frontier.

Significantly, Khan Sahib wanted the British government to make some sort of announcement that would satisfy his party. He knew that its political posturing notwithstanding, Congress 'can't get on without' the British linkage. It should follow that all that was required to bring them together was 'something to show that there was trust' between HMG and India.[47] Hence, what was needed was a declaration of intent about India's political future more or less in conformity with what the Congress had been demanding.

In the wake of the Belgian surrender on 28 May 1940, Cunningham asked Khan Sahib if the latter would serve on a defence committee that the governor proposed to establish. Khan Sahib, the Governor noted, had 'a certain amount of difficulty' in the matter and although he 'would be ready to do anything', he was afraid of the party high command. All the same, the ex-premier 'agreed to come to my meeting' and persuade Congress members 'to perform any task allotted to them' with a view to preserving the peace and good order of the province.[48]

In the course of protest demonstrations launched by the Congress Party throughout the country in the wake of its individual *satyagraha* campaign, (October 1940–December 1941) large-scale arrests were effected. On 14 December 1940 the slogan shouters in Peshawar including Khan Sahib

> had been told to go home. They were quite non-plussed at not being arrested, and Dr Khan Sahib said to Iskander (Iskander Mirza, then Deputy Commissioner, Peshawar): 'But you can't do this' when Iskander took him home and handed him over to Mrs Khan Sahib.[49]

Sharply criticized by Linlithgow's government in New Delhi for not arresting Khan Sahib and others, Cunningham's response was low-key. Even as he had 'expected something of the kind, though not so promptly', he succeeded in fobbing off New Delhi with a 'polite reply' satisfied in his own mind that 'our policy is right'.[50] By end-December, the worst of the storm appears to have blown over for

> The attitude of most by-standers (at the Congress meetings of protest and shouting of slogans) has been one rather of amusement than interest. It is also commonly believed that Congress leaders, with the possible exception of Abdul Ghaffar Khan, are really in secret concord with Government.[51]

Cunningham's diary entry for 16 January 1941 records how innocuous Congress sloganeering was. Bhanju Ram, one of the ministers in the Khan Sahib cabinet who hailed from D I Khan, the governor noted, 'only came out on to the steps of his house, shouted the slogans once or twice and then retreated indoors'. There was a consensus of opinion, Cunningham recorded, that 'it would have been unwise to arrest anyone'.[52]

Later, on 7 March 1941, the governor noted that Khan Sahib and 'other would-be satyagrahis seem to have given up their efforts entirely.'[53] On 14 July, Cunningham found Khan Sahib 'in good form' and 'as friendly as ever'.[54] When his daughter Mariam Khan Sahib's engagement to a non-Muslim pilot in the Royal Indian Air Force was announced, there was no dearth of condemnation by the orthodox Islamists and the political enemies of the Congress. One could sense though where the governor's sympathies lay with a note in his diary that there was 'already a lot of propaganda' against the proposed marriage, 'instigated, I suppose, by Muslim League against Khan Sahib'.[55]

Towards end-July 1942, New Delhi was 'getting nervous'[55] about Congress activities all over the country and wanted George Cunningham 'to arrest everyone and notify everything as unlawful associations'. The governor's immediate reaction: he wanted 'to ignore hot air' and would not arrest people 'before Congress have shown their hand'. And that too 'only if force or violence were used'.[56]

Nor did the bugbear of the Quit India movement (launched on 9 August 1942) make any apparent dent. Cunningham's diary entry for 19 August would demonstrate how lightly he took the threat:

> I sent Khan Sahib a message a few days ago that if he meant to start on the slogan 'English leave India', he must come and say it to me first, in which case I would take him at his word and go off to England, taking Mrs Khan Sahib with me.[57]

As a matter of fact, a week prior to the formal launching of his party's Quit India movement, Khan Sahib 'came to bridge and was in very good form'. The governor asked him 'why Gandhi was taking this absurd line' to which Khan Sahib's laconic response was: 'what else can they do?'[58] Under pressure from New Delhi that the All-India Congress Committee and its working committee 'must be proclaimed' as a banned organization all over India, Cunningham's response was that this would be of 'no practical value'. For his part, he would not notify the provincial Congress committee, 'as they want me to do, certainly not to begin with'.[59] Satisfied that he was on the right course, Cunningham pursued his normal routine: 'went off to Kurram on the 4th, saw a full jirga of upper Kurram tribes . . . only the fishing was a failure'.[60]

On 12 August, the governor-general sent Cunningham a telegram saying 'I ought to arrest' all Congress leaders 'forthwith'. In reply, the governor 'put off with a soothing telegram'. It was widely noticed that the governor had not changed his earlier tour plans because of Congress. Thus he took, as arranged, a fishing holiday in Kashmir, 19 August through 10 September, and went along with his other schedule as well.[61]

How lightly he viewed the political threat may be gauged from his diary entry for 13 September 1942:

> Congress had a meeting today in which they are said to have decided to picket courts intensively and by force if necessary. Date unknown. As Khan Sahib, however, had promised to come and dine and play bridge with me tomorrow it is difficult to believe they really mean business.[62]

The ex-premier did come to dinner and bridge wearing, Cunningham noted, a shirt 'with the faintest suggestion of pink' which, the governor deduced, 'satisfied his (Khan Sahib's) obligation to the Red Shirts'. Cunningham's clear perception was that Khan Sahib 'himself was against all kind of trouble' but he was somewhat at the mercy of Abdul Ghaffar Khan, Qazi Ataullah and others 'who are trying to push him into the forefront in order to get him into trouble'.

Cunningham, for his part, reasoned that it was prudent 'to allow him (Khan Sahib) to remain in the forefront, as we know that he will do nothing extreme'. Meantime, thanks to his refusal to be provoked, the governor was glad serious trouble over picketing of courts had receded.[63]

Even on the eve of arresting Badshah Khan (at Mardan, on 27 October 1942), Cunningham was not sure 'if this was (either) wise or necessary'. Meantime, the governor's informants gave him to understand that Khan Sahib was 'considering ways of gradually reducing Congress activities to vanishing point'. At the same time, the ex-premier was not altogether inactive, undoubtedly because of his firm conviction that before long his party would 'have won their battle with Government and be in power again'.[64]

All in all, it was a happy combination of a governor who was not easily rattled and an ex-premier who was far from being a political activist. Between them, they kept the Frontier at peace. Cunningham undertook tours through Peshawar and D I Khan districts—'the heart of Abdul Ghaffar Khan's country'—where he was 'enthusiastically received and heard never a cry of "Inqilab" '.[65]

Nor was Cunningham's low-key if deliberate, and non-confrontationist, approach to men and events, confined to his dealings with Congress on the political front. For in his day-to-day contacts with New Delhi too, he kept his cool and rarely, if ever, was the one to precipitate matters. Much the same held true for his dealings with the tribes across the province's administrative boundary where, during World War II years, he was to come into intimate contact with Olaf Caroe, then Foreign Secretary in the External Affairs Department. Some of Cunningham's diary entries are sufficiently eloquent in this regard and make for interesting reading:

28 April 1940

Got a telegram from Caroe saying that a conference would be necessary in Simla to discuss the future of the Ahmadzai salient. I wired back and said that a conference would be completely pointless.

14 May 1941

Discussed with Caroe all the various schemes for which the Government of India have offered me more money on the 'secret services', etc. side. . . . Being somewhat alarmed the Government of India, as usual, are feeling very generous.

4 April 1943

In the afternoon a very good jirga of all the Kurram tribes. I had hoped to be able to announce to them there would be no increase in their land revenue. Caroe had been stupidly obstinate about it and in the end the Viceroy gave them a general promise that their revenue would not be much increased; it really came to the same things but has less effect.

6 April 1943

Jirga of all the Maliks . . . I spoke to them for sometime, roughly on the directions indicated by the Viceroy. Caroe had been most troublesome about this speech . . . I had soothed him by 'stiffening', as he put it, the Viceroy's reply but I didn't keep to this in talking to them.

11 July 1944

Sheikh (Mahbub Ali) arrived . . . I tried to get his views on the future administration of the Frontier in the event of Dominion Status being given to India. His contribution was that there should be a Frontier state comprising NWFP, Baluchistan, and probably part of Sind and the Punjab (in some rather vague way, but I gathered financial) HMG would be partly responsible.

17 July 1944

(Discussion on Frontier administration after Indian independence) with Nishtar.[66] He said the NWFP should definitely not be under an independent government. He assumed that it would be part of Defence, possibly under the Viceroy or Commander-in-Chief. When I asked him if it would be a good thing for the tribes to be brought under the provincial government, subject to the Governor's individual judgement, he said he thought it would be an excellent idea—better than having it purely under Defence.

Happily for the province, all through 1943 and 1944, the tribal situation continued to be peaceful or, as Norval Mitchell was to put it, 'by Frontier standards extremely satisfactory'.[67] At an Orakzai jirga at Hangu (3 April 1943):

> They said their piece and I [GC] spoke to the jirga on His Excellency's general directions, although I did not keep very closely to the text. At the end, some men got up and tried to start asking for doubled allowances, but I told the Viceroy they were only praying for the success of the British arms![68]

George Cunningham's personal role in managing the Wazirs and the Mahsuds during the critical phase of the war, in 1943-4, deserves a mention. With the help of a distinguished band of political officers, he displayed an innate skill and wisdom in this endeavour. The odds were unfavourable especially in that the Fakir of Ipi was a major source of trouble, generously funded, and resourced as he was by Japanese as well as German agents. Indian politicals on the other hand had to forswear all military operations because of the exigencies of the war in the campaign in Burma which had threatened the safety of the Raj in the east.

In the event, peace was maintained and even though Ipi was using his 'malign influence' in North Waziristan, nothing of consequence emerged. Happily for the governor and his province the 'inflammatory material' around the old boundary dispute between the Mahsuds and the Wazirs near Razmak 'did not actually ignite'.[69]

III

From the tribes and their jirgas, it may be useful to turn to political developments in the settled districts if only to round off the picture. Broadly, in consonance with the Raj's overall policy of installing non-Congress governments in provinces where the Congress had quit office, an effort was mounted in the Frontier too. The tactics employed in Assam, were replicated. In Peshawar, by April 1943, the number of effective members of the Provincial Legislative Assembly had slumped to 35—with 8 Congress members behind bars and 7 unfilled, vacant, seats. In the event, the League leader, Aurangzeb Khan, managed the support of 22 members and in a ramshackle coalition with some splinter Hindu-Sikh groups was sworn in, in May 1943.[70] Cunningham noted that the new ministers were 'almost painfully anxious to fall in line with every suggestion' he made and the premier 'profuse in his promises of loyalty and desire to administer wisely'. Far from advising him, Aurangzeb Khan sent every file back with the inscription: 'I solicit the advice of HE the Governor'.[71] Cunningham, therefore, found himself giving one or another of his ministers 'a piece of my mind', telling them, he wanted 'deeds and not words' while the latter went back 'rather pale' after the dressing down.[72]

Soon the ministry's contradictions began to surface. In July, it lost two Hindu seats in byelections but damage was contained in that one of the newly elected members was already behind bars.[73] In August, there was a serious talk of ousting the League premier by forming a 'central party' that would take office. Happily for Aurangzeb, Cunningham was hostile to the idea which he labelled 'impossible . . . at present'.[74] Nor had the League been averse to 'a good deal of dirty work' on the eve of a session of the legislature scheduled for August. To no one's surprise, the ministers lacked in public esteem: 'they could not keep secrets, pandered to their friends and were of doubtful honesty'.[75] The governor himself told the premier that he listened 'too much to petitions instead of sending them to the concerned officer for report, (and) interfered regarding postings and promotions', while allowing MLAs to meddle in the day-to-day administration.[76] Earlier, he had warned Aurangzeb that 'it was beneath the dignity' of ministers to interfere in petty details of administration 'such as giving permits for export of grain, sugar etc'.[77]

Cunningham's plain speaking to his League premier was remarkable for its bluntness:

> I told Aurangzeb this morning that he really must start releasing some of the MLAs in jail. I told him that the whole province was being *badnamed* over the thing. He said he would consult his colleagues but I told him that I really meant it. There is no doubt that the name of the Muslim League administration is simply mud nowadays owing to the scandalous way in which they buy votes.[78]

A couple of months later with Aurangzeb still dilly-dallying and dragging his feet as it were, the governor was not a little upset:

> Having promised me ten days ago that he had actually released four of the Congress MLAs he has now, I have learnt, said that he was keeping them on parole in order to get an agreement out of them and may send them back again. I told him I would refuse to agree to a further 'cat and mouse policy' like this. He showed me the draft agreement he was trying to get out of them, a ridiculous agreement asking them, as a 'People's Party' a rather vague chance of being allowed to start some cooperative stores. I told him that he must let me know definitely on 1st June the action he proposed. I spoke to him in terms not usually used to a Prime Minster.[79]

Thanks to its internal bickerings and extraneous pressures, the uneasy League-Akali coalition was finding it increasingly difficult to continue.

On 12 March 1945 it suffered a decisive defeat in the legislature, worsted by a convincing margin of 24 to 18. Two days later, Khan Sahib came to inform Cunningham

> that Abdul Ghaffar Khan and he had decided to form ministry. He wanted me to release Abdul Ghaffar Khan at once but I refused until he had himself taken office. He is evidently going to have difficulty with Abdul Ghaffar Khan over the appointment of Qazi Ataullah. Dr. Khan Sahib thoroughly distrusts the Qazi.[80]

As it was, the 3-member Khan Sahib ministry, sworn in on 16 March, did *not* include the Qazi. Cunningham was pleased no end that his earlier decision not to ban the Congress in the province had stood him in good stead. For 'if he had declared the Congress an unlawful association' straightaway, the governor reasoned, 'we could have been in the same trouble as other provinces and Congress would certainly not have formed a ministry here'.[81]

On 20 March 1945, Governor-General Wavell had written to Secretary of State Amery about a sealed letter reportedly sent by Gandhi to Khan Sahib from his Wardha ashram. Earlier, Khan Sahib had made a strong representation to his party leadership. But with some of the Congress leaders still behind bars, it fell to the Mahatma to sort out matters. Allegedly the letter in question permitted Khan Sahib to accept the governor's invitation to form a government in the province.[82]

It is likely that the Frontier Congress had sought this permission as early as February 1945. Gandhi was cagey and 'would not give any definite instruction except that he was opposed to return to Governor's rule'. In other words, he had left the ball squarely in the court of the Khan brothers.[83]

Two developments directly relevant to the formation of the second Khan Sahib ministry deserve to be taken note of. The first was the winning over of some fence-sitters from the Aurangzeb Khan outfit who had crossed over just before the legislature convened for defeating the no confidence motion referred to earlier. One of them, Raja Manocher Khan, was later rewarded with a ministerial office.[84]

Another hurdle remained to be overcome. It was an assurance—not readily forthcoming—that, in office, Congress would 'cooperate wholeheartedly in the prosecution of the war'. After a party deputation had met Abdul Ghaffar Khan in jail and pleaded with him to allow a ministry to be formed, Khan Sahib is reported to have held forth the necessary assurance 'privately' to the governor. This cleared the way for him to assume office.[85]

Although, in retrospect, this might appear as a relatively smooth affair it was, in actual fact, far more complicated. The harsh truth is that the rank and file among Congressmen, and the Khudai Khidmatgars, were far from enthusiastic. They are said to have been 'taken aback' and 'resented' the haste with which the ministry had been formed.[86] Three Congress leaders who had met Badshah Khan in jail—Ali Gul Khan, Arbab Abdul Rahman and Mehr Chand Khanna—carried the clear impression that even though he did not oppose the move, Badshah Khan did not endorse it either. Convinced that it would be a government without real authority, for now that the war had been nearly won, Whitehall would only accept an administration that would toe its line. In the final count, it would thus appear, the Khan Sahib ministry came into office between Gandhi's 'negative assent' and Badshah Khan's studied indifference.[87]

All the same, New Delhi's initial reaction to Cunningham's handiwork in Peshawar was not exactly an endorsement. As a matter of fact, after a number of exchanges at the highest level, Khan Sahib was persuaded to issue a public statement to the effect that 'when I accepted office I did so with the full intention of running the administration . . . at present this involves participation in the general war effort'.[88]

Meanwhile Jinnah who was not unaware of the exchanges between Peshawar and Wardha is said to have been 'livid' with rage over the replacement of a League ministry by a Congress outfit. But 'personal frailty', his biographer informs us, made it impossible for him to journey to the Frontier. One wonders though what difference his visit would have made any way, for the Congress had demonstrated its *majority* on the floor of the legislature while clearly Aurangzeb's *minority* government had survived in office owing largely, if not wholly, to its continued, if unethical, detention of an unbroken phalanx of Congress Party legislators. In any case, Jinnah, as was his wont, let himself go in his message on 'Pakistan Day' (23 March):

> It is not possible that any Mussalman who has got the slightest self-respect and an iota of pride in him, can tolerate a ministry in a Muslim majority province, which takes its orders from and is subject to the control of Gandhi at Sewagram or the Congress who are deadly opponent [*sic*] to all Muslim aspirations and their national damand.[89]

IV

Against the background of warm, almost intimate, relations that had developed between Cunningham and Khan Sahib, the formation of the second Congress ministry was a landmark. 'Neither', a close observer of the political landscape has noted, 'was greatly interested in technical formalities, nor did they care much for all-India issues'. This augured well for the political health of the province for 'as long as Frontier politics retained their informal, almost parochial character', the province remained a model of political calm and tranquillity.[90]

Not long after he had taken office, Khan Sahib complained to the governor about lack of cooperation from the provincial police. He also took the opportunity to confide in Cunningham about 'some interesting things' relating to the Quit India movement:

> when messengers or deputations had come to the Frontier . . . from the extreme Congress groups in Bengal, and had tried to persuade Red Shirts to blow up bridges etc. Khan Sahib said he had refused absolutely to allow this, and I have no doubt this is true. One more proof of how wise we were not to arrest all Congress leaders. He (Khan Sahib) was positive that most of the disturbances was done by these extremist groups in Congress, and was not organised by the real Congress High Command.[91]

As may be evident, the governor found the new ministry 'much more sensible and business-like' than its League counterpart whom it had succeeded.[92] On 12 September 1945, Cunningham had 'a long talk' with his premier on the 'future management of the tribes' when a singular identity of views emerged.

> His [KS's] main points were that they should come under the provincial government; that they should send one or two representatives from each tribe to the Assembly; that we should not impose ordinary administration but that they keep their Serishta going; that the great cause of all border trouble was the hard and fast administrative border and we should aim at linking each tribe with its adjacent district; and there is nothing complicated about the internal organisation of a tribe, nor had there ever been, at any rate no sort of expert from outside is required to investigate this. In fact very much my own views.[93]

A word on the elections in the cold weather of 1945-6. Ever since the breakdown of the Simla conference (June 1945), the Muslim League in the NWFP had considerably boosted its propaganda for Pakistan and the two-nation theory. There was now open talk of '*Mussalmanon ki hakumat*' (literally, 'government of Muslims') while Muslim traders and wartime contractors were sought to be rallied behind the landed aristocracy that was the stronghold of the Muslim League. Contingents of students from the Aligarh Muslim University and the Panjab poured into the Frontier for the League propaganda while Islamia College, Peshawar, and other

Muslim educational institutions were temporarily closed down, to enable Muslim students join the League campaign. There was, the Congress alleged, both overt as well as covert support from British officials. And the League ascendancy appeared only too pronounced in Peshawar, as well as in such non-Pakhtun areas as Hazara.

Jinnah's visit in November 1945 was a big boost to the League campaign. The Quaid's unambiguous declaration that a defeat for his party would reduce Muslims 'to the condition of untouchables' attracted considerable sympathy. Among deserters from Congress ranks who trooped into the League fold was Abdul Qaiyum Khan, then deputy leader of the Congress Party in the Central Legislative Assembly in New Delhi. The League's decision to contest all Muslim seats, 33 rural and 3 urban, showed its overwhelming confidence in securing sizeable electoral gains.[94]

Another plank in the League propaganda was to dub Badshah Khan, as well as Khan Sahib, as agents of the Hindus. Sadly for the League, it did not register; it was perhaps a little too early for the electorate to realise—as the League stressed—that its objective was to keep the province out of the hands of the Hindus or their agents. By the end of 1946, this sort of argument had gained greater force as the relentless process of communalism took a firmer hold on the Pathan psyche. At the start of the year, however, the Pathan voter's principal concern appeared to focus on such issues as food supplies and other controls which the Muslim League ministry had completely bungled. In the event, the voter appears to have given a second chance to the Congress.

In sharp contrast to the boost Jinnah gave to the League campaign, the Congress was handicapped by AGK's initial hesitation, both in terms of ministry formation in March 1945 and the electoral battles waged later in the year. Badshah Khan's personal lack of faith in constitutional or parliamentary activity was well-known and a change of heart to lend a hand to the party campaign came a little too late in the day (December 1945). To start with, his decision not to work for the elections had Gandhi's support. And he stuck to this position despite an appeal by the Congress Party's central parliamentary board which oversaw all election activity.[95] What brought about the change finally was the clear impression Badshah Khan gained that official machinery was geared up for worsting the Red Shirts; that students of Islamia College, Peshawar, as well as the Panjab and Aligarh Muslim universities were working *in tandem* as it were. 'At the behest of British authorities', some colleges and schools in the province had been closed down to boost the League propaganda campaign. Nor was that all. 'Many girls led by the society ladies . . . also canvassed' support and some English women had approached voters in favour of the League.[96] It was the sight of English men and women 'actively participating' in the election campaign on behalf of the League that is said to have finally persuaded Badshah Khan to jump into the fray.

A contemporary English observer has noted that the remark about his compatriots taking an active part seemed interesting although he could not imagine their being involved in any propaganda campaign on behalf of the League.[97]

As Badshah Khan viewed it, issues were unambiguous. For the League, it was a question 'of Hindus or Pakistan, Hindu or Mussalman, Islam or Kafir'. 'Will you choose a mosque or a temple?', the Leaguers had asked the voters.[98] Happily, AGK noted, unlike Muslim voters in other parts of India, the Pathans had political sense and refused to be misled by empty slogans. And even though the Raj and its henchmen had put all their weight on the side of the Muslim League, the latter was worsted at the hustings.

The League's advocacy of Pakistan was pronounced and yet any precise definition of that elusive goal had been scrupulously avoided. All the same, Jinnah's call for the Muslim vote was forcefully echoed by the Pir of Manki who evoked the Shariat and pointed to the faithful's 'only one path': to cast his vote in favour of a representative of the Muslim League. To support the Hindu Congress or any other party, the Pir averred, was tantamount to treachery to Islam; more, it came into conflict with the 'unanimous opinion' of the ulema. In sum, the League's campaign was for the achievement of Pakistan and its propaganda posters openly proclaimed that fact. It portrayed its Congress adversary as 'Hindu agents', bent on enslaving the Pakhtuns and thereby posing 'a challenge to the faith and honour' of every Muslim.[99]

What helped the League no end was the overall communal polarisation which was so evident by the close of 1945. And with a steadily growing antipathy between educated Muslims and Hindus, the League's ranks were unduly swollen.

In sharp contrast to the Muslim League's sectarian approach, the Congress appeal was broad based. The party slogan, 'Pakhtunistan', was vaguely defined as independence from British imperialism against an exploitative Khani elite. It insisted that the Frontier's khans, jagirdars, title-holders were more interested in their own advancement than in the Pakhtuns' national cause. Badshah Khan stressed that the battle was 'between the Nation and the *Firingis*'; that there was, in fact, no third choice. Those who opposed the Khudai Khidmatgars were those who had always supported the British.[100]

It should follow that the Congress lumped the League and the British together to cast doubts on its rival's Islamic appeal. Not only the League but also the image of Pakistan itself, Congress spokesmen stressed, was the creation of the British. Happily for it, Pakhtun ethnic loyalties proved stronger than their communal consciousness for Islam as yet formed a subordinate part of their identity. It would thus appear that the Congress by and large ignored the subject of Pakistan and concentrated on social and economic issues, and the stinking corruption of the Muslim League government of Aurangzeb Khan and of the officials with whom it had forged an unholy alliance.

Understandably, the Congress election strategy was to help, and support, non-Congress candidates wherever its own name was deemed a handicap. Again, the party depended less heavily than did the League on influential family or tribal linkages.

In his fortnightly report of 9 October, Cunningham noted that in comparison with the League, the Congress had 'better organisation and more money'. He added that the League's electoral chances were dependent on the 'effort their central command is now making to improve local organisation'.[101]

Sadly, the rejuvenated Frontier Muslim League was dominated by the same group of people as earlier and they remained as bitterly divided among themselves as ever before. The newly-inducted, renegade and high-profile Abdul Qaiyum's sole guiding principle appears to have been that all League-sponsored candidates should be loyal personally to him. Riddled with disgruntled elements and handicapped by its own ideological pretensions, the League lacked any worthwhile machinery to conduct its campaign. Besides, there appears to have been no co-ordinated effort, with each candidate more or less running his own show.

A further handicap was that most of the League candidates were drawn from the wealthy and aristocratic families who boasted 'grundi' ties, wealth and social standing. A keen observer has noted that the League candidates' list 'read like a selection from a Who's Who' of the Frontier's 'wealthiest, most aristocratic families'.[102] In the final count, the League's propaganda line was that the Congress was interested only in establishing a Hindu Raj in the country and that its Frontier outfit, subservient to the all-India body, was only a minor agent or adjunct of the parent body; the Congress, that it was the champion of the Pakhtun cause against the British and their Muslim League henchmen.

A word here about the election, and electioneering, as viewed by an old Frontier hand, the provincial governor, Sir George Cunningham. On

NEW BROOM SWEEPS CLEAN

Shankar, in the *Hindustan Times* (New Delhi), 7 September 1945.

20 September 1945, the latter recorded a conversation with 'an old friend', Arbab Muhammad Abbas:

When I said that no educated Muslim seemed likely to believe in Pakistan in the sense of dismemberment of India, he said that he never heard of such a foolish suggestion; Pakistan must of course remain under a central Indian Government. I said that if that was so somebody ought to be bold enough to say so publicly, as otherwise the coming elections would be fought on an unreal issue. He said 'Yes' but it was a useful *bahana* to keep up against the Hindus.[103]

A few weeks later, on 17 October, Sardar Ajit Singh 'Sarhadi' told Cunningham that 'no Muslim believed in it (viz., Pakistan) as a dismemberment from the rest of India', a view, the governor noted, which was later confirmed by Ghulam Rabbani.[104] Again, on 3 November, Pir Baksh came to see him, 'the first time for a long while'. 'He agreed', Cunningham inscribed in his diary, that the Pakistan cry was unreal at present, that for the 'average Pathan villagers', a suggestion of Hindu domination was 'only laughable'. Yet the danger was that ignorant Muslim masses might read more into the Pakistan slogan than the League leaders intended. He also agreed with his interlocutor that until Pakistan was properly defined, elections would be unreal and inconclusive.[105]

At Bannu, on 19 January 1946, the governor spent a whole day meeting people. 'The election campaign is fiery', he noted, 'and all the Muslim members are killing sheep in order to get votes. Apparently, ten votes per sheep. One man is said to have killed ninety-three in the last week or two.'[106]

Nor would Cunningham accept at its face value his premier's complaint about the alleged partiality shown by officers in the elections:

He [Khan Sahib] told me with some amusement how Dring a few day ago had referred to the Muslim League as 'our party'. When I remarked that Indian officials seemed now to be all Muslim Leaguers, he said the 'they only say they are Muslim Leaguers to please their British officers'. I can hardly believe there is much truth in that because a lot of officials tell me that they are Muslim Leaguers, and they quite well know that I make no distinction between Congress and Muslim League.[107]

Keen observers of the election scene noted that neither political party, much less its programme of action, seemed to matter much to the average Pathan voter. That the latter's principal orientation was personal factional feeling or the more familiar *parajamba*.[108] In the wake of the latter charge that the 1946 elections did *not* represent a decisive win for the Congress, it is worth noting that the 1945 revision of the electoral rolls of 1937 (with voter qualifications remaining unaltered) had given the right to vote to almost twice the earlier number, or about 20 per cent, compared to a bare 10 per cent in 1937. The new electoral rolls, it has been suggested, included virtually the entire adult male population, barring women and children.[109]

Election results were revealing . The Congress won in 11 out of 12 minority constituencies, losing a solitary seat to the Akali Dal in Peshawar. It captured 19 out of 27 Muslim seats that it contested; its ally, the Jamiat-i-Ulema-Hind, in D I Khan, annexed 2 while the League took 17 seats. In the Frontier's Pakhtun regions, Peshawar, Kohat, Bannu, Tank tehsil of D I Khan, the Congress Party won in 17 out of a total of 19 territorial constituencies that it contested, losing the other 2 by slender margins. It also lost the landholders' seat in the Peshawar valley. The aggregate of the Congress and the League votes in these constituencies speaks eloquently, of the Pakhtuns' preference for Congress. Overall, the party garnered 51.9 per cent votes in the Pakhtun constituencies and 57.71 per cent in the 20 seats that it contested.

The figures for the League were 39.40 and 37.45 per cent respectively. It should follow that the League emerged as representative of the province's non-Pakhtun Muslims: winning 8 out of 9 seats in Hazara; 2 out of 3 urban seats and in both the landholders' constituencies. From Hazara alone it took 10 out of the League's overall tally of 17 seats.[110]

These figures notwithstanding, the Congress Party's victory was not as 'decisive' as its protagonists suggested, nor the League's defeat as total as its detractors charged. From its pre-election tally of 27, the net gain for Congress was only 3, and with the Jamiat's support, 5.[111] But it may be noted that the franchise was restricted, with only about 20 per cent of the provincial population having the right to vote and only 71 per cent of those eligible exercising that right.

Later, in the post-election period as the Muslim League demand for Pakistan grew ever more strident, the Congress claim that it had won the 1946 elections with the Pathans decisively rejecting Pakistan was not deemed exactly valid. 'This interpretation of the result', it has been suggested, 'was hardly correct' for the elections had been fought 'on other issues and the appeal of Pakistan among the masses was not really put to the test.'[112] This argument sounds specious at best; nor does it stand close scrutiny. The harsh truth is that from the Quaid downwards, the Muslim League had tom-tomed its undying allegiance to Pakistan's cause. That the call did not arouse the average Pathan voter to put the League into power was there for all to see. But the issue had been raised and put to the test.

Contrary to their public professions, the Congress ministers, a contemporary observer noted, were 'much more prone' to intervene in executive decisions than 'in my particular experience', did their Muslim League counterparts. Thus, whereas Aurangzeb Khan had been 'soft and almost sycophantic' in his relations with British officials, the Congress ministers were tough and tended to be fearless, often reckless, in making accusations of administrative inefficiency or corruption. Oddly though, a committee on corruption set up by the Khan Sahib ministry was later allowed to go defunct. This, in the long run, was probably unfortunate because over the next few years relations between the government and its officials, especially Muslim, 'became more and more strained'. 'And it would no doubt have cleared the air' if the allegations on corruption had been investigated and action taken.[113]

This was especially true in the case of the unresolved accusations against Sheikh Mahbub Ali, Deputy Commissioner of Kohat, which were a factor in the charges levelled against him in his capacity as Political Agent, Malakand, during Jawaharlal Nehru's October 1946 visit to the tribal areas. Later the Congress government forced out a distinguished civil servant (viz., Arthur Wooller) who allegedly was the first victim of its political campaign. The incident itself made a British civil official seriously ponder whether there was 'really much future' for any of them in the province.

Noble highlights the case of Bhanju Ram, Finance Minister in the second Khan Sahib administration, who had passed on to him (Noble) an 'oral instruction' about the disposition of cloth quotas for the district of D I Khan from where the minister hailed. For a time, Noble dodged the minister's emissaries and later when Bhanju Ram sent for him, excused himself on the plea of a prior engagement. Undeterred, the minister issued written instructions. Noble pleaded that these were 'not compatible with agreed policy lines' and when Bhanju Ram decreed a deadline by which his orders be carried out, played for time.

Rattled and at his wits' end, he sought out the chief minister on telephone. 'There was', Noble later recalled, 'an immediate explosion of fury on the telephone—rage directed not against me, but at the FM. . . . It was unfortunate that the latter could not hear it.' Khan Sahib was blunt and brutal: 'That man [viz., Bhanju Ram]', he declared, 'is a fool, I tell you: he is corrupt. Do nothing that he tells you.' The phone was slammed down. Noble was relieved no end: 'I did nothing', he noted, 'with a very light heart'.[114]

Nothing in his experience had 'such a strong sense of corruption' as the Bhanju Ram case, Noble later confided in his memoirs, and was happy was most apologetic: I had, regrettably, a previous engagement. Sharply, he had the nerve to push me: "Is it important? With whom are you engaged?" "Sir, I have to see the Brigade Major". Fortunately for me, this was a personage of sufficient standing to give pause even to ministerial authority at this stage in India's political history. I guessed that the Minister was wondering whether behind the meeting with the Brigade Major there might be some important matter affecting the Brigade Commander or even Army District Headquarters, matters into which he would have no authority to pry. He rang off abruptly. I heaved a sigh of relief: I was indeed to meet Major Wilson - on the first tee of the golf course. We had a regular series of excellent week-end games.

Next morning, I was in a dilemma. I knew that even a Scotsman's Sabbath was no defence against this particular minister when he was under pressure from contractors in his home town. It was my normal practice on Sunday to work quietly in the bungalow, and to write my letters home, but I felt too edgy to settle, and decided to put off the evil hour of confrontation by going out without telling my servants where I might be found. Having walked to the Club and sat for a long time by the pool I returned after lunch, still hot and frustrated, to find the Minister's orderly lurking in the shade of a tree in the garden. He had a letter, summoning me at once to the Minister's presence. There was now no escape. We had an uncomfortable interview, in which I made it clear that the orders he was instructing me to issue to the D.C. D.I.K. were not compatible with agreed policy guide-lines. I was given a deadline for the issue of the letter. (For some reason that now escapes me, timing was a factor in the affair, and I had been playing for time deliberately).

Next morning, the revised instructions were drafted, but I sat at my desk staring at the letter awaiting my signature, pondering what I should do. Not to sign was to disobey a Minister's order. I had made my objections very clear, and he had gone as far as he dared to make his instruction formal and specific. I decided that there was only one possible step: that was to ask for the Chief Minister's instructions. If he took action against me for disloyalty or disobedience, that would be that. Suddenly, it dawned on me that the thing to do was to ring him up: if I followed the proper procedure, which was to ask through his office for an interview, Bhanju Ram would certainly be alerted, and Khan Sahib's mind would be filled with all sorts of allegations unpropitious to me. I knew perfectly well that any formal action by me would be keenly observed within my own office and undoubtedly reported to the Finance Minister or his minions. So, without preliminaries, and without going through the usual channels, I contrived to get the Chief Minister on the telephone. He sounded surprised and even a little flurried, possibly puzzled about why a youthful Under-Secretary should be addressing him on the telephone. I simply said that I required his advice, as I had been given an instruction by the Honourable Finance Minister which I regarded as inconsistent with H.C.M's policy; I did not wish to disobey H.F.M. but would like to have H.C.M's assurances that this would not be incompatible with policy, and that policy had not been changed. There was an immediate explosion of fury on the telephone - rage directed not against me, but at the Finance Minister. It was unfortunate that the latter could not hear it. "That man is a fool, I tell you! He is corrupt! Do nothing that he tells you!" The telephone was slammed down. I had not even begun to tell Dr. Khan Sahib what it was that Bhanju Ram ordered me to do. I did nothing, with a very light heart.

I heard no more on the matter from Bhanju Ram, and for a long time had no interference from any other minister. Not very long after, there was a Cabinet re-shuffle, and Bhanju Ram was dropped, being replaced by a very much sharper man, Mehr Chand Khanna, formerly leader of the Hindu Mahassabha party in the Frontier, who had at last allied himself to Congress. The change had nothing to do with the trivial incident which I have described, but perhaps I was lucky in my timing of my phone call. At any rate, the story tells a good deal about relations between the I.C.S. and Ministers in the Frontier - and even more about Dr. Khan Sahib.

Later in my experiences in posts in the Secretariat there were to be other pressures from Ministers and some uncomfortable encounters, but none that I recall in which there was such a strong smell of corruption. It was inevitable that as the months passed in an atmosphere of expectations of independence frustrated by mistaken tactics and the stubborn selfishness of politicians' motives, ministers should question the actions and intentions of British officers who were now clearly subordinated to their authority for the first time in the history of the province. None of them ever seriously embarrassed me by trying to that none of the ministers 'seriously embarrassed' him by trying to involve him in 'dubious transactions or suggesting that the dishonesty of others had any connection with me'. There was, he none the less concludes, 'as much corruption and political bias' in governmental actions under Khan Sahib as in the 'bad performance' of Aurangzeb's Muslim League government.[115]

The third Khan Sahib ministry, sworn in on 9 March 1946 was largely, as its critics rightly charged, a family affair of AGK. The premier, Khan Sahib, was his elder brother; the revenue minister, Qazi Ataullah's daughter had been married to one of Badshah Khan's sons; the education minister, Yahya Jan, was his son-in-law. To add to this familial pattern, the newly elected member to the Central Legislative Assembly (to fill the vacancy caused by Abdul Qaiyum's return to the Provincial Assembly) at New Delhi was Ghani Khan, AGK's eldest son.

The solitary outsider was Mehr Chand Khanna, a front-rank Hindu politician of the erstwhile Hindu-Sikh Nationalist Party some of whose members had supported Aurangzeb Khan's ministry. Khanna had moved over to Congress on the eve of the 1946 elections and now emerged as finance minister in the Khan Sahib government. He was soon to become the principal target of Muslim League propaganda which charged that through him Hindus dominated the Frontier Congress and its government.

The transformation from the old ministry to the new was smooth as well it might, for the governor and his chief minister had established an excellent personal rapport. Two entries in Cunningham's diary may be rated as typical:

7 January 1946

Council meeting . . . in the middle Khan Sahib was called off by Mrs Khan Sahib who had slipped on a potato peel in the kitchen and refused to be lifted until Khan Sahib came and picked her up himself.[116]

27 February 1946

Dr Khan Sahib came and had a long talk in the morning. He seemed unperturbed at the rumours of possible dissensions in the Congress Party and also of trouble possibly spreading here from down country. He and Mrs Khan Sahib came to dinner and were in great form. . . .[117]

This was on the very eve of Cunningham's own departure and handing over of charge to his successor. Before he superannuated (2 March 1946), Sir George Cunningham had served the Frontier for exactly nine years.

'The solid and imperturbable conduct of the administration' under him was the subject of common comment. More, he was regarded with deep affection and respect by everyone including the most perfervid politicians, and the value of his service at the time was by some authorities estimated 'as the equivalent of two or more divisions of troops'.

His biographer noted that Sir George's 'absolutely dominant personal prestige' in the eyes and minds of six million Pathans, both cis- and trans-border, meant that when he told important men not to do something 'they simply did not do that thing'. A man of medium height with very broad shoulders, he gave 'the impression of invincible rightness', and within the limits of justice 'could be ruthless', qualities that the Pathans, 'appreciated and deferred to', no matter what their political views.[118]

On 1 March Caroe had arrived to take over as the new governor. Cunningham inscribed in his diary: 'Long talks with Caroe who seems a bit nervous of the job.'[119]

Apart form Cunningham's own impressions, a contemporary observer noted that there was 'an uneasy apprehension of the undercurrent of political instability' on the eve of Caroe's assumption of office. Not because of doubts about Caroe, as because of the 'familiar staunchness' for which Cunningham's record stood. 'After so many years', he was no longer there 'to calm and settle us.'[120]

V

Nervous or otherwise, Caroe's first encounters with his council of ministers were far from auspicious. For even though dazzled by the personality of his chief minister—'he is the most impressive Indian I have ever met'—he viewed his cabinet as no better than 'a family affair', and was far from happy about its doings. Thus within a week of his taking over, the governor was reporting to New Delhi: 'I have been shocked to find that the Ministers and particularly the Chief Minister are in the habit of trying to influence cases before the courts.'[121] Caroe found this to be 'extremely dangerous'.[122]

It may be of interest to note that the third Khan Sahib ministry took the oath and assumed office on the very day (viz., 9 March) Caroe wrote to the governor-general complaining about the excesses of his premier and his ministerial colleagues. The new governor had been himself sworn in less than a week earlier.

Noble has suggested that all this illustrated Caroe's 'extraordinary emotional capacity' that led him into 'misjudgments'. He truly liked Khan Sahib—as did Cunningham and most British officers. And yet that emotion hours in that beautiful situation would have been paradise! I still remember clearly how depressed I became. There were plenty of kind friends who tried to cheer me up, but the quiet relaxed atmosphere of the hill station was always one of family happiness, and this summer I was too conscious of my family's absence. I stayed with Dudley De la Fargue, who was now Chief Secretary. I had not know him well. He was kind and cheerful in a rather sardonic way. His own family had gone home to Britain, and his languid manner, which could exude charm when the mood took him, did nothing to jolt me out of my dejection. Oliver and Elizabeth St. John, living down in the cottage by Government House (he was still Secretary to the Governor) did their best to cheer me up, but they were having their own trouble at the time. Elizabeth suffered from severe headaches, attributed to sinus trouble and the altitude, but in fact probably the symptom of a neurological illness that too few years from then was to be fatal. As always, it was the Cunninghams themselves who did me most good. They truly were uniquely gifted in their handling of relationships with all the officers in the province. They brought me, the most junior, into the same relaxed circle of friendship that embraced the most senior; one was always alert to respect the dignity of their status, yet never felt patronised by them. They both seemed to have marvellous insight into one's feelings, and to know when and how to probe and when to leave alone. ~~Lady~~ Cunningham's Irish genius could charm secrets out of the most sullen introvert. During that fortnight I was often invited to Government House for meals, or to play bowls, or to join H.E. on his evening walk. Lady Cunningham learned a good deal about Barbara, and when she eventually arrived in Peshawar she was at once brought into the circle of friendship, and helped and encouraged as I always was.

One of my preoccupations for some time had been to find somewhere in Peshawar for us to stay. Accommodation was very scarce, because of the war time expansion of the European population and the number of military families. My post was one of these war time creations which did not have a bungalow associated with it. Soon I saw that the choice lay between a flat in a fairly modern and rather crowded complex or a tiny private cottage in the grounds of the Deputy Commissioner's house. This was originally orderlies' quarters, but these had been converted a few years before to accommodate the wife of a political officer stationed in tribal territory. In 1945 Arthur and Frances Wooller had had the tenancy at the confronted by Khan Sahib's 'stubborn mistakes' seemed to generate violent argument.[123]

The ministerial move to abolish the institution of lambardars by substituting some 'petty officials' in their place annoyed Caroe no end.[124] But is was his ministers' 'unwarrantable interference' with the courts which was to become his 'main preoccupation'.[125]

Some other traits of the chief minister were not welcome to him either:

He too has his durbars and rushes off on enquiries either in person or by deputing parliamentary secretaries when only one side of individual cases has been heard. The tendency is well-calculated to undermine the public service and I often wonder how far it is not deliberate policy on the part of Congress politicians.[126]

Before long, Caroe reverted to the issue of lambardars and put forth the view that the abolition of the institution was the most dangerous scheme on which his ministry had embarked. He dug up some old papers going as far back as 1938 when Lord Linlithgow's government in New Delhi had ruled that, insofar as they were public servants, the lambardars' rights attracted the special responsibility of the provincial governor.[127]

The lambardars apart, Sir Olaf complained that his ministry was always trying to get through ill-considered and unfair decisions in petty establishment cases and 'forcing me to consider whether to exercise my individual judgement or not'.[128]

A little later the governor 'unearthed'

a new form of ministerial interference with the law, consisting of orders by the Chief Minister to the Police to cancel cases before they came into courts—a procedure entirely unwarranted by the Criminal Procedure Code.[129]

To the percipient observer these were irritants enough to cause concern. And yet Caroe somehow seemed to assure himself, and his political masters in New Delhi, that 'in general' his relations with his ministers were 'cordial' and that he had succeeded in inducing them to accept his hospitality.[130] Such references though were few and far between while his almost interminable litany of complaints constituted a recurring theme. Thus:

My ministry continues to stretch the law. Unfortunately they have still in their hands the Frontier Crimes Regulation which allows them to withdraw cases submitted to Sessions and try them by Jirga and they will misuse this power in cases of political complexion.[131]

The governor was not unaware of the unfortunate fact that there was a provision in the law for the appointment of jirgas in the settled districts. And yet in the old days jirgas were always appointed by the deputy commissioner while the right had now been arrogated to himself by Khan Sahib.[132]

Before long Caroe was talking of a 'crisis' situation:

> The matter is one of service protection, tied up with that of interference with the courts. The administration is running down, crime is going up and revenue not coming in, due to rough handling of the administrative machine in its various parts.

And of his chief minister's ways of doing things, the governor was especially sour:

> The difficulty has been brought to a head by Khan Sahib's own predilection for tampering with the law in individual cases. The particular case which brought matters to a head was of attempted murder. Khan Sahib's general procedure is to hold informal durbars on criminal cases whether in the villages or in his house in Peshawar. He sometimes then orders bail to be withdrawn or cases to be retried, or alternately effects compromises, even in murder cases, and does this sometimes when the case is in the trial stage.

Soon there were rumblings of an impending storm,

> My discussions with my Chief Minister are conducted in rather a brusque Pathan manner, but we understand each other very well, like each other, and over this, as always parted in good humour.

Nor was Caroe oblivious of the fact that his ministers had a case of sorts. For

> One must recognise that the ministry are entitled to have the men they want in the key posts, but this must not involve injustice and I must maintain my special responsibility under Sections 52 and 342 of the Government of India Act for postings and transfers in reserved posts.[133]

Before long, there was talk of the chief minister's 'threatened resignation' over the governor's refusal to transfer a particular official. Not that Caroe relished the prospect. For

> If Khan Sahib were to resign, it would be more than unfortunate. Congress with their large majority would no doubt remain in power, and I should have to ask his number two, a very unsatisfactory substitute, to form a ministry.[134]

Somehow the crisis blew over but not without leaving some deep scars. In the aftermath, the governor confessed to 'continue to speak frankly' and urge the minister holding charge of law and order (presumably, Khan

Sahib) 'to observe the decencies and to recognise the dangers of becoming involved with the judiciary'. This though, Caroe recognised, was 'an uphill task'.[135]

Apart from judicial interference, there was tinkering with executive functioning too. It has been suggested that fortified by its success in the provincial elections, the Congress ministry intensified its intermeddling in the executive decisions of officers who had to carry out their policies and take responsibility locally for them. There was a growing lack of confidence between the ministers and the officials, especially at the district level. At the same time, in the provincial capital, the ministry acquired 'a sharper edge' from the sophisticated mind of Mehr Chand Khanna, the new finance minister. And although he and Qazi Ataullah, the revenue minister, had no love lost for each other, their rivalry had the effect of intensifying their intellectual powers with results that could be 'disconcerting'.[136]

Nor was Caroe in general, and the officials in particular, in love with the chief minister's ideological moorings which were pronouncedly left wing. Happily this was neutralised to an extent by Mehr Chand Khanna, the epitome of a successful man of business. There were practical difficulties too. Thus, even though the ministers believed in nationalization of large-scale industry, 'there was no industry for them to nationalise'![137]

VI

Against this backdrop of a mounting swell of acerbity in relations between the governor and his chief minister, another development of some significance now intervened. This was the assumption of office by Jawaharlal Nehru on 2 September 1946 as Vice-President in the Governor-General's Executive Council and as Member Incharge External Affairs and Commonwealth Relations Department. Nehru's portfolio *included* tribal affairs and tribal areas. At the provincial level though, the 'peace and welfare' of the tribes was an additional charge carried by the governor of the Frontier province in his capacity as agent to the governor-general (AGG). It was a vital charge and no one more than Sir Olaf was conscious of the awesome responsibility it entailed. 'If there had been tribal disorder in 1946-47', Caroe wrote years later, 'the transfer of power might well have been impossible.'[138] And in this he was not far wrong. Earlier (1946), the governor had placed on record his very strong feeling and clear perception that tribal affairs should not be handed over to a non-Muslim member of the viceroy's council.[139] The matter had been debated at the involve me in dubious transactions, or suggesting that the dishonesty of others had any connection with me. Apart from Dr. Khan Sahib, whose treatment of me was invariably avuncular and benevolent, the Ministers I saw most were Mehr Chand Khanna and Qazi Ataullah. The former was urbane and sophisticated. Widely travelled, he cultivated a Westernised style, and liked to play host at parties. These could be fascinating social experiences, but sometimes one felt uneasy in the company of subordinate officers, clearly at home in his house, whose normally constrained and courteous manners might be unexpectedly relaxed in circumstances more familiar to them than to me. I have no doubt that the fault lay more with me than with them. For all my liberal views, I was still affected by conventional British attitudes to rank, class and race, and there was something in the well-heeled pretentiousness of the Khanna household that brought my hackles up. But he was often interesting and challenging in conversation, and though I always mistrusted him, I rather enjoyed my dealings with him. He was clever, in the best as well as the worst senses of the word.

Qazi Ataullah was a more frightening proposition. He cultivated the coarse home-spun of the Ghandi tradition, and he was closely associated by marriage to Abdul Ghaffar Khan and by politics to the latter's Khudai Khidmatgar movement (the Red Shirts). One would never expect him to have any social intercourse with a European officer. His public career had been dedicated to the view that they were out of place in India. His manner was cold and severe. There came an occasion when I was visiting Bannu on official business, and he turned up at Circuit House. I was summoned to tea, and put through a most severe cross-examination about my business in Bannu, then about my work in the department in general, and finally about my views on such broad issues as world socialism, and about education as the salvation of the underprivileged. At the beginning of this conversation, I felt very much on the defensive but gradually it became more relaxed, as though barriers on both sides had been dismantled. His philosphy struck me as less home-spun than that of A.G.K., more derived from books he had read but never discussed very deeply with contemporaries. Afterwards I never felt so nervous about him again, though I realised that he was a potentially dangerous opponent, and a man who would never relax in the exercise of power. Altogether, a man to be wary of; but of his good intent I was now less suspicious.

It was in the nature of my new job that there would be unpleasantness in

Memoirs of Sir Fraser Noble (p. 249).

highest level of government and even though there was a measure of unease over the prospect, no viable way to split or divide the charge in the department of external affairs could be worked out. Nor was Nehru altogether unaware of these behind-the-scenes confabulations.

As has been briefly noted, the subject of external affairs *included* relations with the tribes of the Frontier, as well as with sovereign States overseas. The Frontier tribes were *not* British Indian citizens but protected persons whose independent status was recognised in a series of formal treaties historically binding on the British government in London and the individual tribes. Relations between the tribes and the British government were conducted between tribal jirgas and agents of the crown. The political officers who deputized for the crown were responsible to the provincial governor in his special charge as AGG, commonly referred to as the viceroy's 'other hat'. In this capacity, the governor was completely free from any responsibility to receive advice from his provincial ministers whose authority covered only the settled districts.

The pace of developments in the wake of the assumption of office by the Congress Party in New Delhi was hectic. And, as may be obvious, larger all-India issues and personalities were involved far beyond Sir Olaf's capacity to influence from his small if uneasy perch in Peshawar. He did not know Nehru personally but was determined to start on a good wicket:

> I wrote Nehru a short private letter of good wishes when he took office saying that I had been over six years in the External Affairs Department and it was more than thirty years since I first saw NWFP and I was sure he would find it all intensely interesting if difficult.[140]

And intensely interesting and amazingly difficult it proved.

Not long after he had taken over, Nehru announced his intention of paying a brief visit to Caroe's province and its frontier areas. Nor were reasons far to seek. As a matter of fact, a week or two before he took over, bombing operations had been launched against an offending tribe in Waziristan which continued even after he assumed office, and without his or his government's knowledge. Many a critic averred that the intent was to queer the pitch for Nehru and his party. The operations halted before long but raised important issues of policy. Senior officers in the External Affairs Department suggested that Nehru visit the area and meet local officials. A suggestion with which he 'cordially agreed'.[141]

A caveat though need to he entered. G C L Crichton, then Deputy Secretary in the Foreign Department, who was detailed to accompany the Honourable Member on his visit to the Frontier, confided in a friend that he rated the exercise as a 'death ride' and could foresee 'how futile such a gesture was' on the part of so prominent a member of the Congress Party and of the government. In retrospect, the visit turned out to be much more than futile.

Mitchell's own perception was clear and beyond the shadow of a doubt. To him, the events of those few days were 'a clear warning of the determination of the Pathans not to be yoked' to the Hindu governors of India.[142]

A word here on the August-September bombings of the tribal areas. Briefly, it all started on 21 June 1946 when the Political Agent, South Waziristan, J.O.S. (Jos') Donald (whom the writer knew intimately during his one-year, 1944-5, sojourn in D I Khan) was kidnapped. A victim of identity mix-up, he was waylaid by the Bromi Khel tribesmen, a section of the larger Shaman Khel Mahsud clan. The Bromi Khel's principal demand was for a larger share of government allowances as well as foodstuffs doled out to the Mahsuds, a demand the latter had stoutly resisted. Without the knowledge of their larger fraternity, the Bromi Khel took the law into their hands, forced issues and kidnapped Donald. They released him a couple of weeks later but refused to pay the indemnity government demanded for their misconduct. This invited aerial and artillery bombardment towards end-August and early September; their political repercussions led to Nehru's visit to the tribal areas in October.[143]

It is interesting to reconstruct the story of Donald's kidnapping and its aftermath from Olaf Caroe's fortnightly letters to the governor-general. To start with, Donald was kidnapped on 21 June by the Shabi Khel Mahsuds at a place on the Takkistan road, about 20 km below Razmak.[144] He was travelling with a close escort of Mahsud Maliks and Khassadars—who evidently betrayed him. For normally such an escort was quite capable of protecting its political agents against anything but a large tribal *lashkar*. The Shabi Khel, the governor added, had always been 'a centre of mischief' and had lately harboured some hostile Mullas and Pirs while Donald, whose father had spent much of his time in Waziristan, carried a 'good deal of his father's aura around him'. The Shabi Khel who had taken the political agent in mistaken identity for the garrison engineer had, for the record, treated him 'well and hospitably'.[145]

Within ten days Donald returned, thanks to the efforts of Packman, then Resident in Waziristan who 'did all the jirga work'. Donald was brought to Nathiagali, the governor's summer resort in the Murree hills, and stayed with Caroe for a few days. He was pressed not to return but insisted that he would, 'urging the moral compulsion that is taught to a rider after a fall'. Reluctantly, he was allowed to, but only for three months. A few weeks later, he shot himself while a letter, telling him of his transfer, lay unopened on his desk. Caroe was convinced that Donald himself 'was to blame' for taking his own life; Wavell too 'seemed to think so'.[146]

On 23 July, Caroe reported that a conference had been held in Rawalpindi with the army's northern command and the corresponding air group to map out the timing and strategy for punishing the Shabi Khel.[147] A couple of weeks later the governor intimated that the 'air prescription' of the tribe was 'going steadily on' and that reactions so far, both among the tribes as well as the rest of the province, had been small. Air action was such a well-known expedient in dealing with such situations that he doubted whether it would lead to 'any formidable political reactions' on the present occasion.[148]

On 23 August, Caroe reported that while air strikes had inflicted a lot of damage on the offending section of Shabi Khel, it was agreed that attacks be mounted on some of the other villages which were implicated so that they could 'bring their influence to bear' in favour of a settlement. Happily, he added, there was as yet no sign of political interest in the province 'in respect of what was happening in Waziristan'.[149]

In his letter of 9 September, Caroe reported that the Mahsud terms for settlement were not good enough so that the 'demolition one by one of some more Shabi Khel villages' was called for. To get results, 'we ought to be patient' he counselled the governor-general, and reminded him that 'it took us a year to deal with the Afridis' in 1930-1. And added that we 'must not expect quick results' now.[150]

Sadly for him, patience was in short supply. For the *Tribune* of 7 September spilled the beans. It carried a brief press statement by Abdul Ghaffar Khan intimating that he had 'just learnt that mass aerial bombardment' had been going on in Waziristan which was bound 'to create administrative difficulties and obstructions' for the new government in Delhi. He added that 'under no circumstances can one agree to this wholesale slaughter'. To contain the damage likely to flow from Badshah Khan's statement, the Associated Press of India was 'authoritatively informed'. More, the same issue of the paper reported prominently on its front page, that there had been 'no mass aerial bombardment nor wholesale slaughter' that the attacks were undertaken 'as a punishment to some sections of tribesmen in a limited area in Waziristan and after giving full warning'.[151]

Caroe for his part hastened to add that there had been no question of wholesale slaughter to which the Frontier leader had referred. 'As a matter of fact', he informed the governor-general, 'there had been no loss of life' except on two occasions when bombs dropped outside the prescribed area. And in both cases compensation had been paid.

Pushed to the defensive, Caroe added that the Mahsuds had admitted that the Shabi Khel had brought this 'just punishment' on themselves; that there had been 'no sign whatever' that they resented it or apprehensive of the present trouble 'spreading to them, let alone to other tribes'; that not only Donald but his Indian staff also had been kidnapped. More, he warned that if the new Indian government were going to 'set their faces' against the use of the air arm, 'they will let themselves in for military operations on a heavy scale' in Waziristan.[152]

Reasons for the bombing, a contemporary observer noted, were 'very complicated and deeply rooted in the lore and conventions' of tribal ways and the 'rules of the game' between them and the British political authorities. He reveals that Wavell himself had felt dubious about the ethics of the decision to bomb and sanctioned it only after a personal conference with the air officer commanding-in-chief, who had satisfied him both on the ability of the Royal Indian Air Force 'to hit the chosen targets and on the suitability of these targets'.[153]

It is also important to underline that the bombardment was *not* directed at human beings but at the 'towers' individually identified for destruction as punishment for particular subsections of the tribe. Again, ample early warning was given for the evacuation of the vicinity. In this case, the Mahsuds are said to have been amazed that aeroplanes could achieve such accuracy. In actual fact, 'Typhoons' had been used for the first time on the Frontier, firing rockets. Previously such towers had been extremely resistant to bombing.[154]

The precautions taken and the warnings given notwithstanding, it is only fair to note that the use of air power under the strict regulations of the grey book was deemed reasonable and effective up to a point. Indiscriminate or inhuman bombing was taboo. All the same, it had always roused strong passions in debate, both in England as well as in India. Was it a surprise then that Nehru felt 'uneasy' about the air actions mounted against the tribes even as he took over his new charge?

Nor was Nehru's personal unease or embarrassment the sole problem. In wilful misrepresentation of ground realities the propaganda blast unleashed against the new member in the governor-general's council heavily underlined the canard that the bombing was an effort of the Hindu Raj—which Nehru's new government allegedly represented—to make the tribes knuckle down. More, that the Khan brothers had hobnobbed with Nehru whose Hindu co-religionists were busy perpetrating untold atrocities on Muslims in Bihar and elsewhere.

Nehru's proposed visit was by no means his first to the Frontier even though, in retrospect, it proved to be his last. Earlier, in October 1937 and again in January 1938, he had visited the province and received a warm, even enthusiastic, welcome. Apart from the Khan brothers' ancestral home at Utmanzai, Nehru had during these visits repaired to the Khyber Pass as well as nearly all political centres in the province. To signal their warmth, the Afridis had kept 'beacon fires burning' at several points on the hill tops all through the night and which could be seen for miles around. In his speeches, Nehru had been critical of the Raj and its tribal policy which, he argued, had inflicted a great deal of damage and destruction, and yet not shaken the morale of the Pakhtun people. Again, the tribal territory had been invaded in furtherance of imperialist gains, nor was there any justification whatever for the huge waste of men and resources in which the Raj indulged. Both visits had been a resounding success with Nehru receiving tumultuous welcomes. 'At one place 300 tribal riflemen had surrounded him' while one of the Maliks offered him a goat—a signal honour; another placed his son at Nehru's feet. During his drive at Kohat, the Afridis honoured him by spreading costly red carpets on the road.[155]

In comparison to his earlier sojourns, Nehru's October 1946 visit was a study in contrast. The 1946 visit, as has been suggested, was undertaken at the request of Badshah Khan to enable Nehru to see things for himself; much the same advice, it may be recalled, had been given by senior officials in the external affairs department. In sum, the bombing of the tribal areas synchronising with the formation of the interim government had provided the occasion, with popular imagination wrongly holding Nehru's new regime responsible for the holocaust.

The visit was anathema to Sir Olaf Caroe in Peshawar. As early as 29 September, the governor had let it be known that he strongly deprecated the visit and dubbed it as 'a deliberate partisan approach to tribal problems'. Worse, in its wake, Caroe feared, he may not be able to 'discharge my responsibility for maintaining the tranquillity of the border'.[156] The governor's warning notwithstanding, knowledgeable officials in Delhi were satisfied that Sir Olaf was taking an exaggerated view of the matter, and that it was 'quite impossibly out of date' to suggest that Nehru keep away from the tribal areas. Governor-General Wavell was similarly persuaded and noted that 'we cannot obviously prevent visit'.[157] On the eve of the visit and, on Caroe's initiative, Wavell asked Jinnah to exercise the utmost restraint on his Muslim League hotheads in the province.

In retrospect, it is interesting to study the respective stance of the three major players. To start with, Caroe pleaded with the governor-general that Jinnah 'in generous fashion' should tell his followers that in so far as Nehru will be a 'guest' of the people of the Frontier, no 'counter demonstrations' be staged either on his arrival or during his tour.[158] Writing to Jinnah, Wavell urged that in view of the impending announcement of a Congress-League coalition government at the Centre, the Quaid would recognise 'how undesirable' it was that there should be 'hostile demonstrations against a member of the Government'.[159] Inimical, if not singularly hostile to such suggestions, Jinnah's brief if laconic reply was that in so far as the people of the Frontier viewed Nehru's visit 'with disfavour', it would be advisable to postpone it to a later date. He affirmed none the less that no instructions had been issued to the provincial League to stage demonstrations. This was being less than honest. For the Quaid had, in fact, given his 'approval' for such demonstrations.[160]

Whatever his other fears or failings, Caroe's assessment of the delicacy of the prevailing situation at this most critical juncture would be hard to falter. And times, for sure, were out of joint. On the morrow of Wavell's invitation to Nehru to form the interim government (6 August), Jinnah had announced the observance of 'Direct Action Day' and scheduled it for 16 August. In Calcutta, this black day was witness to the shameful 'Great Calcutta Killing' which, on conservative estimates, claimed 5,000 lives, with another 15,000 grievously wounded on the town's blood-stained streets.[161] This was only a curtain-raiser for worse things in Bihar—and later in the Panjab, and the Frontier itself.

Meanwhile, on 9 October, Caroe travelled all the way to Delhi to dissuade Nehru from his announced visit. Not that it helped.[162] Nehru noted that the governor had felt rather perturbed over his visit and 'did not like the timing of it'. For his part, in a letter to Khan Sahib, Nehru explained that he was not going 'for party or narrow political purposes but rather as a representative' of the new interim government to convey 'our friendly feelings' to the tribal people, and have informal talks with them. 'I do not propose', he affirmed, 'to discuss with them any detailed matters of policy or to commit myself in any way at this stage. I want to hear what they say.'[163]

Sadly for him, there had been a singular transformation in the ground reality. Until 1946 for instance, tribal interest in the Frontier's provincial politics had been slight, ranging from relations with Afghanistan, Persia and Turkey, and of course Russia to the strategies of the war against Germany and Japan. When, however, in the summer of 1946 it was realised

15A. Background to Nehru's Frontier visit.

Nehru visited the Frontier in the fortnight between Letters 15 and 16 in this series. On October 9th the writer went down to Delhi to try to dissuade him, using the argument that a visit at that juncture would not strengthen, but weaken, the Frontier Congress Government, for the flags of Islam would be unfurled. If Nehru wanted a united India, it would be wise to play a waiting hand. The Frontier Government was losing ground, and would lose further ground. (In the writer's mind, though not on his lips, was the parallel of the Emperor Akbar's Brahmin favourite, Birbal, sent by Akbar to control the Pathan tribes and killed by them in the passes of Swat and Buner in 1586). Nehru would not listen, saying that his friends told him he was more than half a Pathan by nature, and that it was his duty to back up his friends, the Khan brothers.

At the time the writer did not know that exactly the same advice was given to Nehru by Maulana Azad, the leading Muslim on the Congress High Command, and, it seems, by Gandhi himself. This is clear from Azad's own book.

Sir Olaf Caroe's Mss (p. 79A).

that the *Hindu* Nehru had assumed control of the advice given at the centre to the viceroy about tribal matters, their concern about Indian politics began to stir. The notion that there might be a *Hindu* master of their affairs, so long dismissed from their thoughts as ridiculous, now acquired a new significance. And the existence of a provincial ministry at Peshawar constituted by the Khan brothers who, their detractors never tired of insinuating, gave their children in marriage to infidels quickened tribal interest in the message of the Muslim League and its protagonists.

Nehru should have stuck to his resolve to keep out 'narrow political purposes'. Sadly, as his biographer affirms, Nehru's overt intent to see things for himself in the tribal areas was only a plausible excuse for the visit. Its clear purpose, S Gopal avers, was to 'undertake a flag march, as it were' across terrain which had 'cast its spell' over him.[164] Apart, no doubt giving a well-timed boost to the sagging morale of his beleaguered Congress colleagues. This too, in normal times, would have been understandable. But times were, in fact, far from normal what with a ballast of hostile, highly motivated propaganda that the bombing was only the first fruit of the Hindu Raj. In a fast developing milieu of mounting communal frenzy in other parts of the country, this wild canard vitiated the atmosphere no end. In the event, as he and his friends viewed it, Caroe's charge that the visit was 'a deliberate partisan approach' to the tribal problem may not have been very wide of the mark.

Caroe apart, Wavell too was far from enthusiastic about the visit. Initially, he had asked Nehru to consider taking a Muslim colleague with him 'to show a united front'. Nehru reacted, Wavell recorded in his *Journal*, 'without any enthusiasm, as was natural'. The viceroy, convinced that he 'could not well stop him', gave such comfort as he could to Caroe who, first in the line of battle, was 'chiefly concerned'. Both Caroe as well as Wavell had hoped that a Congress-League coalition government in New Delhi would assume office *before* Nehru set out on his tour and that 'a mandate from a coalition' would be a great gain.[165] Sadly for them, the League came into the interim government only *after* Nehru's return from the tour. In retrospect though, it is doubtful if it would have been any help, considering the overall political climate and the way the coalition was to function in actual practice.

It may be of interest to recall that Nehru's own colleagues, both in and outside of government, had been less than encouraging. Maulana Azad notes that there had been conflicting reports from the Frontier about the popular support which the Congress ministry in general, and the Khan brothers in particular, enjoyed. Nehru felt, Azad records, that he would been friendly long before. The orderly who met me at his house (the same house from which John Nicholson started his march on Delhi in the days of the mutiny of 1857) was another old friend. When our greetings were completed and I asked for the D.C., my friend said "spo tah tale dai", which means in Pakhtu "he has gone to the dogs". I had not spoken Pakhtu for six years and failed to catch the significance of the words. They seemed to comprise a good deal of prejudice and disrespect. Slowly, however, with the orderly's help, I understood. At this late date in the history of India the Peshawar Vale Hunt was still going strong. John Dring, D.C. Peshawar, was Master. And at that evening hour he was down at the kennels.

The Muslim League commanded overwhelming support from Muslims throughout India. Yet, as I have mentioned above, the Congress Party in the Frontier Province had secured a comfortable majority in the general election of January 1946. The flood of events, however, was soon to show that their hold on the people of the frontier was not based on fundamental political loyalties. While the Deputy Commissioner of Peshawar was in his spare time directing hounds and hunt members in perfect safety over the countryside, the horrific virus of communal riots in Eastern Bengal spread quickly north-west. The province of Bihar saw massacres of Muslims. Meerut in the United Provinces saw massacres of Hindus. So the mischief advanced north-west like an infection.

In October 1946 I went to Delhi, in my capacity as Financial Secretary, to attend two conferences as the representative of my Minister, Mehr Chand Khanna. I stayed as the guest of a friend in a house which was being shared by four or five senior officers of the imperial secretariat. One of these was Lieutenant Colonel G.C.L. Crichton, Deputy Secretary in the Foreign department. He came in early on my first evening and announced that he was off on his "death ride". He referred to the decision of Pandit Jawarhalal Nehru to visit the Frontier Province with his Deputy Foreign Secretary in attendance. Crichton, as an experienced frontier officer, knew how futile such a gesture was on the part of so prominent a member of the Indian Congress Party at that time. In fact it turned out much more than futile. The Muslim League staged a very aggressive demonstration tour the Frontier areas and assess the situation for himself. And as a matter of fact, both Azad and Gandhi—who, the Maulana affirms, 'supported my view'—opposed Nehru's plan for fear that it would give the 'dissident elements' an opportunity to organise opposition. There was the additional fact, Azad maintains, that a majority of officials in the Frontier were allegedly arrayed against the Congress.[166] According to Wavell, Sardar Patel too lent no countenance to Nehru's plans for a visit.[167]

The visit itself started on 16 October when Nehru arrived at Peshawar to a very large, and hostile, demonstration by the Muslim League and its supporters. He had to be escorted through the backdoor to prevent any embarrassing situation. Accompanied by Khan Sahib and Khan Abdul Ghaffar Khan, Nehru flew to Miranshah on 17 October; his meeting there with Waziri tribesmen was also attended by his two companions. Amid shouts of 'we do not want Hindu Raj' and would not tolerate any interference with our independence, the noisy demonstrations were repeated at Razmak which made Nehru remark that the jirgas assembled made for poor representatives of the people of the Frontier. From Razmak, the party flew to Tank and then on to an unscheduled visit to Jandola where the tribesmen gave Nehru a warm reception and brought in sheep as presents.

Earlier, at Miranshah, AGK is said to have accused the tribes of being mere pawns of the political department, mouthing words they had been tutored to utter. This made the members of the jirga so angry that they reportedly left the meeting without hearing Nehru.[168]

Later at Razmak, the Mahsud Maliks gave their visitor 'a very hostile reception' telling him that if they had any grievances, they would turn to Jinnah, and would have nothing to do with his Congress Party. Nehru wondered aloud as to why they were being so uncooperative considering the liberal allowances they received from New Delhi and accused them of being petty pensioners and slaves of the British. The Mahsuds stoutly repudiated the accusation, insisting that it was not they but the Raj who did their bidding. One of the Wazirs later wrote to Jinnah to confirm that he was the one 'who had made a speech' at the Mahsud jirga where apart from the resident and the political agent, Khan Sahib and AGK were present in the course of Nehru's visit to Razmak. Later, and for a change, the minuscule Shabi Khel (at Jandola) expressed satisfaction that they would receive compensation for the losses suffered in the recent raids.[169]

The Ahmadzai Wazirs lined the road at Wana, waving black flags. Their jirga became refractory and was ordered to be controlled by armed infantry. This deeply annoyed the tribe who, in retaliation, refused to attend. In the event, Nehru had to leave without seeing them.

At Tank, some hostile Muslim League sympathisers threw stones at Nehru and his convoy. The impromptu visit to Jandola, as noticed earlier, was marked by 'a small but friendly' Bhittani jirga.[170]

On 18 October, Nehru visited the Khyber. At Jamrud, the Afridis sitting a little away from the road 'waved shoes' and indulged in some sniping. After tea at Torkham, on the Indo-Afgan border, the convoy reached Landi Kotal. The tribal people squatting on the road there threw stones at Nehru's convoy, whereupon the political agent's guards opened fire to disperse the crowd. The glass screen of the car used by Nehru was broken, though no one was hurt. The Afridis had refused to see him; a small section who wanted to parley with their visitor, was overawed by the rest.[171]

The following day (19 October) Nehru was to arrive at Malakand. The Political Agent, Sheikh Mahbub Ali Khan, a great friend and admirer of Cunningham, had visited Peshawar on the eve of Nehru's visit to confer with the governor. AGK had been averse to the Malakand visit, but Nehru, keen on keeping to his itinerary, refused to budge. At the political agent's post, where the party camped overnight, a Khudai Khidmatgar leader had warned Badshah Khan that Mahbub Ali 'had collected a lot of goondas', clearly implying that Nehru's party should take adequate precautions. Next morning, a Red Shirt volunteer had arrived to inform Badshah Khan that a big tribal gathering had been kept ready to thwart Nehru's progress. Confronted with this information, Sheikh Mahbub Ali protested ignorance and insisted that as a Pathan he could not be 'so treacherous as to deceive' his visitors.

And yet that was precisely what he appears to have done. Throwing precaution to the winds, and relying implicitly on the Sheikh's word, Nehru and his entourage started on their return journey without even waiting for the police escort to arrive. The Sheikh was part of the convoy to start with but slipped away before long, leaving Nehru and his motorcade to fend for themselves. Even as they proceeded apace, the waiting crowd threw stones and later blocked the road by pulling a truck athwart. 'A stone hit me on the back', AGK recorded, 'and I felt dazed.' Meanwhile Khan Sahib snatched his jamadar's revolver and threatened to shoot any intruder whereupon the crowd dispersed. Later, he browbeat the truck driver who cleared the road.

Nor was that the end, for even as the convoy reached Dargai, there was a big crowd waiting to throw stones at Nehru and his party. 'I pushed my hand to shield Jawaharlal', Badshah Khan recalled, 'from a stone aimed at him. Another man lifted an earthen pot filled with night soil and threw it at us.' They made a detour, avoided the hostile country and reached Peshawar. AGK was to complain later that had he been given a free hand to make arrangements, all these ugly scenes and worse would have been avoided.[172]

Two small footnotes may be in order. To start with, Tendulkar's narrative based on Badshah Khan's version of events retailed earlier needs to be balanced by those of 'Benjie' Bromhead, Political Agent, Miranshah; Robin Hodson, then acting Political Agent, South Waziristan; and Major Mohammad Khurshid, his counterpart in the Khyber. Again, the courageous intervention of C G S Curtis, then Deputy Commissioner, Mardan, needs to be heavily underlined. It was he who insisted on diverting the party from the main road at the foot of the Malakand pass along a subsidiary canal road, away from the waiting hostile demonstrators. As a matter of fact, Curtis had been deputed to escort Nehru through his district to Malakand but when the latter drove off earlier than scheduled, he was temporarily left behind (answering, as he said, a call of nature). And even before he effectively caught up with the convoy, near the bottom of the pass, they were in trouble with Khan Sahib brandishing his revolver.[173]

It was believed that in diverting the party from its scheduled route, Curtis had saved Nehru's life. Sadly though, his reward was bitter: unfairly criticized and transferred from his beloved district work to an uninspiring job at the secretariat. His morale badly shaken by what he deemed to be unjust criticism from Nehru, and failure of support from Caroe. He later tendered his resignation. Nor was he alone. Every other political officer/agent, albeit not to the same degree, was suffering from a genuine lack of confidence as well as studied resentment at what they all viewed as Nehru's unkind if disingenuous remarks.[174]

As was to be expected, Indian press reports gave a prominent place to Nehru's 4-day visit to the tribal areas. And invariably made front-page headlines. Most stories underlined a 'plan to kidnap' Nehru; of the 'tutoring' of jirgas which made it impossible for him to meet independent tribesmen 'without the presence and influence' of the political agents (25 Mahsud leaders at Razmak made this allegation in a letter to Nehru and the latter confirmed receiving seven such letters); of the Political Department's anxiety to see Nehru's tour 'cancelled' *ab initio* and when it did take place 'mislead ignorant tribesmen' about its real purpose. Reporters also suggested that the highest political quarters in Peshawar 'knew what was going to happen even before' Nehru left on his Waziristan journey. And highlighted his statement that the Political Department may have 'hinted at' what it wanted and 'don't need to organise' things.

As between 19 and 23 October, the *Tribune* carried three leading articles: 'Pandit Nehru in No Man's Land' (19 October); 'It Must Become Tribesmen's Land' (20 October); and 'Bureaucratic Infection and Tribal Sore' (23 October). The burden of the paper's song was predictable. The opening gambit

> the behaviour and utterance of the hand-picked persons, who constituted the jirgas . . . acted like a trained and tutored lot. The hidden hand that brought about the ugly demonstration (at Peshawar) . . . has become fairly visible.

Interestingly enough the preceding editorial took an Associated Press of America correspondent severely to task for his suggestion that the firing at Peshawar was 'reckoned an unusual event' and that the general impression was that it was 'meant to show the tribesmen's opposition' to Nehru's visit. No wonder the paper rated as blasphemy the same correspondent's view that the 400 headmen gathered at Razmak by the Political Agency were 'truly representative' of the entire population of North Waziristan. And charged *inter alia* that the correspondent in question had been 'used as a publicity agent' of anti-Congress vested interests. More, it dismissed as 'sheer innuendos and insinuations' his considered opinion that in the Waziristan affair, Pandit Nehru had been the 'sinner' and the Political Department 'sinned against'.

The Indian Premier's (as it called Nehru) task was in fact, the editorial concluded, clearly cut out for him: 'remove the British imperialist incubus, make tribesmen really breathe freely, and link them up as a truly independent unit' with their Pathan brethren of the Frontier Province.

A day later, the *Tribune* was at it again:

> Pandit Nehru was destined before long to open a new chapter in the history of the relations between India and 'No Man's Land' . . . [and] convert this British Imperialism's Land into what may be called the Really Independent Tribesmen's Land. (20 October)

If only to reiterate what had been said earlier, the paper reverted to its theme song:

> Those who had allowed British Imperialism all these decades to keep them (the Frontier tribes) trammelled and to suck their blood merrily, smelt a rat in the visit of Pandit Nehru and the Khan Brothers and attacked them and inflicted injuries on their bodies. Every blow hurled at them was obviously a nail driven into the coffin of the Muslim League-British Imperialism Alliance. (The *Tribune*, 23 October)

For his part, Caroe had little doubt that the demonstrations against Nehru had been 'League organised'. Mercifully, the tribals were not armed but in so far as they gathered on the hill sides, the 'temptation to throw stones' proved irresistible.[175] This was dangerous because of crashing glass; no wonder Nehru and his companions sustained bloody noses, and chins.

Apart from police and constabulary guards, Nehru's convoy had to be escorted by troops. The position by the end of the tour, Caroe informed the governor-general, was such that Nehru 'could not go anywhere', outside of Peshawar Cantonment, 'without strong escorts of police and troops'. This was all the more striking in that the governor could boast of his moving about the province 'entirely without escort'.[176]

Though Nehru made no direct charge that all the political agents had been guilty, he did, however, point out that those in the Khyber (viz., Major Mohammad Khurshid) and Malakand (viz., Sheikh Mahbub Ali Khan), as well as the deputy commissioners of Peshawar (viz., John Dring) and Mardan (C G S Curtis), both English, had been 'unable to prevent' hostile demostrations.[177] Cut to the quick, Caroe's retort was that if Nehru believed that 'our Indian subordinates' were 'powerful enough' to organise opposition of this nature, 'he would believe anything'.[178]

This apart, Caroe was unhappy on other counts as well. He had warned Nehru not to take with him the leaders of one party, in this case, the Congress—which he did. Later, his own secretary in the external affairs department echoed much the same point of view, insisting that 'all of us' had always stressed the 'overall necessity' of a 'non-party approach' to the tribals. Proforma, Nehru too had endorsed this view. Yet, as Weightman underlined, 'HM (Hon'ble Member) was accompanied on his tour by the leader of the Congress party in the Frontier and by the Premier of the Congress Government of the province.'[179]

Partly to offset Nehru's partisan, one-party approach, Caroe had—on the eve of his tour—allowed Muslim League propagandists, including the better-known Mullah of Manki, a free run of the tribal areas. Since Nehru's tour, the governor had argued, was 'obviously intended to push the Congress cause', it would have been wrong to put any restraint on the Mullah.[180] As it was, Manki's tour proved to be the launching pad for a virulent campaign of calumny and hatred of which Nehru was to reap a bitter harvest.

Caroe had also been critical of Nehru's inept handling of tribal sensibilities by calling them 'pitiful pensioners', and read him and his colleagues a lesson or two in man-management:

These people—and in this criticism I include people like Khan Sahib—are far too intense to deal with tribesmen. They do not understand that a steady quiet bearing, turning off to a smile or a joke when tempers get frayed, is the proper way to deal.

The tribes, for their part, Caroe remarked, were far from happy with 'a Hindu coming down to talk to them from a position of real authority' and told Nehru that they rated Hindus as 'tenants and serfs' and therefore would have no truck with him. Caroe was outraged too by hostile and unfair comments on the political service. He charged Indian political parties of being 'far more authoritarian than any ICS officer had ever been', and commented on their tendency 'towards one-party rule and, when in power, to over-ride the law'. He was intrigued too by the fact that 'at critical junctures' Nehru set out on his own 'with preoccupied and published ideas', which made it difficult for him to adjust his attitude later.

Nor was the governor overly impressed with his visitor, being left with the clear impression that 'this politician of worldwide repute' was 'entirely without any element of statesmanship'. Further, matters such as 'timing, adjustment and quiet approach and a decision after weighing a great issue' were 'beyond' his ken.[181]

It wasn't the first time, that Caroe reverted to his by now time-worn theme song. Nehru's appointment with its power over tribal affairs, he reiterated, had been anathema to the Muslim League and persuaded the latter to send the Mulla of Manki—with Caroe's tacit approval (if not active connivance)—to rouse the tribes. If the present arrangement, with Nehru incharge of tribal affairs, was to continue, the governor further warned, there was bound to be disorder. The possibility of tribal risings, posing a grave danger to the peace of the country as a whole, was always there. His remedy, therefore, was to treat the tribes 'at least during the first part of the interim period' like the princely states and 'place their affairs in the portfolio of the Viceroy himself'. It was necessary, Caroe cautioned, that the 'nettle be grasped' and tribal affairs taken out of Nehru's hands, and, as a first step, to deal with 'all these matters in Council', thereby depriving Nehru of ploughing 'his lonely furrow'.[182]

At his end, Nehru had been unhappy too. On the morrow of his return from the tour he unburdened himself of all that had happened. At Peshawar airport: 'I cannot imagine that they (concerned officials) could not have stopped this exhibition of crude violence . . . if they had so wished'; the encounter with the tribal Maliks in Waziristan 'left a feeling of doubt in my mind . . . (that) there was no inherent improbability (about the whole thing) being stage managed'; at Jandola 'where my programme had been fixed rather suddenly, I had a warm welcome'; at the Khyber, 'no steps seem to have been taken to avoid' hostile demonstrations. At Malakand, 'whether it was incompetence or something worse', the political agent had shown himself 'to be completely unfit for any responsible charge'.[183] Above all, Nehru told Caroe and in no uncertain terms that

> there is a hiatus between you as Governor and the AGG and the provincial government and those whom they represent. There can be no cooperation when there is this lack of confidence in each other and a desire to pull in different directions.[184]

Reverting to his being placed incharge of tribal affairs, of which Caroe had (behind the scenes) made such a hullabaloo, Nehru revealed that before he took over he had been given to understand that his induction would be 'unwelcome' to the tribal people. Later, some meetings or jirgas in the tribal areas had expressed their disapproval. 'It was curious', Nehru concluded, 'that the tribal people should agitate themselves about a fact which was not publicly known and indeed which had not been finally decided upon.'[185] Unknown to him, Wavell had commented: 'It was always quite obvious that the Tribes would react strongly towards anything that suggested Hindu domination.'[186]

As if to dispel fears of alleged Hindu domination, Wavell mapped out his own tour of the tribal areas a few weeks after Nehru's return. 'The idea'—of domination by Hindus—'which is what they took Nehru's visit to imply is anathema to these people', the viceroy confided in his *Journal*. Besides, the morale of the services was low and there was a good deal of mistrust between them and the ministry.[187] Worse, the political officers in the tribal areas were 'extremely sore' at their treatment by Nehru and his party. They were planning an exodus as it were 'to get out as soon as possible', regardless of consequences. This, Wavell thought, would be tragic for here was a body of men 'as devoted to India as any in the services'.[188]

For British officers, Fraser Noble underlines, the immediate consequence of Nehru's visit was to impair their confidence and undermine their 'influence'. They were seen by the tribes to have been unable to curb 'the insolent arrogance of this Hindu' whose place amongst them should be no better than that of a suppliant *hamsaya*, dependent on their protection.

This apart, Nehru's accusations, Fraser Noble continues, left a bad taste. In certain cases they were really made against men who had, in fact, saved his skin, if not his pride. Thus, Gerald Curtis, Deputy Commissioner, Mardan, whose interventions after Nehru and his companions had been roughed up in Malakand, certainly saved Nehru's life, was so enraged by allegations against the political service officers that he wrote formally to the governor asking to be relieved and allowed to resign. He warned that the authority of the (political) service was being so undermined by the ministry that the time had come 'for us to leave them to sort out the mess for themselves'.[189] Fraser himself quit even though he would have wished to stay on, especially when Khan Sahib had specifically 'wanted me to be told' that he (Khan Sahib) would like him to continue. Sadly, it was too late for him to change his plans; nor may Khan Sahib be in a position to help for 'he may himself be in prison' before long.[190]

It may be of interest to recall that there was a clear and contrary perception. Badshah Khan for one had, from the very outset, accused the Political Department of masterminding the hostile demonstrations against Nehru. The objective, the Khan had little doubt, was to teach Nehru a lesson for his daring to defy its dictates; in other words, in refusing to call off his visit.[191] Jansson who later verified with people involved in the demonstrations as to the tenability of the charge has concluded that by and large, Badshah Khan's accusation stood confirmed.[192]

The Muslim League's objective could not have been clearer: to discredit Khan Sahib in general and the Frontier Congress in particular, in Nehru's eyes and estimation, and give a lie to Congress propaganda that the Pakhtuns did not favour the call of Pakistan; that they indeed did.

Many a small detail relating to men and events got filled up later. Some men had been paid Rs. 200.00 each, then a princely sum, 'to snipe at' Nehru's plane when it landed at Razmak; the Muslim League trouble-makers received 'moral and other support' from Muslim officials all through. The junior officers were 'for all practical purposes in league with' Muslim officials; their British bosses, even when unsympathetic to this stance, were thwarted by their (Muslim) subordinates. Again, the conspiracy among the Afridis was at the behest of Col. Khurshid, then Political Agent in the Khyber Agency.

Of all that happened, the Malakand incident caused by far 'the most acrimonious controversy'. It is true that proforma Justice Clarke, the Madras High Court Judge, acquitted Sheikh Mahbub Ali of the charge of negligence of duty but Wavell was far from convinced and 'retired him'. As regards the Sheikh's complicity, several persons believed he was responsible for the demonstration and expressed the view that such a clever and shrewd man should never have allowed this to happen had he not wanted it. Three young men who were part of the anti-Nehru demonstration later confided in Jansson that 'this was their own ideas and nobody else's'; in the final count, they would suggest that the Sheikh was not responsible for the demonstration. All the same, Jansson concludes that the Sheikh 'could have prevented' the whole melee, but 'did not protect' Nehru and his party 'as he could have done'.[193]

Nehru had made a public accusation that while others were not allowed to go into the tribal area, mischief mongers were permitted to propagate the lie that Hindu Raj was being established and that his government was responsible for the aerial bombing of the tribal area.[194]

The end-result of Nehru's visit remained a subject of lively, if contentious debate. Jansson has expressed the view that in its aftermath, the tribal areas were 'definitely drawn within the orbit' of Indian politics. The religious sentiments of the Pathans were now fully aroused, and 'fanned by officials, students and regular Muslim Leaguers', weighed heavily in vitiating the atmosphere in favour of Pakistan. Understandably, those among the tribals who were inclined towards the Congress now found their position 'increasingly difficult'.[195]

Apart from its wider ramifications Nehru's visit had a powerful impact on the far from pleasant relations between the governor and his council of ministers. Caroe himself was to note that in the aftermath of Nehru's visit, these relations were 'seriously affected' and were now 'less cordial' than before.[196]

Officials in Nehru's own external affairs department refused to endorse what they viewed to be his 'emotional approach'. This added to a 'lingering belief' that the subconscious objective of the British was 'to impede progress'. If the 'gloomy prognostications' of Weightman 'about danger to the peace of the border' came true, then Nehru would be justified in believing that the old Political Service had engineered it all. If, on the other hand, 'peaceful conditions continued' Nehru would be confirmed in his doubts of the Political Service's 'ability to appreciate the psychology' of the tribal people.[197]

As briefly noticed, not long after Nehru had left, Governor-General Wavell visited the Frontier for five days (14-19 November). He took the opportunity to address a jirga of the Afridis at Landi Kotal and another of the Ahmadzai Wazirs at Wana. While the Afridis were, Wavell noted, 'dignified and impressive', the Ahmadzai were 'more communal and less dignified' in their outlook. Wavell had also motored by Nowshera, Dargai and the Malakand pass to Chakdarra, at the junction of the Dhir and Swat valleys. At the Malakand pass he had looked 'at the scene of the assault' on Nehru and his party.

Broadly, the tribals had told the viceroy that their treaties were with British government and as long as the Hindu-Muslim conflict continued British India, they would have nothing to do with its interim government.

Both in South Waziristan and the Malakand agency, strong support was expressed for tribal independence—and for Pakistan. Wavell's non-committal response to their jirgas underlined that the freedom of the tribes would be respected and that they would get every opportunity 'to state their case' and 'make their own terms' with any future Indian government.[198]

NOTES

1. Tendulkar cites from the accounts furnished by AGK and Khan Sahib and reproduces excerpts from a summary of the 350-page report of the Peshawar Enquiry Committee set up by the Indian National Congress under the chairmanship of Vithalbhai Patel. For details see D.G. Tendulkar, *Abdul Ghaffar Khan: Faith is a Battle,* Popular Prakashan, Bombay, 1967, pp. 65-76. Cited hereafter as Tendulkar.
2. Olaf Caroe, 'From 1947 On', 38-page unpublished *Caroe Manuscript*. Cited hereafter as *CM* 2.
3. 'India in 1930-1931', cited in Tendulkar, pp. 73-4.
4. Fraser Noble, Comments on PLM's TS. Cited hereafter as Comments. The TS was mailed to Sir Fraser in Edinburgh and the comments were made, in hand, on the draft itself. This was June-August 1994.
5. HRS, 'Unrest in the Peshawar District, 1930-32', *Journal of the Royal Central Asian Society* (cited hereafter as *JRCAS*), 19, 4 (October 1932), pp. 624-42. 'HRS' (identity withheld by the journal) presents what would appear to be a highly coloured official version. How well-informed he was of the ground reality may be gauged from the fact that Khan Sahib is referred to as 'brother-in-law' of AGK!
6. Sir William Barton, 'The problem of law and order under a responsible Government in the NWFP', *JRCAS*, 19, 1 (January 1932), pp. 4-21. Also see 'Proceedings of the Indian Round Table Conference', second session, London, 1932, p. 416, cited in Amit Kumar Gupta, *North-West Frontier Province Legislature and Freedom Struggle 1932-47,* New Delhi, 1976, p. 23, n. 47. The work is cited hereafter as Gupta.
7. Olaf Caroe, *The Pathans, 550 BC-AD 1957,* Macmillan, London, 1956, rpt., 1965, pp. 421-7.
8. For details see chapters 'Breach of Truce: 1931', 'Ordinance Raj: 1931-2' and 'State Prisoner, 1932-4', in Tendulkar, pp. 124-63.
9. *George Cunningham's Diary* (cited hereafter as *GCD*), entry for 22 March 1937.
10. *GCD*, 29 March 1937. At the end Cunningham confessed to 'rather an exhausting day'.
11. *GCD*, 19 June 1937.
12. Ibid., 24 July 1937.
13. Gupta, p. 77.
14. Olaf Caroe, *The Pathans*, p. 426.
15. Norval Mitchell, *Sir George Cunningham, A Memoir*, Willaim Blackwood, Edinburgh, 1968, p. 63. Cited hereafter as Mitchell.
16. *GCD*, 31 August 1937.
17. Ibid., 9 September 1937.

18. Ibid., 17 Septemebr 1937.
19. Ibid., 2 October 1937.
20. *GCD*, 28 October 1937.
21. Ibid., 19 November 1937.
22. The Congress high command constituted what came to be known as the Asaf Ali Commission whose *Report on NWFP and Bannu Raids* was published in 1938. In the meantime, the NWFP government of Khan Sahib constituted an official committee under Olaf Caroe to report on the matter. For details, see Gupta, p. 105.
23. Under the Government of India Act 1935, the superior services, viz., the ICS and the Indian Police, posted in British Indian provinces, fell within the purview of the governor's 'special responsibility' and to that extent were immune from ministerial control.
24. Tendulkar, pp. 266-7.
25. The Teri Bill related to the rights of the Nawab of Teri, Baz Mohammad Khan, a Muslim League MLA, to collect certain dues from his tenants. At one stage, the Khan Sahib ministry was prepared to resign *en bloc* if Cunningham who viewed the Bill's provisions as injudicious, refused the Royal assent. Matters were, however, sorted out through a compromise: Cunningham returned the Bill to the Provincial Assembly with amendments which were both acceptable to the ministry and compatible with his own convictions. For details, see Mitchell, p. 69.
26. 'Legislative Assembly Debates: NWFP', V, 17 March 1939, cited in Gupta, p. 105.
27. Cited in Gupta, p. 106, n. 198.

    The reference to two Hindi publications has not been verified; that to a document in the 'Transfer of Power' volumes has remained unsubstantiated.

    In actual fact, Cunningham's report to the governor-general is critical of Khan Sahib's 'foolish statement' on the failure of the Cripps Mission. Khan Sahib was equally foolish to refuse Sir Stafford Cripps' invitation to see him. The governor ascribed the first to Khan Sahib's gullibility in acting as the 'mouthpiece' of others but in reality to his disappointment. For, 'in his heart of hearts' he was 'undeniably anxious to lead the Ministry again.'

    As to Khan Sahib's refusal to see Cripps, when invited, Cunningham attributed it to his (Khan Sahib's) lack of assurance: 'he was terrified', the governor added, 'to answer awkward questions'. On the second count, the governor had his feelings conveyed to him 'through Mrs Khan Sahib'.

    For details see 'Extracts from Governor's Report, No. 8 of 23 April 1942', *Transfer of Power*, I, HMSO, London, 1970, Document 673.
28. For details, see Gupta, p. 106.
29. In February 1938, Governor-General Lord Linlithgow instructed the governors of UP (Sir Harry Graham Haig) and Bihar (Sir Maurice Garrier Hallett) to reject the advice of their respective premiers (UP, Govind Ballabh Pant; and Bihar, Sri Krishna Sinha) to release the remaining political prisoners accused of serious offences. Whereupon the two premiers tendered their resignations. Later these were withdrawn after the governor-general gave an assurance that the agreed policy of gradual release, after examination of each case, would continue to be adhered to. At one stage, the episode threatened to develop into a constitutional crisis leading to the resignations of all Congress governments—including that of NWFP. For details see Tara Chand, *History of the Freedom Movement*, 4 vols., New Delhi, 1961-72, iv, p. 248. Also see 'Ministerial Resignations in U.P. and Bihar', in N N Mitra (ed.), *The Indian Annual*

Register, January-June 1938 (Calcutta, 1939), pp. 307-11. The Register was published bi-annually from 1930 to 1946.

Inter alia, Khan Sahib had told Cunningham that if the Congress central leadership pressed him to resign, he and AGK 'would go and argue the point' at the plenary session of the Congress at Haripur, *GCD*, 17 February 1938.

30. *GCD*, 19 April 1938.

The premier informed the governor that the Peshawar Board and the Congress leadership had 'gone against his own wishes' in the matter but he 'could not flout their orders unless he actually resigned his ministry'.

31. Loc. cit.
32. *GCD*, 4 July 1938.

Earlier, on 1 July too, Cunningham had 'a long talk' with Khan Sahib who 'seems to be in very good form'. Ibid., 1 July 1938.

33. *GCD*, 16 August 1938.
34. Ibid., 31 August 1938.

The officials, named and un-named, included Laughton, Russell and Smith.

35. *GCD*, 20 September 1938.

Europe had gone through a major international crisis following the Munich pact (September 1938) and the war clouds seemed to be gathering thick and fast.

36. *GCD*, 2 March 1939.
37. Ibid., 15 May 1939.
38. The Congress ministry headed by Khan Sahib quit on 7 November 1939; on the eleventh, the governor assumed full powers and prorogued the provincial legislature. It is incorrect to say (Gupta, p. 121), that this was done by Cunningham. In actual fact, the latter had proceeded on home leave (9 August through 2 December 1939), and Sir Arthur Parsons had acted as governor in an officiating capacity. It was to him that Khan Sahib submitted his resignation.
39. Irwin paid George Cunningham a warm tribute in a personal letter saying how much he (viz., Irwin) owed to his 'steadiness and wisdom' especially inasmuch as 'everybody outside had the most implicit trust and confidence in you'. This, the former governor-general continued, made 'his own work to go on smoothly'. Irwin to George Cunningham, 21 April 1931, cited in Mitchell, p. 55.
40. Cunningham had been Political Agent, North Waziristan, 1922-3.
41. Mitchell, pp. 56-7.
42. *GCD*, 31 August 1937.
43. Mitchell noted that Khan Sahib 'did not allow' his political views to affect his social activities 'more than he could help'. This was in sharp contrast to the 'rigid refusal' of the Congress Party.

In confidence, the premier once showed Cunningham a telegram he had received from Badshah Khan, then in Calcutta, asking ministers not to attend investitures at the Government House. The governor noted that Khan Sahib was disappointed and gave him (Cunningham) the clear impression that he disliked being disciplined by the party high command, *GCD*, 28 October, 1937. See also Mitchell, pp. 64-5.

44. Mitchell, p. 69.

Earlier, Cunningham noted that 'I think he (Khan Sahib) finds Bhanju Ram rather a trial in some ways.' Bhanju Ram Gandhi who hailed from D I Khan was Finance Minister in the first and second Khan Sahib ministries. For details see *GCD* 28 October 1937 and 4 July 1938.

45. Khan Sahib in conversation with Sir George Cunningham, 16 December 1939. Cited in Mitchell, p. 75.
46. *GCD*, 12 December 1939.
    Cunningham's informant was none other than Malik Khuda Baksh 'who was carrying on as Speaker until further orders'. He was a Congress legislator.
47. *GCD*, 16 December 1939. See also Mitchell, p. 75.
48. Ibid., 30 May 1940. See also Mitchell, p. 79.
49. Cunningham had been touring in the Kohat district where the news was relayed to him. For details see *GCD*, 14 December 1940. See also Mitchell, p. 83.
50. *GCD*, 16 December 1940.
51. Ibid., 24 December 1940.
52. Ibid., 16 January 1941.
53. Ibid., 7 March 1941.
54. Ibid., 13 July 1941.
55. Ibid., 20 April 1942.
    Mrs Khan Sahib and her daughter, Mariam, had come over to the Government House for lunch after the engagement was announced.
56. *GCD*, 29 July 1942. See also Mitchell, p. 97.
57. Mitchell, p. 96.
58. *GCD*, 2 August 1942.
59. Loc. cit.
60. Mitchell, pp. 97-8.
61. Mitchell records that there was virtually no trouble within the province and that the governor was 'more bothered' by alarmed orders from the Government of India 'than internal trouble'. Cunningham noted that the Congress-sponsored Civil Disobedience movement (1941) was 'not going too badly' and although liquor shops had been picketed, people 'can apparently get what they want'. In any case, since it hurt nobody and was 'a good face-saver' for Congress, he did not 'propose to stop it'. How serious the Frontier Congress was about its Quit India movement may be gauged from the fact that Khan Sahib had left for Kashmir on 19 August, a bare ten days after the movememt had been launched. For deatils see *GCD*, 19 August 1942. See also Mitchell, p. 98.
62. *GCD*, 13 September 1942. See also Mitchell, pp. 99-100.
63. Ibid., 15 September 1942. See also Mitchell, p. 99.
64. For his assessment of Khan Sahib and what he was about, Cunningham's informant was Jamil Ahmad, one of the governor's confidants. *GCD*, 27 October and 4 November 1942.
5. Early in December (1942), Cunningham had toured in the south of the province where the 'results had been very much the same'. For details see Mitchell, p. 101.
5. Sardar Abdur Rab Nishtar was a member of the Aurangzeb Khan ministry (1943-5) and later, as a Muslim League nominee, Member for Communications in the interim government.
. Mitchell, p. 106.
GCD, 3 April 1943.
Mitchell, pp. 108-9.
For details of the arithmetic leading to the formation of the Aurangzeb Khan ministry see Gupta, pp. 133-5. The author maintains that it was essentially a League-Akali coalition which was a product 'of political manoeuvres' with the ministerial party

being supported by 19 members in a house of 43; in the event, its fate 'depended solely on the continuing detention' of Congress MLAs.

Jansson is less than sure if the League ministry 'ever had had a majority and even if it did, this majority was never stable'. Erland Jansson, *India, Pakistan or Pakhtunistan; the Nationalist Movements in the North-West Frontier Province, 1937-47*, University of Uppsala, 1981, p. 130. Cited hereafter as Jansson.

71. The Aurangzeb Khan ministry was sworn in on 25 May 1943. *GCD*, 26 May 1943.
72. *GCD*, 19 July 1943. See also Mitchell, pp. 103, 106.
73. Ibid., 27 July 1943.
74. Ibid., 7 August 1943.
75. Ibid., 13 August 1943.
76. Ibid., 14 and 25 October 1943.
77. Ibid., 23 October 1943.
78. Ibid., 27 March 1944.
79. Ibid., 27 May 1944. See also Mitchell, p. 110.
80. Ibid., 15 March 1945.
81. Ibid., 16 March 1945.
82. For Wavell's letter to Amery, 20 March 1945, see *Transfer of Power*, V, HMSO, London, 1974, Document 327. See also Ibid., Document 374.
83. Gandhi, it is clear, 'preferred leaving things to local initiative'. Pattabhi B. Sitaramaya, *History of the Indian National Congress*, S. Chand & Company, 2 vols, rpt., New Delhi, 1969, II, p. 531.
84. Jansson, p. 144, n. 13.
85. V P Menon, *The Transfer of Power in India*, Orient Longman, Bombay, 1957, p. 180. See also Cunningham to Colville, 2 May 1945, *Transfer of Power*, V, Document 433. Sir John Colville was then acting governor-general.
86. Gupta, p. 161 relies on Muhammad Yunus, *Qaidi ke Khat*, 2nd edn. New Delhi, 1984, p. 161. Sadly for Gupta, Yunus makes no mention of the statement attributed to him. See Yunus, p. 167.
87. Badshah Khan was against forming a ministry but cut off from recent happenings in the province as well as outside, he let the ministerialists have their own way. For details see Gupta, pp. 160-1.

    The expression 'negative assent' is from the *Tribune*, Lahore, 26 March 1946.
88. Cunningham to Viceroy, 7 May 1945, cited in Jansson, p. 144, n. 18
89. Stanley Wolpert, *Jinnah of Pakistan*, OUP, Delhi, 1988, p. 243.
90. Jansson, pp. 144-5.
91. *GCD*, 16 June 1945. See also Mitchell, pp. 112-13.
92. Ibid., 20 April 1945.
93. Ibid., 12 September 1945.
94. For details see Gupta, pp. 176-7.
95. Tendulkar, p. 367.
96. Loc. cit.
97. Fraser Noble, Comments.
98. Tendulkar, p. 367.
99. Stephen A. Rittenberg, *The Independence Movements in India's North West Frontier Province*, Ph.D. thesis, Columbia University, 1977, p. 326. Cited hereafter as Rittenberg.

    Rittenberg's thesis was published in book form, under the same title, at Durham

(USA), in 1988. In the absence of the book's availability, the thesis copy at NMML has been used.

100. Rittenberg, pp. 328-9. See also Jansson, p. 150.
101. Governor's Report, No. 15, 9 October 1945, cited in Rittenberg, p. 321, n. 14.
102. Rittenberg, pp. 321-2.

Of the League's nominees 'there were 5 big Nawabs, 1 Knight, 7 Khan Bahadurs, 3 rich military contractors, 2 army recruiting officers and at least one person known to have participated in the communal riots in D I Khan'. Gupta, p. 174.

103. *GCD*, 20 September 1945. See also Mitchell, p. 114.
104. Ibid., 17 October 1945. See also Mitchell, p. 114.
105. Ibid., 3 November 1945. See also Mitchell, p. 114.
106. Ibid., 19 January 1946. See also Mitchell, p. 120.
107. Ibid., 17 February 1946. See also Mitchell, p. 120.

John (later Sir John) Dring was then deputy commissioner in Peshawar.

108. Cunningham, Governor's Report, 24 January 1946, cited in Jansson, p. 151.
109. Jansson, p. 151, n. 55.
110. A detailed, constituency-wise, analysis is provided in Jansson, 'The 1946 Elections', Appendix III, pp. 255-63.
111. Gupta, p. 179.
112. Jansson, p. 152.
113. Fraser Noble, Memoirs, pp. 244-5.
114. Ibid., pp. 246-8.
115. Fraser Noble, Comments.
116. *GCD*, 7 January 1946.
117. *GCD*, 27 February 1946.
118. A Norwal Mitchell, Memoirs, MSS Eur D 944, IOL & R, pp. 244-6 (252-4).

There is an overlap in Mitchell's paging; the figures within brackets indicate a consistent numbering adopted by the India Office Library & Records; those preceding are Mitchell's own. To avoid confusion, all subsequent references are to IOL & R numbering.

119. *GCD*, 1 March 1946.
120. Fraser Noble, Memoirs, p. 266.
121. Caroe to Wavell, 9 March 1946 in Olaf Caroe, 'A Price for Freedom', unpublished manuscript comprising 31 fortnightly reports of the governor to the governor-general commencing 9 March 1946 and ending 23 June 1947 besides an exchange of telegrams relating to Caroe's exit from office (Caroe Manuscript cited hereafter as *CM*).

The *Tribune*, 3 March 1946 carried a long piece, 'Legends Around Frontier Premier: Dr Khan Sahib, Old Woman & Her Chicken', by the well-known leftist politician, Yusuf Meherally.

122. Caroe to Wavell, 9 March 1946, *CM*.
123. Fraser Noble, Comments.
124. Caroe to Wavell, 23 March 1946, *CM*.
125. Ibid., 10 April 1946, *CM*.

A fortnight later when he reverted to the subject, Caroe sought a clearer directive from New Delhi:

> If possible I should be grateful for a line on the question about the Ministry's interference with the Courts. I expect this question has arisen in the past with

other Ministries and I should like to hear anything that Secretary to the Governor-General (Public) and for the Home Department have to say. Caroe to Wavell, 23 April 1946, *CM*.

126. Caroe to Wavell, 8 May 1946, *CM*.

'He too' is explained by a reference to the neighbouring province of the Panjab:

> I was interested to hear of Jenkins' difficulties with Bhim Sen Sachar for the latter's behaviour is an exact repetition of what we have to put up here from Dr Khan Sahib.

In the Panjab, Sir Evan Jenkins was governor and Bhim Sen Sachar, a Congress minister in an uneasy Unionist-Congress coalition government under Malik Khizr (later Sir Khizr) Hyat Khan Tiwana.

127. Caroe to Wavell, 23 May 1946, *CM*.
128. Ibid., 9 June 1946, *CM*.
129. Ibid., 9 July 1946, *CM*.
130. Ibid., 9 July 1946, *CM*.
131. Ibid., 22 August 1946, *CM*.
132. Ibid.
133. Ibid., 23 September 1946, *CM*.

Caroe had notified New Delhi that he wanted to take a firm stand on the issue:

> Over this matter of executive interference with the magistracy it is necessary to stand firm and it is to be noted that this interference has been made the chief plank of opposition attacks on the Congress government in this province. The Government are exposing surface all along and the position is becoming scandalous.

134. Caroe to Wavell, 23 September 1946, *CM*.
135. Caroe to Wavell, 11 October 1946, *CM*.
136. Fraser Noble, Memoirs, p. 269.
137. Ibid., p. 280.
138. *CM 2*, p. 3.
139. Caroe to Wavell, 23 October 1946, *CM*.
140. Caroe to Wavell, 9 September 1946, *CM*.
141. Reply to a short notice question in the Legislative Assembly (New Delhi) on 29 October 1946 in *Legislative Assembly Debates*, Official Report, VII, New Delhi, 28 October 1946–11 November 1946, cited in *Selected Works of Jawaharlal Nehru*, Second Series, I, Jawaharlal Nehru Foundation, New Delhi, 1984, pp. 331-5.
142. Norval Mitchell, *Memoirs*, pp. 255-6.
143. For details of Donald's detention and the negotiations leading to his release as well as the 'intermittent bombing' between 10 August and 10 September see Charles Chenevix Trench, *Viceroy's Agent*, London, 1986, pp. 321-2.

In a tragic end, Donald shot himself (24 September) 'through a misguided sense of shame' at 'having made a nonsense' of the cloth ration and having been 'humiliated' while his bodyguard 'stood idly by'. Loc. cit.

144. Trench, op. cit., p. 321.
145. Caroe to Wavell, 23 June 1946, *CM*.
146. Caroe to Wavell, 9 July 1946, *CM*. See also Caroe's note 3, in ibid., p. 52-A.

See also n. 143 of this chapter.

147. Caroe to Wavell, 23 July 1946, *CM*.
148. Ibid., 9 August 1946, *CM*.

149. Ibid., 22 August 1946, *CM*.
150. Ibid., 9 September 1946, *CM*.
151. Both statements were carried together prominently on the front page. For the texts see the *Tribune*, 7 September 1946.
152. Caroe to Wavell, 9 September 1946, *CM*.
153. Fraser Noble, Memoirs, p. 290.
154. Ibid., Comments.
155. For details including Nehru's own impressions, see Tendulkar, pp. 220-8.
156. Olaf Caroe to governor-general, telegram, 29 September 1946, *Transfer of Power*, VIII, Document 382.
157. Minutes by G E B Abell, Private Secretary to Viceroy, and Wavell, 30 September 1946, in ibid., Document 383.
158. Caroe to Wavell, telegram, 15 October 1946, in ibid., Document 459.
159. Wavell to Jinnah, 15 October 1946, in ibid., Document 461.
160. Jinnah to Wavell, 15 October 1946, in ibid., Document 468. For the Quaid's attitude see Syed Waqar Ali Shah, *Muslim League in NWFP*, Royal Book Company, Karachi, 1992, p. 116.
161. For details see *Tara Chand*, IV, pp. 447-84; *Wavell's Journal*, pp. 334-5, 338-9; Parshotam Mehra, *A Dictionary of Modern Indian History 1707-1947*, OUP, New Delhi, 1985, pp. 196-7.
162. Wavell noted that after his meeting with Nehru where disucussion 'seems to have been amiable', Caroe had 'quite failed to shake N. (Nehru) in his intention to make the visit' and that he (Caroe) was 'chiefly concerned' because Badshah Khan was going to accompany Nehru. *Wavell's Journal*, entry for 9 October 1947, pp. 355-6.
163. Nehru to Khan Sahib, 10 October 1946, *Selected Works*, second series, I, 1984, pp. 306-7.
164. Sarvepalli Gopal, *Jawaharlal Nehru: A Biography*, OUP, Delhi, 3 vols., I, 1979, p. 333.
165. *Wavell's Journal*, entries for 4 and 9 October 1946, pp. 355-6. See also Caroe to Wavell, 11 October 1946, *CM* and n. 157 of this chapter.
166. Abul Kalam Azad, *India Wins Freedom*, New Delhi, 1949, pp. 169-70.
167. *Wavell's Journal*, entry for 21 October 1946, p. 361. Wavell who had a talk with Sardar Patel that evening noted: 'He (Patel) said that he had advised Nehru not to make this N.W. Frontier trip.'
168. Tendulkar would suggest that it was Nehru who 'heatedly' dismissed about a hundred headmen and told the rest 'I am amazed how you people who get government money and act as they like, talk of freedom.' Tendulkar, p. 387.
169. Jansson has suggested that the Mahsuds told Nehru that their allowances were 'only taxes for roads and land used by the government'. He also mentions that 'not all the Mahsuds showed themselves as hostile'. Jansson, p. 183.

    For the Waziri Malik see Malik Muhammad Hayat Khan to M A Jinnah, 26 February 1947, No. 38 in *Jinnah Papers*, I, 1.
170. Caroe told the governor-general that the Bhittanis, 'a tame little tribe', were not real tribesmen and had been brought there by a dismissed tehsildar. Caroe to Wavell, 23 October 1946, *CM*.
171. Tendulkar, pp. 387-9, reproduces AGK's own graphic account of Nehru's visit; Jansson, pp. 184-5, has drawn on the accounts furnished to him by one Gulab Khan

for Nehru's visit to South Waziristan and one Faridullah Shah (who had earlier served as Assistant Political Officer) for his visit to the Khyber agency.

172. For details of Nehru's reception on his visits to Waziristan, the Khyber and Malakand agencies, based presumably on eye-witness accounts of the concerned political agents, see Charles Chenevix Trench, *Viceroy's Agent,* Jonathan Cape, London, 1987, pp. 323-7.

Also Caroe to Wavell, 23 October 1946, *CM*. The entire report deals more or less exclusively with Nehru's tour seen through a critical, if unsympathetic eye. For a pro-Nehru version, based on Badshah Khan's rehearsal of events see Tendulkar, pp. 384-94.

173. Trench has given a vivid account of all that happened at Miranshah where there was pandemonium when Nehru, AGK and Khan Sahib 'lost their tempers, arguing with each other, and outside the ring were the Wazirs howling foul abuse'. At Razmak, the Mahsuds behaved no better: 'You have the effrontery to call us slaves of the British: We've never been anyone's slaves, and we are not certainly going to be yours!' At Wana, the Ahmedzai Wazirs 'refused to meet' Nehru and 'chased away some of the bazaar Hindus who had come to garland him!' Trench, pp. 323-7.

174. Fraser Noble, Comments.

175. Caroe to Wavell, 23 October 1946, *CM*.

176. Loc. cit.

177. Nehru was categorical that he did *not* 'personally saddle' the political agents with 'responsibility for much that happened' but averred that 'their basic approach to my appointment and visit' was such as to 'add to that hostility'. Nehru to Caroe, 16 November 1946, *Selected Works,* second series, I, 1984, pp. 337-42.

178. Caroe to Wavell, 23 November 1946, *CM*.

179. Weightman's note of 6 November 1946 was in reply to Nehru's of 24 October. *Inter alia*, Weightman strongly repudiated the suggestion that there had been any official resistance to Nehru's tour and defended the existing frontier policy. Referred to in 'Further comments on tour', *Selected Works,* second series, I, pp. 343-5.

Wavell noted that the commander-in-chief (Sir Claude Auchinleck) was 'disturbed' at the effect of Nehru's visit. At the same time though he was unhappy with the political system 'which has been going downhill for the past twenty years and has completely failed to change with the times', *Wavell's Journal*, entry for 4 November 1946, p. 372.

Wavell's own comment: 'I discussed with Weightman this morning Nehru's tour and his foolish and unrealistic note about it. Weightman said that Congress are 'gunning for' Olaf Caroe and will have him out if they can.' *Wavell's Journal*, entry for 6 November 1946, p. 373. Reference is to Nehru's 'Note on my tour . . .', 24 October 1946, *Transfer of Power,* VIII, Encl to Document 520.

180. Caroe noted that 'neither the Mullah of Manki nor any other important League propangadist' repaired to Waziristan and that the Mullah 'had been active only among the northern tribes around the Peshawar district'. Caroe to Wavell, 23 October 1946, *CM*.

181. Loc. cit.

182. Caroe to Wavell, 23 November 1946, *CM*.

183. In January 1947, the Government of India appointed Justice R. Clark of the Madras High Court to conduct a judicial enquiry into charges framed against Mahbub Ali

Khan relating to his conduct during Nehru's visit to Malakand. In his report of 28 February 1947, the judge exonerated Mahbub Ali holding that the charges against the officer were 'not established'.

184. Nehru to Caroe, 28 October 1946, *Transfer of Power*, VIII, Document 520.

185. Nehru indicated that he had received 'many complaints' against Mahbub Ali; that there were reports of his having encouraged people 'to misbehave towards us'; that Caroe had told him (Nehru) about Mahbub Ali's case being investigated by the Frontier government's anti-corruption officer. Above all, that his past record was 'not inspiring'. And yet he would not allow these reports to 'influence my judgement'.

    Abell noted that Nehru's letter represented 'a considerable climb-down' and should 'hopefully give some encouragement' to Olaf Caroe. For details see Nehru to Caroe, 16 November 1946, *Transfer of Power*, IX, Document 46.

    Wavell commented that 'it was a sensible letter' which showed the best side of Nehru. 'It is certainly as far as Nehru is expected to go and I think does considerable credit to his honesty and good feeling.' He expressed the hope that Caroe would accept 'this "amende honorable" in the right spirit'. For details see Document 52, in ibid.

186. Wavell's minutes in the margin of his copy of Nehru's letter. *Transfer of Power*, IX, Document 52, n. 4.

187. Wavell to Sir Francis Bourne, governor of CP and Berar, 20 November 1946, Extract, Document 65, in ibid.

188. Wavell to Pethick Lawrence, 22 November 1946, Document 77, para 6, in ibid.

189. Fraser Noble, Memoirs, pp. 291-2.

190. Fraser Noble, Comments.

191. Rittenberg maintains that the accusations against the Political Department 'overlooked much more important reasons' for the tribes' hostility. These included communal riots in Bombay; the tour of the Pir of Manki; aerial bombing of tribal areas. Above all, the visit revived the hitherto implausible—the possibility that the British would be replaced by the Hindus with independence. 'As Caroe put it, it seemed like the coming of a second Birbal.' Rittenberg, p. 349.

192. Jansson, p. 188.

193. Loc. cit.

194. Tendulkar, pp. 389-94, reproduces the texts of the Khudai Khidmatgars' address and Nehru's reply to it.

195. Jansson, p. 189.

196. Caroe to Wavell, 23 November 1946, *CM*. One of the manifestations of bad relations, Caroe indicated, was his ministers' refusal to attend an investiture at the Government House. Khan Sahib was 'wishful to attend and had held out hopes that the other ministers might also do so, but it is clear that they might have consulted Nehru when he came here and got the order to keep away'.

197. Weightman to Abell, 15 February 1947, *Transfer of Power*, IX, Document 405.

198. Jansson, p. 189. See also *Wavell's Journal*, entry for 19 November 1946, p. 377.

    Wavell's tour of the Frontier lasted for five days; from 'midday' on 14 November to 'just before lunch' on 19 November.

CHAPTER 3

Mountbatten, the Third June Plan and Caroe's Dismissal

THE PERIOD between Nehru's tour of the tribal areas in October 1946 and Caroe's unceremonial exit in June 1947 was witness to a remarkable transformation in the political scenario in Peshawar. Events outside the Frontier too had by now begun to have a direct, if powerful, bearing on developments.

Two of the more important ones need to be taken note of here. The failure of the Simla Conference (June-July 1945) underlined the considerable clout that Jinnah and his Muslim League had by now come to wield. It was the Quaid's unrelenting opposition to the viceroy's proposal on the composition of an interim government which brought a well-meaning initiative to a cruel end. Nor was Wavell prepared to venture ahead without Jinnah's nod.

The ensuing general election throughout British India in the winter of 1945-6 gave a powerful boost to Jinnah's claim to be recognised as the 'sole spokesman' of Muslim India. In the short run though, the formation of non-League governments in the two Muslim-majority provinces of the Panjab and NWFP posed a major challenge. In the Frontier, as has been noticed, the Congress-Khudai Khidmatgar combine had won an absolute majority in the Provincial Assembly and Khan Sahib returned to power for the third time in a row.

In the Panjab, the situation was a little more complicated for even though the Muslim League had demonstrated strong electoral support, the Hindu and Sikh legislators of the Congress had joined a predominantly Muslim, though ideologically secular and non-sectarian, Unionist Party to form a coalition government. To Jinnah and his supporters, it was plain as a pikestaff that both these predominantly Muslim provinces had to be wrested from non-League control. Even as the Quaid's arithmetic was being worked out, Whitehall had despatched a three-member Cabinet Mission (March 1946) to help break the political logjam. Failing to make any headway, it had by May announced a (Cabinet Mission) Plan to work out a compromise between the conflicting demands of the Congress and the Muslim League. The Plan envisaged a three-tier Indian Union. At the federal centre would be a union of India embracing both British India as well as the Indian princely states; its jurisdiction, limited to the spheres of foreign affairs, defence and communications. All other subjects, and all residuary powers, were to vest in the provinces and the princely states; the latter, to retain all powers other than those ceded to the union. British Indian provinces were free to form groups, with executives and legislatures in each group determining the provincial subjects to be taken in common.

A constituent assembly, representative of the British Indian provinces as well as the princely states, was to convene. After some preliminaries, it was to split into three sections: 'A', 'B' and 'C'. Group 'A' provinces, predominantly Hindu, were Madras, Bombay, UP, Bihar, CP & Berar and Orissa; Group 'B', predominantly Muslim, Panjab, NWFP and Sind; Group 'C', with miniscule Muslim majorities, Bengal and Assam. Each section was to settle a constitution for the provinces included in it and decide whether any group constitutions were to be framed, and if so, with what provincial subjects.

As soon as the new constitutional arrangements came into operation, it would be open to any province to opt out of any group in which it had been initially placed. Such a decision was to be taken by the legislature of the province, *after* the first general election under the new constitution.

Pending the implementation of the Cabinet Mission Plan, it was proposed to establish an interim government at New Delhi having the support of major political parties. Ideologically, the Congress Party was unwilling to be reconciled to the decentralisation of power, the communal veto and the possibility of provincial secession which the Plan envisaged. Hence its insistence that the grouping of provinces was optional or voluntary—neither mandatory, nor compulsory. The Frontier Congress, on the other hand, objected solely to the province's inclusion in group 'B' where Panjab's overwhelming legislative strength, they argued, would pose a grave threat to the identity of the Pathans and the political supremacy of the Congress in the province.

Congress opposition to grouping manifested itself into a demand for self-determination, for on 21 May, Badshah Khan said as much. Congress, according to him, was agreed to the fullest measure of provincial autonomy and even to the right of self-determination. It was the Muslim League, with its insistence that the provinces join grouping, that was opposed. The provinces, he pleaded, should be allowed to act of their own free

Shankar, in the *Hindustan Times*, 31 March 1946.

will. Besides, the very idea of grouping NWFP with the Panjab was revolting to the former; this would ensure that the Frontier got a raw deal, and that the province would have no future for the Panjabis considered the Pathans to be 'Kaffirs'. The Congress, Badshah Khan pointed out, had always stood for Pakhtun nationalism; the League did not.

The Frontier Congress stance, as retailed earlier, was no surprise, for keen observers of the political scene suggested that a direct relationship could be posited between the political conditions in India and the Khudai Khidmatgars' emphasis on Pakhtun autonomy; the greater the chances of Pakistan, the more militant would be the Frontier Congress' brand of regional autonomy.

As to the interim government, the Muslim League insisted, that it alone had the right to nominate its Muslim members—a claim Congress stoutly contested. In the final count, the League withdrew its support to the Cabinet Mission Plan and announced non-participation in the interim government as well as the proposed constituent assembly. In the wake of its repudiation of the Plan, the League fell back on extra-constitutional means to coerce or browbeat the Raj. 16 August (1946) was declared to be Direct Action Day. In Calcutta alone, as has been pointed out, its observance led to large scale violence which claimed, on conservative estimates, no fewer than 5,000 killed, 15,000 wounded and a hundred thousand rendered homeless.

The 'Great Calcutta Killing', had powerful repercussions on other parts of the country: Muslims rioted against Hindus in Noakhali in East Bengal (second half of October); Hindus had their reprisals against Muslims in Bihar (end-October/early November). Bombay was in the grip of a mass frenzy which, among others, claimed a number of Pakhtun casualties; the Pakhtuns had constituted a small, though significant minority group in the great metropolis. With the 'Great Calcutta Killing' as a backdrop, an interim government headed by Jawaharlal Nehru was sworn in on 2 September 1946. To start with, it did not include any representative from the Muslim League; they joined in only six weeks later. Sadly though, even its joining the government did not register any change in the League's attitude which remained obstructionist, and stridently anti-Congress.[1]

II

A word on the Frontier Muslim League which, until the mid-1940s, had remained largely an adjunct of the traditional alliance between the Raj and the big khans. It had little by way of ideological underpinnings; less by way of any credible programme. By 1940, however, things were beginning to change for Pakistan had emerged as a live issue. In its wake, quite a few political heavyweights, hitherto aligned with the Raj or the Congress, scrambled to jump on to the League bandwagon.

Prominent among those who defected from the Congress mention may be made of Arbab Abdul Ghafoor Khan, at one time a close associate of Badshah Khan and briefly General-Secretary of the Frontier Provincial Congress Committee (FPCC). Another big 'catch' for the League was Abdul Qaiyum Khan who, in 1937, had succeeded Khan Sahib as the NWFP's solitary representative in the Central Legislative Assembly at New Delhi, and later rose to be Deputy Leader of the Congress Parliamentary Party—a position of considerable visibility, though of no great power. In the League, Abdul Qaiyum's gain was immediate: in the February 1946 elections, he won a seat in the Provincial Assembly at Peshawar on the League ticket, and soon emerged as leader of the Muslim League Party in the provincial legislature.

Among the better known, two other defectors who switched loyalties were Ghulam Mohammed Khan, a former President of the FPCC and Rab Nawaz Khan, at one time Chief Commander of the Khudai Khidmatgars. For the League, Rab Nawaz was to organise its paramilitary brigade, the Muslim National Guards.

Government officials in the Frontier, as elsewhere in the country, were by definition as it were pro-British and anti-Congress. With an upsurge in the communal divide so marked in the 1945-6 general election, they swore fealty to Jinnah and his Muslim League. Jansson singles out the specific instance of Iskander Mirza who as Deputy Commissioner of Mardan in 1937 'did all he could to oppose' the Congress and had been 'most deeply involved' in the formation of the rival Muslim League organisation. Later, he used his influence in favour of the Muslim League; a support so blatant as to compel Khan Sahib to have him posted out of the province (1946).[2]

Another prominent Muslim official who lent active help to the Muslim League cause was Major Abdur Rahim. He too followed in the foot-steps of Iskander Mirza.[3] As a matter of fact, the phenomenon was so clearly pronounced that in October 1945, Sir George Cunningham noted that in the wake of the failure of the Simla Conference, 'well-educated Muslims of the senior official type, who never took much interest in politics, are becoming almost rabidly anti-Congress, and therefore, pro-Muslim League'.[4] Hindu officials, despite their generally pro-Congress leanings, were in no way a counterbalance to the influence of their Muslim

*(4) Their landlord was Iskander Mirza, then D.C. Peshawar - much later to be President of Pakistan. "Recently, he had been transferred from the Province. It was true that he had himself requested a transfer, but it was also well-known that Dr. Khan Sahib and his Ministers had been very keen that he should go. He had been D.C. in 1942 during their civil disobedience campaign, and had outmanoeuvered and humiliated them on several occasions. During the Muslim League Ministry, his personal links with the League's high command had become evident, and his contempt for Aurangzeb the Chief Minister helped to undermine his authority. When Jinnah sent a Commission to Peshawar to enquire into the provincial Ministry's shortcomings, Liaqat Ali, the League Secretary and Jinnah's first Lieutenant, stayed at the D.C.'s house."

Memoirs of Sir Fraser Noble (p. 260).

colleagues. As to the British, their broad leanings towards the Muslim League were pronounced.

Sir Olaf Caroe's alleged sympathy for, if not actual collusion with the Frontier Muslim League, was a subject a acute controversy; few in the Congress doubted his political predilections and covert, if not overt, support to the League cause.

Among the religious leaders, mention may be made of the young and fiery, then barely 25-year-old, Pir of Manki Sharif. His large retinue of *murids* boosted the Muslim League cause no end. A Pakhtun, well-known in the predominantly Pakhtun area around Peshawar, he served as a 'very effective counterbalance' to Abdul Ghaffar Khan. The Pir took an active interest in organising his *sajjadanashins* and in the 1946 elections lent solid support to the Muslim League cause through his *Anjuman-i-Asfia.* Jansson affirms that to him, 'more than any single person', goes the credit for the success of the Pakistan movement in the Frontier.[5]

Students too lent a big hand. The Frontier Muslim Students Federation took an active part in the 1946 elections. They later were to emerge as 'a dominant group' in the Pakistan movement.[6]

By 1946-7, the League's National Guards too began to play an important role. The Guards wore uniforms, were organised on paramilitary lines and usually armed with spears and lathis. Drawn from all sections of society, they gave the Pakistan movement in the Frontier a broad base and widespread acceptability. It should perhaps bear a mention that in seeking these means to achieve their legitimate political ends, the Muslim League were only following the example set by Congress; that the 'Green' National Guards had long been preceded by the 'Red' Shirts.[7]

In discussing any reorganisation of the Frontier Muslim League, two aspects need to be kept in mind. One, many of its new entrants were youngmen who gave it a fresh look. There was the 25-year-old Secretary, Muhammad Ali Khan and a year younger to him, Arbab Nur Muhammad Khan who was to be the party treasurer. Two, there were a number of heavy-weights among the Congress deserters who trooped in. Apart from those listed earlier, there were Mian Abdul Shah, one of Badshah Khan's close associates since 1931; Muhammad Ramzan Khan, a member of the organising committee of Abdul Ghaffar Khan's Afghan jirga and a former President of the FPCC, Ghulam Muhammad.[8]

The Pir of Manki's tours, often in the company of Muslim League activists, were a big draw. He and other *sajjadanashins* were allowed a free run of tribal territory on the specious plea that they had *murids* there.[9] This was a great advantage to the League because ordinarily politicians were debarred from visiting tribal areas. A common propaganda stance that the Pir took was that the Congress ministry in the Frontier was corrupt, partisan and anti-Islamic.

Expectedly, the over-arching objective of the Frontier Muslim League was to break the Congress stranglehold on a predominantly Muslim majority province. By 1946-7, it nearly succeeded, emerging as less of an organisation and more of a movement fed on religious and political passions aroused by the sharp communal divide all over the country.

At the all-India level, the sequence of communal killings retailed earlier destroyed any hope whatever of a political settlement that may stop short of partition. In the Frontier, it accomplished in a few months what the League had hitherto failed to achieve over many years: a stark communal polarisation with a massive swing of public opinion away from the Congress and in favour of the Muslim League. The latter now became ever-more strident in its call for the achievement of Pakistan.

Large-scale rioting in different parts of the country exposed the contradiction between the average Pathan's communal and political loyalties: as a cleric in the Kohat district put it: 'We woke up to the danger of Hindu domination' and the transformation came 'very suddenly'.[10] Highly exaggerated tales of atrocities on Muslims lent countenance to the basest of human instincts. It was openly propagated that 'all Muslims would unite and organise and should prove to the Hindus' that the blood of every Muslim would be 'definitely avenged'.[11] Of all places, the riots in Bombay and Bihar, where there were small but affluent pockets of Pakhtuns, had a particularly noticeable effect—for the worse—in the Frontier, with the Muslim League and its agents provocateurs exploiting the situtaion by using blood-stained clothing, torn pages of the Koran and skulls of alleged Muslim victims of Hindu atrocities.[12] Some of these were paraded in public to corroborate these wild, gruesome accounts.

On the morrow of rioting in Bihar, Olaf Caroe wrote to the governor-general (13 January 1947) that Abdul Ghaffar Khan was on his way there 'not, I think, for his ostensible purpose of seeing Bihar, but to be able to say later on that all this (viz., communal rioting in Hazara and Peshawar) happened during his absence.'[13] As a matter of fact, in the wake of the rioting in the Frontier, Sardar Patel told the Mahatma that out of 31,000 Hindus and Sikhs (as against 900,000 Muslims) 20,000 had fled; as many as 40-50 had been killed besides cases of arson and looting on a large scale. 'Bihar', he told Gandhi, 'is being avenged in the Frontier. . . . Badshah (Khan) has gone to Bihar where nothing is happening. But he will do as he thinks fit. . . . Dr Khan Sahib is in a predicament. The Muslim League is making poisonous propaganda.'[14]

In the context of the Muslim League upsurge, the role of the tribes too deserves a mention. The Raj had all along advised them to stay clear of party politics in British India until a general agreement concerning the country's future had been knocked into shape. Both Wavell (November 1946) and earlier Caroe, had categorically assured the tribes that 'no one would interfere with their freedom' and that they could 'make their own terms' with any future government of India. The essential thing was 'not to tie themselves' to any political party, for their interests were 'bound up with India as whole'.[15]

Gradually, however, the tribes became actively involved in the subcontinent's politics and on the side of the Muslim League. This came about largely because, it would appear in retrospect, of Nehru's visit; their Muslim identity; the influence of the Pir of Manki Sharif; and the pronouncedly pro-Muslim League stance of Muslim officials. Tribal support proved crucial for the League in winning the final rounds of its political battles in the Frontier. It has been suggested that the idea 'to stress the independence' of the tribes emanated originally from government employees who, not yet certain about the country's eventual partition, intended to use it 'as a lever' for the Muslim cause.[16]

In sharp contrast to the League, the Congress had all along desired in some way to unite the Pakhtuns of the tribal areas with those of the settled districts,[17] and spoke disparagingly of tribal allowance-receivers as the Raj's toadies who had buttressed its rule. As will be noticed presently, the League to start with, had no tribal policy worked out; later Jinnah promised that the tribes would be left, as hitherto, to their own devices.

Quite clearly, the tribal leaders supported a political outfit from which they hoped to gain most. As the Congress was opposed to the Raj, such tribes as were hostile to British rule were inclined to show some sympathy, however indirectly, for its broad objectives. A key role in determining the political affiliation of the tribes was played by members of the Political Service, the political agents and their assistants. They could turn and twist the issues in any manner they or their masters wished, and posed crucial questions in a language that answered to British interests.

A few weeks after the arrival of the Cabinet Mission, in March 1946, Caroe gave 'his general impression' that the tribes were 'very much on the Muslim League side'. All the same, he underlined that he accepted this stance 'with a good deal of caution'.[18] The launching of 'Direct Action', also called the Civil Disobedience movement (February-March 1947), by the Muslim League in the Frontier was not without its powerful impact either. To repudiate the insinuation repeatedly urged by their detractors, that they were toadies of the Raj, the League mounted a vigorous campaign asking its members to renounce their British-bestowed titles. This did make an impact, for by end-September, the tally of those who fell in line was 17 Khan Bahadurs and 27 Khan Sahibs. More, as the campaign for Pakistan gained in momentum, many an old Raj loyalist came out openly and defiantly on the side of the Muslim League. A small minority though did hold out and quit the League rather than incur the opprobrium of opposing the government in power.[19]

An unintended, though significant, result that flowed from Nehru's visit was that the tribes were now drawn within the orbit of Indian politics and had to think out their policy approach *vis-a-vis* the future constitutional setup in the subcontinent. In doing so, their religious sentiments, 'fanned by officials, students and the Muslim Leaguers', weighed heavily in the balance in favour of Pakistan. Here the Pir of Manki Sharif and his band of Muslim League zealots touring the tribal areas with urgent exhortations to the faithful to work for the attainment of the goal of Pakistan made no mean contribution. Understandably, those among the tribes who had hitherto leaned towards the Congress found their position increasingly untenable and began to talk in terms of 'independence' or, alternately, stress their Afghan links.[20]

III

The Khan Sahib government, with its convincing legislative majority at Peshawar and the unstinted support of the Congress Party in the interim government at New Delhi, left the League with few options except to resort to extra-constitutional means to dislodge it from power. An erosion of its support base at the popular level was thus the only way of weakening the authority of the provincial administration. In this 'holy' crusade, the League had few scruples in employing any weapons or means that came handy.

Nature too seems to have lent a hand in terms of what appeared to be an impending famine. Already there had been an acute shortage of food, especially in the settled districts of Bannu and D I Khan, and in the tribal areas of Waziristan. The Rabi (spring) crop in 1946, had been far from satisfactory; and the Kharif (autumn) in 1947, a virtual washout. A bad situation was further aggravated by a large and unprecedented influx of *powindas*, driven from across the Afghan territory by paucity of food supplies at home. Just about this time, Nehru's visit had left the Khan Sahib government rudely shaken. For the League's propaganda mills,

Nehru allegedly stood for Hindu domination, and the Khan Sahib government was in an unholy collusion with him. More, Nehru's Hindu coreligionists had perpetrated untold atrocities on a hapless Muslim minority in Bihar, and in Bombay. Exploiting the resultant human misery, compounded further by an acute food shortage, the League was to gain maximum political mileage. *Inter alia*, it openly alleged that Hindu shopkeepers had been diverting their food grain surpluses to the black market.

Even at the best of times, the Frontier was not exactly a foodgrains surplus province; for most part, it just about managed to scrape through. During 1944-5, when crops failed, it was bailed out by allocations of grain from the Panjab under a fiat of the central government. This had helped avert famine. All the same, during the mid-1940s, quantities of grain found their way into private hoards, rather than grain mandis. The Muslim League government, then in power, had no alternative but to introduce controls. This was not to the liking of the big landlords who were the League's natural constituency. In so far as the ministers' real purpose was to abuse, and exploit, the power which the apparatus of controls vested in the executive—rather than to secure the best interests of the consumer—the resentment of the landlords was understandable. To no one's surprise, the Congress Party, then in opposition, exploited the popular discontent and vociferously condemned the system of controls.

In 1945, the main problem had been eased by the high yield of the harvest but in the following year foodgrain production was low. Meanwhile the Muslim League had been dislodged from power and the Congress was back with a convincing electoral win. One of the immediate priorities of the new government was to manage the grave food situation. Sadly for it, the scarcity of foodgrains in the Frontier was replicated elsewhere in the country. In the event, New Delhi warned Peshawar that it must plan to reduce its food imports. Forced to fend for itself, the provincial government decided upon a tighter, stricter, form of procurement: it fixed a higher (procurement) target for each district and imposed a compulsory levy on individual landlords. This entailed a lot of complicated paper work, a less than fair or equitable assessment of the individual levy and no end of resentment by the individual landlords.[21] Before long, Fraser Noble who was the province's Foodgrains Procurement Officer concluded that the scheme, 'constructed meticulously' on paper, ignored harsh ground realities; and that the Khan Sahib outfit ignored the fundamental change that had come over the political landscape. It refused to face the harsh truth that the landlords who had stoutly resisted the imposition of controls by their own party, viz., the Muslim League, were far from willing to oblige their known political enemies, the Congress. This became doubly dangerous in the light of the pronouncedly hostile communal tack which the League had now taken. Consequently, in the large surplus districts, which also happened to be the major Congress-Khudai Khidmatgar strongholds, such as Mardan and Peshawar, the Muslim League's propaganda line 'began to take more effect'.[22]

Even as the food situation worsened, a rash of communal riots broke out. On the night of 7-8 December (1946), trans-border tribesmen attacked the village of Battal in Hazara district and burnt down the bazaar. A couple of days later, they torched the village of Oghi (also Orghi). A number of Sikh rural folk had settled in the hills below the *ghalis* in this area as small-time cultivators since the times of the Sikh ruler, Maharaja Ranjit Singh (r. 1799-1839). Owing to poor communications and the mountainous nature of the terrain, reports of these orgies received at headquarters were patchy at best. But probably, Caroe estimated, there were 20 odd murders and some forcible conversions, with a number of evacuee houses burnt down. Most of the survivors, therefore, fled to neighbouring Panja Sahib at Hasan Abdal just inside the Attock district of the Panjab while others made their way to Kakul, Abbotabad, Havellian and Haripur.[23]

The Khan Sahib ministry and Governor Caroe came under heavy attack from all sides: from Hindus and Sikhs, for weakness and inadequate protection and Caroe especially, for instigating the disorders; and from the League, for tyrannical repression of local Muslim patriots. The governor was persuaded that many among the minority community felt that a Muslim ministry, i.e. a Muslim League outfit, 'would afford a surer guarantee of minority safety' than did the 'present epicene organisation'.[24]

The Hazara raids appeared well-organised, apparanetly 'instigated' by mullahs across the border working on fanatical tribes to avenge the anti-Muslim riots in Bihar. Thus began an exodus of over 10,000 Hindus and Sikhs to Kashmir and the Panjab.[25]

The Khan Sahib ministry's knee-jerk reaction was to ban public speech, processions and rallies in Abbotabad and other towns of the Hazara district. At the same time, a Public Safety Ordinance was promulgated to check rumour-mongering while collective security fines were to be imposed for the protection of evacuee property.[26] Additionally, tribes responsible for the raids were asked to pay an indemnity which they eventually did. This obviated the need for going across the border to chastise them. Needless to say, numerous arrests were made.[27]

Predicatably, the Muslim League exploited the situation by exhorting the people to defy executive authority, especially in terms of the restrictions imposed on public speech and political rallies. A case that was to gain considerable notoriety was the forcible conversion to Islam of a pregnant Sikh girl who was also coerced into marrying one of the gang members responsible for the murder of her husband. As a result, the Sikh evacuees threatened not to return to their homes, a move that was bound to slow down any reversion to normal conditions.

The Hazara Sikh girl's case was magnified out of all proportion.[28] She had been brought to Peshawar and Khan Sahib put her up in his own house: 'unwisely as I think and as I told him', reported Caroe to the governor-general.[29] To silence the critics, she was produced before the district magistrate where she swore that she wanted to rejoin her faith. To squash wild rumours that this was false and that she was being coerced, the premier had invited Abdul Qaiyum and other League leaders to hear her testimony.[30] Even though persuaded of the truth, they refused to yield the political high ground they now occupied. Khan Sahib, they charged, was not behaving as a true Muslim. Having allowed his own daughter to marry a non-Muslim (her husband, Jaswant Singh, who was a pilot in the Royal Indian Air Force, was actually an Indian Christian, *not* a Hindu, as the League charged) he was now privy to a *Muslim* girl reverting to her Sikh faith!

On 24 February, a mob had assembled at Peshawar ostensibly to free the Sikh girl, whom, they alleged, Khan Sahib was now sheltering. In the guise of a procession, of 'at least 5,000 men', they marched towards the Government House, broke the police cordon and came right up to the road in front of the Governor's house and into Khan Sahib's garden. Having broken loose they now besieged the house on all sides.

The police did not exactly mutiny but, going through the motions of loading their rifles, 'quietly disobeyed orders to fire'. Meanwhile the mob broke some window panes and threw stones—but 'did not succeed in storming the house'. It was presently dispersed with tear gas shells, having first been halted in its tracks by the 'defiant imprecations' of Khan Sahib's cockeny wife 'for whom', Fraser Noble recorded, 'we all felt unbounded admiration'. Nor did Khan Sahib cower. 'Brave as a lion', he stood up to tell the crowd what he thought of them and 'refused to give away any points'.[31]

Later when the Sikh girl's conversion was revoked, the Muslim League exploited the situation no end, alleging, *inter alia*, that the case bore a striking resemblance to that of Islam Bibi in the 1930s which had led to the rising of the Fakir of Ipi.[32]

Meantime there had been large-scale demonstrations, and processions, in Peshawar and elsewhere in sympathy with what had been happening in the Panjab. The saving grace though was that, in sharp contrast to the Panjab, the Frontier had so far steered clear of violence.[33]

Just then a byelection to the Provincial Assembly in Peshawar was to prove to be a benchmark of sorts. Traditionally, the Kamalzai rural constituency in Mardan, had been a stronghold of the Khudai Khidmatgar movement; the seat though was then held by a Muslim League MLA, Sir Mohammad Akbar Khan, the Khan of Hoti. Somewhat of an eccentric if also a known Raj loyalist, the Khan was by far the most important and wealthiest of landowners in Mardan. He, and not a few others of his class, had found their influence gradually eroded as new political forces, channeled through the party organisations of both the Congress and the League, displaced the authority of large landowners as powerful allies of the Raj. The byelection was caused by the Khan's resignation from the legislature and his membership of the Muslim League in that he had refused to heed the latter's call for renouncing his British titles. This, to him, was blasphemy: disloyalty towards, and betrayal of, his British masters.

The election campaign in Mardan, in which the Congress had fielded its earlier (i.e. 1946) candidate against a comparatively weak League nominee, was fought on a straight issue: the League, for Pakistan; the Congress, for united India. When the Khan Sahib ministry had promulgated its Public Safety Ordinance to contain growing violence in Hazara District, the League had announced the formation of a 'War Committee' under the leadership of the Pir of Manki. *Inter alia*, the Committee blamed the Hindu and Sikh blackmarketeers for the Hazara disturbances and urged the offenders—whom it projected as the Mujahideen—to refuse to pay fines, and instead rise in opposition to the authorities and wage a holy war, tactics which a contemporary observer had dubbed as 'despicable'.[34] The Pir had none the less postponed action on his call pending the results of the Mardan byelection. Writing to the governor-general on 8 February 1947, Caroe had confided: 'I rather expect myself that Congress strong as they are in villages, will pull it off.'[35]

As a matter of fact, it did not, and this despite resort to some questionable means. Thus Fraser Noble who was in Mardan on the polling day, recalls how Mrs. Yahya Jan, wife of the education minister and a daughter of Badshah Khan, visited a booth for women and seeing that the vote was going against the Congress sat on a ballot-box and refused to budge, defying the authorities to remove her. Before Peshawar could be contacted for orders, polling was over for the day!

'The Congress debacle was a surprise to everyone, including both the parties', wrote the governor a fortnight later, and this despite the fact that the Khan of Hoti, had declared his neutrality. The Congress made a 'struggle to win' in an area where it had a good deal of backing.[36]

Nehru's analysis of the result was not without its merits. 'There was', he conceded in a communication to the governor-general, 'a slight increase in the Muslim League majority' (from 189 to 558) but the total voting had gone up too, from 16,539 to 17,294. 'Both the candidates increased their pool' though the increase on the Muslim League side was somewhat greater. On the whole, he concluded, 'it might be said that there was no change'. In the event, Nehru stoutly repudiated the charge that the Khan Sahib government had lost public support.[37]

Whatever gloss Nehru and the Congress may have put on the result, it was clear that a year earlier—at the time of the general election in February 1946—the League had, on the whole, failed to convince the average Pathan that a vote for Congress meant a vote for Hindu-controlled India. It was now obvious that Abdul Ghaffar Khan had lost considerable ground. Not many in the Frontier bought his argument that Pathans could control their destiny in an alignment with Hindustan whereas within a Pakistan grouping they would be exploited and absorbed by the Panjabi majority.

The Mardan byelection result was declared on 15-16 February; four days later, on 20 February, a protest demonstration at Mardan led to the arrest of Abdul Qaiyum Khan as well as Samin Jan (president of the Frontier Muslim League) for defying prohibitory orders. The governor had viewed the arrests as 'entirely justifiable'.[38] None the less they were to provoke a demonstration in Peshawar which among other things demanded the release of the Muslim League leaders.

Thus, it was that the Frontier Muslim League, 'partly stimulated' by developments in the Panjab, and partly yielding to the cry of 'Islam in danger' over the incident of the Sikh girl from Hazara, launched its political offensive. The Peshawar demonstration, in retrospect, was to prove its opening shot.

IV

Before long the ugly confrontation between the Premier and an unruly mob was by no means an isolated incident. The editor of the Quaid's 'Papers' refers to the Muslim League's 'vigorous' Civil Disobedience movement launched to dislodge the Khan Sahib ministry and 'increasingly undermine its authority and popularity'.[39] Presently, the movement gathered strength and worse things were in store. Sadly, the legislature too was completely paralysed, for almost the entire League opposition were behind bars. All this while the governor was telling his ministers that there had been 'a swing away from them' during the previous year which made it imperative for them 'continually to assess their position with the electorate'. This position, he was certain, would 'gradually grow weaker' in the absence of a reconciliation with the opposition. For public opinion, he warned, was 'falling away' from the Congress.[40]

The Muslim League's 'one line of propaganda', as the correspondent of the influential *Civil & Military Gazette* (Lahore) put it, was that the Khan Sahib government, of three Muslims and one Hindu, was 'a mere stooge of Hindu Raj like the Vichy government in 'free' France'. What was more, the League propaganda was 'falling on very fertile ground'. Against this, 'how strong was AGK today' to withstand the Muslim League onslaught? This 'crucial question', he argued, could only be decided by an election.

The Congress disdain for fresh elections was well-known but its reasoning that as it had been voted to power only a year back did not hold for:

> those elections were not fought on the issue of Pakistan and were moreover before the visit of the Cabinet Mission to India, and over-riding all . . . (was) the compelling fact that the British Prime Minister's statement of February 20 (1946) had completely changed the political situation.

Among other things the correspondent emphasised that in the Frontier, the 26-year-old Pir of Manki had 'made Islam and the Muslim League one'. He also had 'his trump card' of the Sikh girl up his sleeve and with a bodyguard of 600 'six-foot Sheiks, armed to the teeth' was planning to 'lead the fanatic tribes' into Peshawar 'on this issue'.[41]

Ideologically too, the position of the Khan Sahib government was becoming difficult, if not indeed impossible. For the influence of the north-western Panjab on the east and of the tribes on the west, all declaiming against Hindu domination, was 'certain to squeeze' Congress out before long. For, as Caroe saw it, Congress was 'not natural here'.[42]

Even though the disorders in the Frontier hitherto (February 1947) had, mercifully, not approached the Panjab ravages in fury, there had been, as the governor put it, 'butchery of defenseless minorities' in the villages around the Peshawar and Hazara districts and some forcible conversions.[43] Fraser, an eye-witness, has suggested that while there was no evidence of 'butchery' in the villages around Peshawar—as had been the case of Sikh villagers around Hazara—there were quite a few communal murders in Peshawar city. Worse, in several cases, Hindus and Sikhs were sought out in spite of efforts made by their Muslim friends to protect them. The butchery threat, Fraser Noble adds, was much worse in D I Khan and its Tank sub-division.[44]

On 21 March, part of Manshera township in Hazara district was burnt down, even though there was a company of troops in the place.[45] The incident was largely a spill-over from the Panjab and pointed to an already mounting tension and uneasiness. For the earlier Peshawar demonstration on 24 February was symptomatic of worse days ahead. On 6 April, Peshawar was placed under a round the clock curfew with a few hours in-between for people to collect essential supplies.[46]

The arrest of Muslim League leaders, among them Arbab Abdul Ghafoor and Fida Mohammed, in the wake of the Peshawar demonstration, proved to be a signal for the movement to spread. The official ban on meetings and processions, referred to earlier, was observed more in the breach than compliance. The Pir of Manki who played no small part in spreading the movement avoided arrest for almost a month; he was not to be nabbed until end-March when matters had already reached a sad pass. Congressmen alleged that the Pir enjoyed government's protection; critics averred that the ministry was afraid of the serious consequences his arrest would provoke. In actual fact, it was Caroe's advice to the government to stay its hand largely because he viewed the Pir less 'an agitator' and more 'an organiser', who could be a help in restoring communal harmony! All the same, the Governor's rating of the Pir was not exactly flattering: 'quite pleasant but nothing much more . . . I would not see in him one who is in due time going to become the Abdul Ghaffar Khan of the other side. He is however only 26 and may develop.'[47] In restrospect, one may add, that the Pir failed to. His rise was meteoric; his eclipse, equally sudden. Within a year of Pakistan's birth, the Pir had faded away.[48]

It may be of interest to note that a report in the *Tribune* datelined Peshawar, 31 March, 'From our own correspondent', suggested that with his arrest 'the long rope' given by the Frontier Government to the Pir's activities had at last been cut. It added that 'some sections of people' held that if 'this Mullah' had been arrested earlier 'in the first batch of Leaguers', the movement would have died 'its natural death'. Among different stories about his non-arrest was Khan Sahib's statement that the Mullah 'had friends in the higher circles'.[49]

Meantime the Muslim League's parallel 'civil disobedience' movement in the Panjab had succeeded in pulling down the provincial government of the Unionist-Congress coalition (2 March 1947). Rated a great triumph, it served as a big morale booster for the party leadership in Peshawar. Here, interestingly enough, even though there appeared little by way of planning, the League campaign did not flag. This was the more remarkable in that a number of prominent League leaders were behind bars. Initially, the parent all-India Muslim League had been quite sceptical about what its Frontier unit was up to. But as the latter's campaign gathered in strength and gained momentum, the central body lent its provincial outfit a measure of moral and organisational support.

On 10 March, a bare week after its triumph in dislodging a non-League government in neighbouring Panjab, the Muslim League staged a demonstration in Peshawar to disrupt the budget session of the Provincial Legislative Assembly.

Anticipating trouble, the premier had asked for army units to be present with clear instructions that, on no account would the demonstrators be allowed to upset the business of the legislature. Despite an earlier warning that the government had posted military guards around the Assembly chamber and that nobody should go there, a crowd had collected on the railway line near the chamber and tampered with the track. The magistrate on duty tried to persuade them through requests and appeals and right from 9 a.m. to 1 p.m., the troops were checked from firing. Yet the crowd would not behave; instead, it attacked the troops and started stoning the police. It was only then that the army were compelled to open fire.

In an appeal issued to its citizens, the deputy commissioner of Peshawar remonstrated:

> If at all you want to stage demonstrations against the Government in power then adopt peaceful ways and means, which are more effective. At all times you can get chances to lay your grievances before the Government through your representatives.[50]

His, sadly, was a lone voice in the wilderness.

All said and done, it was a bad show, what with the opposition in and outside the legislature in jail and with the army resorting to firing which resulted in the loss of two killed and several injured. 'So much,' Caroe told the governor-general, 'for democratic processes!'[51] Even though the ministry managed to carry through the budget session, in retaliation for what happened around the Assembly building, an irate mob ravaged through the town, killing twenty Hindus and Sikhs and burning their houses and property. Before long, the contagion caught on; killings and arson became routine and spread to other districts.

I, F.Noble Esq. IC.S. Joint District Magistrate of Peshawar, acting under Section 130 of the Code of Criminal Procedure, required No A11150 Rank Capt. Name J.G. Collins of the "D." Coy Unit 1st B^{ln} The Royal Garhwal Rifles to disperse an unlawful assembly at 09.40 o'clock (approximately) on the tenth day of March 1947 at Peshawar.

Countersigned by J.G. Collins, Capt, my signature, inscribed with a very nervous hand on a military notebook, is clumsy and barely decipherable. Underneath, more firmly and clearly, I had written "09.40 hours".

Four sepoys moved forward to within twenty paces of the forbidden line, and took up firing positions, and waited. The crowd wavered, and I thought they were going to retreat. Suddenly, more stones were thrown, and there was a rush forward - not from the front ranks but from further back. Four shots*(4) were fired on command; an extraordinary silence followed; for several seconds the scene seemed to freeze; then a backward movement started and in a minute the line was clear, except for some men carrying others behind the running mob. All the shots had struck low, below the knee as the manual prescribes. But at that range, the damage was severe. Two of those who were hit subsequently died. As Mohammed Jan had foreseen, they were elderly zamindars, not active political agitators, who had probably come into town for the tamasha. The mob's leaders had discreetly melted away when the soldiers took up firing positions - perhaps to cast the stones that caused the crucial last flurry of movement over the line. Thankfully, the young students also had retreated or turned aside.

I was too busy at first to feel unduly concerned - relieved that the threat to the Assembly had been repelled, as the Ministers had ordered, but preoccupied by the inevitable consequences that followed at once in the city - the looting and burning of Hindu property, and stabbing and beating of anyone who looked as if he might not be Muslim. But the horror of the experience stayed with me, for the order to shoot had been given, not to stop a communal riot, but to save the face of an unpopular Ministry and to fulfil their expressed instructions. I did not find it easy to argue with myself that if we had stood aside and let the crowd advance, more men would have died at the gates of the Assembly, perhaps even some of the elected representatives of the people."

Memoirs of Sir Fraser Noble (p. 311).

Fraser Noble has suggested that in the progress of the League campaign for murder and mayhem, these episodes were now a daily occurrence. The one on 10 March proved to have 'a symbolic influence' on the Muslim League's Civil Disobedience campaign, and the inevitable consequences followed: looting of anyone who looked as if he might not be a Muslim! For himself, Noble was emotionally shaken:

> the horror of the experience stayed with me, for the order to shoot had been given, not to stop a communal riot, but to save the face of an unpopular Ministry and to fulfill their expressed instructions.[52]

In the weeks that followed, the army was active in aid of civil authority in Peshawar. But the 10 March firing was 'the only instance' when its fire power was brought to bear on an ugly situation. This saved a great deal of bloodshed in consequence. In the days and weeks of night curfew and tear-gas that followed, the army patrols were not challenged while their co-ordination with police activity was 'a superb demonstration' of fine planning and first-class training.[53]

On 2 April a train was stopped near Kohat and attacked by men in Muslim League uniforms. And as the official fortnightly report for the second half of April put it, the general picture was one of processions, picketing and interference with the running of trains. This, in turn, invited police lathi charge, use of tear-gas and even arrests. There were occasional murders of Hindus and Sikhs apart from more serious outbreaks. Bomb blasts and sabotage of roads and bridges was not unknown. There was an atmosphere of uneasiness everywhere and fear in the minds of the minorities.[54]

Serious riots broke out in D I Khan on 14 April when 18 people were reported killed and 900 shops and private buildings torched. From D I Khan the riots spread to Tank which was invested by Mahsud tribesmen from across the border. The raiders burnt down practically the entire town. The conflagration spread far and wide. This was to pose a serious threat to stores of grain and other commodities. And inasmuch as southern Waziristan depended upon Tank for its food supplies, ramifications were bound to be widespread. Caroe, away to Delhi for a governors' conference, 'and kept awake all night by decoded cypher telegrams', rushed back to visit both Tank as well as D I Khan. Accompanied by General Messervy, then GOC, Northern Command, Caroe's objective was to see what could be done 'to restore confidence' in the Derajat where the most serious problem now was agrarian.[55]

Meantime, the League's highly decentralised and largely spontaneous disturbances in 1942, the Frontier police had not had that handicap. Now, whenever a lathi charge was launched on a crowd of demonstrators, Hindus and Sikhs were attacked elsewhere in the city. (There had been about twelve of these occurrences each leading to a crop of stabbings and arson). The police could not be everywhere, and must be reinforced, because they were becoming exhausted. They were not even adequately fed during long hours on active duty.

During the critical first three days of the trouble the military had acted helpfully and effectively in aid of the civil power, keeping the outskirts of the city and its suburbs, and the approaches to the cantonment, clear of demonstrators, but there was a limit to their usefulness and their ability to help in circumstances of general unrest. The army was properly unwilling to be called in unless there was a specific job for them to do. So after three days they had withdrawn, leaving the police to cope, although they stood by to help on a Friday, when trouble was always likely to break out after the special Friday prayers in the mosques. On that day, in particular, large crowds from the rural areas and even from Tribal territory were likely to be in the city.

The D.C. did not shirk from calling on the Congress Government to respect and make allowances for the criticisms and grievances of the people and to take "initiatives towards clemency and reconciliation". He called courageously for a willingness to participate in open discussion - if only to "allay the doubts and suspicions of those who are levelling unworthy and ill-founded charges against Government". It must have been a difficult document to draft in the circumstances - and events were soon to show how empty an exercise it had been. I have pencilled notes of a meeting of senior officers held to review the happenings on the following Friday (7th March). Those present, besides the D.C. and myself, were the Senior Superintendent of Police (S.S.P.) the P.A. (Khyber Agency), the City Magistrate, the Assistant Inspector of Police (in charge of training) and the Deputy Superintendents in charge respectively of the City Police and the force of Additional Police based in the District (D.S.P. City and D.S.P. A.P.). The S.S.P. was a key figure throughout these months. He was Sardar Abdur Rashid, an exceptionally bright police officer, not many years older than myself, who in the first phase of independent Pakistan had an outstanding career, becoming a senior

Memoirs of Sir Fraser Noble (p. 305).

ventured to agree with my view, and for the present it was decided not to bring the F.C. in with such specific instructions.

We also discussed ways of trying to reduce ingress to the city on Fridays, for it was after Friday prayers in the mosques that Muslim tempers were on their shortest fuse. It was suggested that we should close the shops of all communities; stop the cattle fair which was held on the Grand Trunk road a short distance out beyond a well known warehouse; close all Government offices inside the city, like the Tahsil, the courts of the Tahsildar and Naib-Tahsildars; and simply prohibit all entry through the city's numerous gates after the start of Friday prayers. I was very nervous about most of these suggestions, opposing them partly because they would interfere with the legitimate business of many people and would cause more bad temper and fuel the rising tide of criticism of the Congress Minsitry. The idea of closing shops reminded me of the notorious August public holiday which had been declared in Calcutta in 1946 and had left too many malcontents of both communities with too much time on their hands, leading to the awful Calcutta killings which had marked the earliest worsening of the communal situation after the failure of the Cabinet Mission. In my view, the best policy was so far as possible to allow business as usual, and try to protect the minorities.

A note written that evening after the meeting shows what my thoughts were. "The signs are that the spread of communal rioting in Punjab has definitely made our dangerous situation extremely delicate. I agree that we **must** concentrate on preventing actual communal rioting rather than on mere political demonstrations, if our police are really stretched. Are they? It is now again almost too late to put force to the test. On the whole, I think that up to date it has been wise to use force so judiciously, in fighting against a legitimate political cause, albeit one using illegal methods. But for this argument to be correct it is essential to get set in motion efforts at a settlement. Almost any attempt to negotiate would do, but in the absence of such an attempt the odds are heavily against a preservation of 'peace'. The move at this stage must come from the strong side - i.e. Government. The difficulties are obvious - the leaders (on both sides). We must use the dangers of the Punjab troubles as a lever of persuasion on our Ministers - but we must also find new leaders on the other side who can negotiate decently".

Memoirs of Sir Fraser Noble (p. 307).

campaign gave the province little peace. Behind the scenes, large groups of Muslim students and almost all Muslim officials played a key role: the former engaged in small-scale terrorism, the latter, in subverting state authority and hobnobbing with the law breakers. A sympathetic police force meant that illegal demonstrations were not taken serious note of. At the same time, both overt and covert support from the police and state functionaries made the crisis look somewhat less than real, even 'artificial'.[56]

Together with Muslim students, Muslim National Guards led demonstrations, supplied volunteers and co-ordinated activities. Some teachers at Islamia College (Peshawar) are known to have lent a hand in making explosives; the Pir of Manki provided some financial assistance.[57]

With the League's top leadership behind bars, new leaders emerged and replaced their arrested comrades. Thanks to police laxity and alleged connivance, the incarcerated leaders remained actively in touch with their followers outside. And the movement did not appear to lose its edge, its strength or momentum. Jansson's considered view that 'illegal demonstrations were dealt with very leniently if at all' bears testimony. He cites the instance of a deputy superintendent of police at Peshawar cantonment, one Faizullah Khan, who when ordered to make a lathi charge, let his men 'beat the ground and their own buses'. Faizullah Khan, it is now known, used to attend meetings where measures 'to be taken against the activists' were discussed! Later, he would dutifully inform the students as to what the government proposed doing.[58]

The Muslim National Guards were a paramilitary outfit and roughly a counterpart of the Khudai Khidmatgars. Upfront, they led demonstrations, recruited volunteers and took a prominent part in all League-sponsored activities in general. Khurshid Anwar, a high profile functionary of the Guards, played a prominent role in this context. His almost two-month sojourn (28 February to 24 April) was to prove eventful. Armed with a generous supply of explosives, he advocated large-scale sabotage and organised an underground movement to bomb government buildings. Interestingly enough, he managed his supply of explosives through the police school at Hangu; his mole was the chief drill inspector who also imparted instruction in the use of explosives. There was help too from a professor of chemistry at Islamia College, Peshawar.[59]

Khurshid Anwar was also to play an important role in organising and sustaining Muslim women demonstrations which caused the Khan Sahib government no end of embarrassment and were indeed hard to counter. There were then no women police and letting loose men in uniform on women agitators would have been outrageous. The highest of government functionaries were thus reduced to pleading with these fair sex demonstrators, to disperse. And when they did not, ignored them; or, closed down for the day.

Additionally, these women demonstrations caught the Frontier Congress in a cultural trap, for Pakhtun values came in the way of employing force, even though there were the worst of provocations. The role of women in the League agitation was limited because participation by the weaker sex in public events is anathema in Islamic eyes and most Pathans make for staunch Muslims. Male activists, therefore, keen on relief from what was now a daily ritual, conceded occasional days when it would be women's turn to keep the police force on tenterhooks.

On the first occasion, a group of women had marched over the railway bridge towards the cantonment where they worked their way through and around the barricades. The police force proved to be helpless spectators—a fact that emboldened the demonstrators no end.

A few days later women processionists marched to the civil secretariat and, brushing aside policemen on duty, flooded all over into the gardens, the courtyards and the verandahs. Administration was paralysed and even some of the ministers had to be rescued!

On 14 April, women protestors, escorted by a large contingent of men, marched to the railway station, close to the site of army shooting on 10 March. For a time, they succeeded in halting railway traffic but in the process a number of demonstrators were injured, some seriously. Happily though, no one was killed. All the same, the incident infuriated the menfolk who turned their anger and frustration on hapless Hindus and Sikhs in the town. Quite a few were stabbed and their shops burnt. A magisterial inquiry into the incident later revealed that the public focus on the railway embankment was compounded by wrath on a train which was viewed as an instrument of government activity, whose operations the League was out to stultify and grind to a halt.[60]

In a letter to the Quaid datelined 'Peshawar, 30 April 1947', Firoz Khan Noon who claimed to have spent a week in the province—his wife had played a prominent role in the women's protest demonstrations—addressed 20 meetings and covered about 250 miles in the districts of Kohat, Mardan and Peshawar, exhorted Jinnah that 'he must press for Section 93'. Noon underlined that in the event of elections 'one of the contesting parties cannot be allowed' to remain incharge and warned of the danger that Olaf Caroe 'may, like Jenkins (Governor of Panjab) become a Ranjit Singh in the NWFP and procrastinate and not hold elections'. He typescript, and there were nineteen pages of exhibits, including formal answers to specific questions put to an expert of the North-West Railway. My final report, which ran to about 8,000 words, almost certainly pleased nobody of importance. The train driver was exonerated, the organisers of the demonstration were criticised, and a number of officials were probably embarrassed by comments on their failure to prevent the accident. As I proceeded with my task, my depsair about the Indian situation grew. In itself the enquiry was important: but its true significance was submerged in the thorny thickets of the political struggle - and public interest ceased as soon as it was realised that my findings would not contribute to the cause of either party. That was quite a healthy lesson for me, for at the start my inflated ego had imagined my investigation to be central to the course of the political struggle. After all, in Peshawar its public focus had been on that railway embankment since the riot of 10th March, and the accident to the women was inflicted by a train, which was seen as an instrument of government, whose operations the League wanted to halt. There was an intriguing symbolism about the affair, which it became my duty to shatter. But in doing so, I felt deflated. Even as I worked on the report, I realised how trivial any single event in the struggle had become - however central apparently for a day or two in a local context - in relation to the hugeness of the upheaval that confronted the attenuated number of those who served the Crown in India.

Memoirs of Sir Fraser Noble (p. 318).

therefore, exhorted the League leader to 'get the Viceroy committed to holding elections'. There was the other possibility, Noon continued, that like Jenkins, Caroe too 'continues to rule' under Section 93. In such an eventuality, however, 'a movement would develop which will finish the Congress forever' and put the League 'at the top'.[61]

The active involvement of women protestors was, thus, 'a new and important element' in Frontier politics.[62]

V

In meeting the manifold challenges it was up against, the response of the Khan Sahib government was 'neither systematic nor severe'. At best, it appeared ill at ease; at worst, increasingly helpless. Chief Secretary Mitchell confessed as much. There was, he conceded, 'no long-term policy for dealing with the situation other than hanging grimly on from day to day and hoping to tire the other side out'.[63] The laxity, in part, stemmed from the government's clear realisation that most of its Muslim officials sympathised with the League and shared all the intelligence official agencies garnered with the party's agitators. The law and order agencies, therefore, could, under no circumstances, be depended upon to enforce harsh measures. Again, administrative surveillance was confined at best to towns, while out in the countryside, the League organisers moved about freely, holding meetings, planning demonstrations and recruiting volunteers with impunity. The long arm of the law, conspicuous by its absence.

The first phase of the Muslim League civil disobedience movement which may be said to have lasted until 10 March was characterised by noisy, yet relatively peaceful, demonstrations. And minor property damage. But no deliberate attempt to sabotage or engage in communal violence. All the same, hotheads in the movement, egged on remorselessly by outside elements, were convinced that sabotage of government facilities and communal violence against the minorities alone would bring the Congress government to its knees. No wonder that, in the second phase of the movement, broadly heralded by the fall of the Khizr government in the neighbouring Panjab, destruction of government as well as private property was singularly pronounced. The aftermath of the firing on the League's procession at Peshawar on 10 March was witness to roving gangs in the towns who 'sought out' Hindus and Sikhs.[64] All the same, all through March communal violence was confined largely to Hazara and Peshawar while stabbing incidents in Bannu, Mardan and Kohat were of a relatively minor nature.

It is revealing that in the early phases of the Muslim League agitation, the nationalist press continued to harp on the theme that it lacked mass support. This much is evident from a leading article in the *Tribune* entitled 'These Frontier Pirs, Mullahs and Nawabs'. It underlined *inter alia* that the League's 'political monstrosity' in the Frontier was 'most staggering'. For here it 'mobilised all the reactionary and medieval forces under its flag and aroused the worst communal passions and got the worst terroristic scenes enacted . . .'

The 'spearhead' of its army in the Frontier province, consisted of pirs, mullahs and nawabs—'the heavily crusted repositories of obscurantism and reactionaryism'—who were in the forefront of the movement. Their game plan, the paper continued, was to make the Frontier Governor 'drive a coach and six through all democratic principles and practices and dismiss Dr Khan Sahib's ministry which continues to enjoy the confidence of the Legislature, which represents the Frontier people'.[65]

It is important to bear in mind that the League agitation's non-violent exterior was purely notional. For all its lip service to *peaceful* demonstrations notwithstanding, there was from the very beginning no attempt to contain violence. To the contrary, this alone, it was argued, would cripple the administration and thereby demonstrate the unrepresentative character of the Congress government. No wonder, members of the League's 'War Council' were readily convinced of the political efficacy of violence.[66]

Beginning in April, the centre of communal disorders moved south and the starting point here was the ten days of gruesome rioting in D I Khan, 15-25 April. Not unlike Hazara, D I Khan also had linkages with the Panjab, of which it was truly a geographical extension. In the event, large-scale rioting earlier in the neighbouring Multan district of Panjab had cast grim shadows over D I Khan. The mounting tension was further exacerbated by the incursions of the Mahsuds from the tribal area with their aftermath of rape and rapine. By 25 April, when the army brought the situation to some semblance of normalcy, the toll had risen to 118 killed. While almost the entire Hindu-Sikh population living in rural areas, appoximating 16,000 and many more in the towns, had moved into refugee camps in D I Khan or spilled over into neigbouring Panjab. By mid-May, an estimated 60 per cent of the minority community in Peshawar, Mardan and Kohat had left the province; the percentages in Hazara and D I Khan being much higher.[67]

A slight lull in the situation in May was occasioned by two developments. One, Mountbatten's visit to Peshawar and the tribal areas around the Khyber (28-9 April)—to which a detailed reference is made later—to an extent eased Muslim League apprehensions about the future of the province. For the viceroy gave broad enough hints that the eventual fate of the province would be decided either through an election or some sort of a test of public opinion, and *not* by the Congress majority in the province's incumbent legislature.[68] Two, Jinnah's joint appeal with the Mahatma for an end to violence (15 April) reinforced by his (Jinnah's) personal efforts with the League's Frontier leadership scaled down the fury of violence. That it tailed off but did not end, underlined both the decentralised nature of the agitation as well as the active involvement in it of non-League elements.[69]

A few details may be relevant. At their meeting in jail on 1 May, in the aftermath of Mountbatten's visit, the Frontier League leadership resolved to continue their agitation until Section 93 rule was promulgated and an election ordered. Four of the leaders were soon paroled to discuss the situation with the Quaid: the Pir of Manki, Abdul Qaiyum Khan, Samin Jan and Arbab Nur Muhammad. Assured that they would win in the proposed election, Jinnah reportedly endorsed their decision to continue the agitation but is said to have asked them to put a stop to killings in the province.

As a matter of fact, the Frontier Muslim League leaders met Jinnah in New Delhi on 3-4 May. In a long statement on 7 May, the Quaid while endorsing their decision to continue the movement, underlined his disquiet on mounting violence in the Frontier and referred among other matters to the League resolution of 29 July (1946) and the meaning of 'Direct Action' 'which is attributed to us maliciously, namely that it is based on the principle of force, violence and bloodshed. This was of course without any foundation and untrue.'

All that direct action meant, the Quaid stressed, was 'social pressure, strike or revolt, constituting moral pressure upon the authority in power to redress our grievances and meet our demands'.

It is illuminating to recall that large-scale smuggling of arms and ammunition to the Frontier was not unknown. Thus a press report suggested that a parcel containing 2,900 cartridges of .303 bore and 'destined for some station in the Frontier' was intercepted at the Amritsar railway station on 10 June. It had allegedly been booked 'from a station in the central Punjab.'[70]

A measure of the bad name that the League was getting for its activities may be gauged from the emphasis in the Quaid's statement on avoiding violence. *Inter alia,* he underlined that the movement should *not* be 'allowed to take a communal turn'; that the fight was not 'against the Hindus or the Sikhs'; that 'we should harm the weak' was 'against all canons of morality and civilisation and the teachings of Islam'. Above all, it was the duty of every Muslim 'to protect the minorities.'[71]

It may be recalled that the agitation was not formally called off until after 4 June in the wake of the 3 June announcement which committed HMG to a referendum in the NWFP.[72]

By mid-May government officials in the rural areas of Peshawar district began to be attacked and village land revenue records destroyed. Demonstrations in the known Congress strongholds of Charsadda and Utmanzai bore eloquent testimony to the agitators' growing clout and ability to challenge the Khudai Khidmatgars even on their home ground.[73]

A slight digression may help put the League agitation into sharper focus. Early in April, Mountbatten had sought out Lt Col Dudley de la Fargue, Chief Secretary to the NWFP government, then in Delhi on his way home on leave. The colonel gave the governor-general his considered view: (*a*) that free elections in the Frontier would return a Congress government; (*b*) that Caroe was biased against the Khan Sahib ministry; (*c*) that his (Caroe's) continued presence in the province posed a threat to British prestige. Hodson has expressed the view that de la Fargue was 'a man of little judgement' who was deeply involved with Khan Sahib and his faction, and more, that his opinion did not weigh heavily with Mountbatten.[74] One may add that Hodson was known to have pronouncedly pro-Caroe leanings. Years later Caroe noted that he was 'very relieved' to get Norval Mitchell as Chief Secretary in place of de la Fargue whom he had found 'quite unreliable and ready to intrigue (*entre nous*)'.[75]

Almost immediately after Mitchell took over as Chief Secretary, the governor persuaded him to draft his 'appreciation of the present situation' in the province. This oft-cited report needs to be looked at more closely. As broadly representative of its contents, two brief passages may suffice:

> It is for all practical purposes a certainty that most of all senior officers at least will crack up sooner or later; and all the sooner as the hot weather comes on. They have been exposed for about two months already to a physical, nervous, and moral strain which they cannot fairly be asked to endure any longer. They have been abused by responsible people (I state a fact) on grounds of disloyalty, which has not helped . . . (while) many of them do hold their private political views. . . . I have failed to find any officer's political views having affected the execution of his duty. . . .

As to 'inferences':

> One frequently reads and hears that the situation, generally or locally, is under control. I believe . . . this not to be correct. . . . Not so the situation as a whole,

regarding which it can only be said that it is being coped with from day to day and from hour to hour.[76]

In forwarding the report, Caroe expressed the view that Mitchell's appreciation was 'broadly correct'. His own idea of 'a conciliation or compromise' by the Congress government was the 'possibility' of a coalition government with the Muslim League leading 'eventually to elections'. At the same time, it was imperative to consider what action was to be taken if there were a real breakdown of civil forces of law and order 'complicated further by tribal aggression'.[77]

Transmitting Mitchell's report along with the governor's forwarding note to the governor-general, the Home Member, Sardar Patel, made a few observations that help to place it in perspective. To start with, he pointed out that Mitchell had 'less then 17 years' standing' as a civil servant; that he had dealt with the situation at first hand 'only for a few days'; that his report was 'got prepared' by the governor 'over the head' of the chief minister; that in compiling it, the comparatively young chief secretary, who was 'apparently the conscience keeper' of a responsible governor, had displayed his 'defeatist mentality'. More, a comparison of Mitchell's appreciation of 31 March (i.e. the intelligence report for the second half of March) with that of 5 April would suggest that 'all demoralisation, danger of breakdown and tiresomeness of the services' came about during those 'three or four miraculous' days. The Sardar added his own irresistible conclusion that Mitchell's report was prepared to serve the purpose of a governor who had made 'no secret of his determination to hand over the province' to a Muslim League Ministry.[78]

In his *Memoirs*, Mitchell has explained the background of his report and this should help put it in sharper focus. He took over as chief secretary on 1 April 1947, his promotion especially requested by Khan Sahib even though it involved the supersession of 'at least two' of his seniors.

On the day he took over, Sir Olaf Caroe asked Mitchell to write for him an appreciation of the political situation in the NWFP. Sir Olaf's thinking, Mitchell would have us believe, was that such an appreciation by an officer who had considerable experience of the Frontier but who had recently not been involved in political affairs could be a valuable support for the arguments which he was preparing for the viceroy in respect of the policy to be adopted for the political future of the province. The main point in that policy was to hold an election on the issue of whether the province should, in a divided India, be assigned to Pakistan or not.

Mitchell had dictated the note to his wife who had typed it out and retained a single copy for him. He delivered it to the Government House himself addressed personally to the governor and sealed with his own seal. Sir Olaf was later to confirm that it had been transmitted to the viceroy 'in a highly confidential manner'.

To his great surprise and chagrin, almost immediately the note became 'more or less' public property in Delhi and gave great offence in Congress circles. Nehru, Mitchell recorded, 'made contemptuous comments about it and its obscure author'. In the aftermath, Khan Sahib, he recorded, was 'noticeably less friendly', while Qazi Ataullah would 'glare at me with burning hatred when we met'.

Writing in 1976, Mitchell felt that 'somewhere there had been a breach of confidence' and would appear to hint at Khan Sahib's complicity. He had 'a deep affection' for the premier and 'then as now' found it 'very hard to bear the thought that he might regard me as treacherous'.[79]

Coming back to the Home Member's assessment as to the governor's motives and motivations, there may be a modicum of truth in what the Sardar said, but for the record Mitchell poured out more of the same to his wife a little over a week later (13 April):

> things cannot go on as they are. The strain on the administration is too great, and in many respects it has already begun to cease to function, such as if the province were the scene of a war . . . the demonstrations are on such a scale and so varied that many activities of government simply cannot be done.[80]

Mitchell and some of his colleagues in the administration no doubt felt that matters would get worse if Congress stuck to office. Disorder would spread to tribal territory which would touch off a tribal war. Caroe was to tell his ministers as much in mid-March: that the provincial government should bring itself in line with public opinion. Mountbatten's own difficulties arose form the growing differences between Khan Sahib and Caroe. Whatever his personal predilections, the viceroy hated to jeopardise his relations with Congress, for it alone seemed to hold out the prospect of resolving the Indian political impasse.

A word on the tribal alignments in the wake of the Muslim League agitation in the Frontier. Broadly, apart from some activist pro-Leaguers among the Mahsuds in southern Waziristan who ravaged Tank and Kulchi in mid-April and the trans-border Hazara tribes in the northern district, tribal incursions into the settled districts were few and far between.[81]

There is now conclusive evidence of the Pir of Manki dispatching his 'emissaries' to Waziristan to put the tribals there wise on 'events in Bihar, Assam, Bengal, Bombay, Lahore and the four corners of India'. As one of them wrote to confirm this to the Quaid, the Mahsuds thanked the emissaries 'from the core of their hearts, wished them well and promised to sacrifice all their wealth and lives' for the cause. They 'praised you (the Quaid) and prayed to Allah for His Mercy on you'.[82] Later, the office secretary of the Waziristan Muslim League at Tank wrote to Jinnah about a joint jirga of the Waziristan tribal Pathans, the Wazirs, Mahsuds and Bhittanis, which convened on 20 March and unanimously passed three resolutions affirming (*a*) that Pakistan was 'their birthright'; (*b*) that Khan Sahib 'if he had a little sense in his head and if he is not a traitor to Pathans' should resign along with his ministry and leave it to the Muslim League to form one; and (*c*) that the Patel Committee on the rights of minorities should 'step down in Delhi' for 'the consequences (of its proposed visit to the Frontier) would be very grave otherwise'.[83]

Attempts by the trans-border tribes to invest D I Khan and Bannu were frustrated by timely intelligence. All the same, pro-League elements among the Mahsuds succeeded in holding a tribal council, marakka, on 20 March which among other things demanded the establishment of Pakistan and the dismissal of Khan Sahib—'the Hindu-hired agent'—and his government.[84] It also called for a boycott of the proposed visit by the Tribal Affairs Committee of the Constituent Assembly in New Delhi. A rival marakka by pro-Congress elements among the Mahsuds failed to come off.[85]

A heavily slanted pro-League 'undated (April 1947)' report by 'Anonym' (*sic*), on tribes of the NWFP, underlined the fact that the tribes were in sympathy with the Muslim League and while some people wished that they take an active part in the present agitation against the Congress government, 'we are resisting' this. If however 'the present tempo' of the revolt continued and 'resort to firing' took place in the administered areas of the NWFP 'then tribes might plunge in'. This though, the report argued, was 'not in our interest' for it would involve 'a clash' with the British government for which the tribes 'are not ready'. All the same, the objective was 'to husband our resources, organise (ourselves) and when the time comes . . . to attack from Kalat to Nandihar'.

The report further regretted that 'nothing much' had been done for the formation of an 'Islamic Confederation of the North-West' and expressed the view that 'a factor . . . which must be tackled as early as possible' was the 'pro-Congress attitude' of the Afghan allowance holders among the Mahsuds. It identified 'three leading Maliks' who reportedly were 'working' in the Congress interest. In this context, the report urged that 'we should build up an organisation' that could contact authorities in Kabul 'quickly'.

To counter the influence of Mahsud Maliks who were 'holding' Afghan allowances, the report counselled the dispatch of 'a goodwill Trade Mission' to Kabul and in so far as the latter wanted 'an outlet' to the sea, it may be possible 'to come to some terms' on this issue.

In a breakdown of pro- and anti-Muslim League elements, the report revealed that Ahmadzai Wazirs inhabiting the Wana area were '100 % (pro) Muslim League'. At the same time it gave the names of three 'important Maliks' in North Waziristan who were pro-Congress and named one 'important' Shabi Khel Malik who was working for the party.

About the Fakir of Ipi, there were contradictory reports. He was said to have recently taken Rs. 30,000.00 from AGK for his *langar*. The writer's impression though was that the Fakir would not support the Muslim League and this despite rumours to the contrary by pro-Congress elements.

The author of the report also revealed that he had had exploratory talks as regards the supply of firearms which were required 'practically all over India'. A beginning might be made by establishing 'a secret arms factory' at Bahawalpur. But difficulties were numerous: 'Will Bahawalpur (state) cooperate? With whom could I work in Bahawalpur. Is Nawab Gurmani 100 per cent reliable'.[86]

The above 'report' by 'Anonym' notwithstanding, it was well-known that the Afridis, always rated as the key to the Frontier tribes had, during World War II years, remained 'steady' and indeed loyal to the British cause. And, in the bargain, secured for themselves maximum economic gains. Happily for the province, their steadiness remained undisturbed during the Muslim League agitation for they kept their counsel and refused to be involved in it either directly or indirectly. Fraser has expressed the view that Sahibzada Muhammad Khurshid, the Political Agent in the Khyber, and A S B Shah, the Deputy Commissioner of Peshawar, 'deserve much credit' for this. In any case, a repetition of the Afridi invasion of 1930 would have proved disastrous in 1947.[87]

It may be instructive to recall that a section of Afridi as well as Mohamand Maliks had lodged a protest against the Quaid's proposed visit to their territory in June. Jinnah was planning such a visit to help the League in its referendum campaign. The tribal leaders warned the Quaid that it would be 'a most unwise step' and indicated that the Government of India alone would be 'responsible for any consequences' that may ensue.[88]

Ahmed in the *Hindustan Times*, 22 June 1947.

Interestingly enough, in a letter marked 'private' and addressed to M.A. Jinnah, Sahibzada Khurshid, alluded to in the preceding paragraph, claimed that the Afridis had refused to negotiate with the 'Tribal Advisory Committee' of the Constituent Assembly and that people 'not only here but down there' accused him of this. 'Perhaps', he continued, 'I do not deserve all this misplaced compliment though I am not unwilling to welcome it.' Among the tribes, Khurshid underlined, the Afridis of the Khyber Agency 'were powerful and important of all and more clever than others'.[89]

To say all this is not to unsay that the Political Agent in the Khyber apart, elements among the tribe themselves did try to influence Afridi Jirgas. None the less, their worst efforts notwithstanding, the much touted all-Frontier tribal marakka, to lay down a common policy for the tribes, failed to mature. The nearest it got to was a 12 May (1947) meeting where the Afridi representatives left before the Mahsuds arrived![90] In the event, in the crucial period before the transfer of power, the various tribes—their pro-Muslim League elements notwithstanding—remained sharply divided along traditional lines. With no united front or a common plan of action ever achieved.

Nor was the Quaid an uninterested bystander. Acknowledging 'the messages of good wishes and greetings' from the tribal areas, Jinnah reiterated that the Muslim League and the Pakistan Constituent Assembly 'will honour and respect their freedom and will always be ready to come to brotherly understanding with them, which will be to the advantage of both . . .'.[91]

VI

Against the backdrop of mounting communal tension and riots during March-April 1947 and in the wake of the Muslim League's Civil Disobedience movement, a major development of some significance needs to be taken into account. This was the running battle and a growing rift between Governor Caroe and his premier, Khan Sahib. The more paralysed and effete the Congress administration became, the greater was the blame that the governor attracted. He was viewed as the arch-enemy colluding with the League, and the bureaucracy, to clog the wheels of governance, and making the ministry ineffective, almost irrelevant. That was all there was to the Muslim League plan with Caroe as its centre-piece.

It may be recalled that as early as March, Caroe was impressing upon his ministers that their representative character was seriously in dispute:

that the position in the House did not represent the position in the country. The minorities have 25 per cent of the members although their population is only 7 per cent of our total and in the country they counted for practically nothing which showed that the ministry had to consider afresh whether they had a majority of Pathans behind them.[92]

The minority logic was quixotic and by no means peculiar to the Hindu-Sikh minority in the Frontier. It applied with even greater force to the miniscule Muslim minorities in Madras as well as CP and Berar. In fact, such a logic was part of the scheme of weightages given to minorities under the 1932 Communal Award which was integral to the Government of India Act 1935. Caroe's real objective in driving home the point though, it would seem, was that until and unless the ministry made a 'substantial move towards reconciliation' with their political adversaries, its position would become weak and even untenable. Nor did his ministers appear to realise 'how far public opinion' was falling away from them.[93] In so far as his warnings did not register, the governor confessed to the 'strange' position of a Congress government:

which has or had—a considerable Muslim backing. But the influence of the North-Western Punjab to the East and the tribes to the West—all declaiming against Hindu-Sikh domination is, I think, certain to squeeze Congress out before long, for Congress is not natural here.[94]

If only Khan Sahib had played the game! And Caroe was not oblivious of the solid traits of his premier's character:

Khan Sahib is a fine old man and packed full of courage. I am fond of him. He has genuine and righteous hatred for the acts of communal passion which have disfigured the League case up here, but in my judgement he entirely fails to appreciate the strength that lies behind the League movement based as it is on the traditional Islamic and Pathan culture determined to shake free, if it can, from any regime that can be represented as financed or dominated by Hinduism.[95]

Nor was Caroe alone in exhorting the Congress government to take steps towards reconciliation with its political foes. As early as March, A S B Shah, then Deputy Commissioner of Peshawar, had drawn up a six-page memorandum with a view to asserting the authority of the government and preventing political bodies from resorting to lawlessness. He had called upon the Khan Sahib government to respect and make allowances for the criticisms and grievances of the people and to take 'initiatives towards clemency and reconciliation'. Above all, he advised a courageous willingness to participate in open discussion so as to 'allay the doubts and suspicions of those who are levelling unworthy and ill-founded charges against the Government'. Sadly though, his advice fell on deaf ears; the whole endeavour, an empty exercise![96]

For Caroe's, as indeed Shah's, reasoning ran counter to all that Badshah Khan and his Red Shirts stood for. Sedulously nurtured over the past two decades and more, the Congress-Khudai Khidmatgar combine in the Frontier represented a considerable mellowing of the traditional Pathan obsession with the cult of the gun, and a certain coming together of the majority-minority communities for the attainment of a common political objective, i.e. end of British rule. The resultant political processes had, as noticed earlier, yielded rich electoral dividends. Apart from its 1937 triumph, the third Khan Sahib ministry was elected to office only a year earlier with a convincing popular mandate.

In refusing, therefore, to be drawn into Caore's parlour, Khan Sahib was reacting the way his, and his younger brother's political culture dictated: refusal to have any truck whatever with all that the League represented, and stood for. All the same, there is no denying that there was a great deal of robust common sense and hard-nosed pragmatism in what Caroe was pleading.

Two things should be obvious and beyond fear of contradiction. To start with, though he may not have been friendly to the Khan Sahib ministry, Caroe was not exactly fond of the Muslim League leadership in the province either, and, barring the Mullah of Manki, rated them 'a miserable crew'.[97] Again, what he advocated and was looking for was a coalition of sorts under Khan Sahib—a Pathan outfit that 'severed its connection with Congress'. By implication, all extra-Pathan linkages were out, with the local Muslim League too delinked from its parent body. It is interesting that, as Caroe saw it, Khan Sahib might have taken the bait:

> I have often told him [Khan Sahib] that this is what I would like to see and I have a feeling that in his heart of hearts, he would welcome it too, but he is too tied to his brother Abdul Ghaffar Khan and through him to Nehru and there is always the money interest. . . .[98]

For a better appreciation of the issues involved a slight digression may be in order. That Khan Sahib's political compulsions may not have been altogether imaginary is revealed by the turn of events long after the curtain had rolled down on the Frontier drama of 1945-7. Khan Sahib's later career would appear to suggest a propensity to compromise at the cost of political principles and life-long ideological loyalties. Put differently, he may be called a pragmatist, a resolute practitioner of the art of the possible. Thus, as early as October 1954, he had mended his fences with Pakistan's rulers to emerge as a minister in Chowdhury Mohamed Ali's cabinet. Later, in close liaison with Iskander Mirza who had taken over as Governor-General, Khan Sahib lent his support to the one-unit West Pakistan scheme under which he was to be Chief Minister for a little over two years, April 1955–July 1957. He also launched his own political outfit, the short-lived Republican Party. It may be pointed out that Abdul Ghaffar Khan and people of his persuasion (which now included the Pir of Manki) were vehemently opposed to the new political configuration as being unfair to the Frontier. For his pains, Badshah Khan was prosecuted and placed behind bars by his elder brother's government.[99]

Writing years later and alluding to this episode, Caroe expressed the view that had Khan Sahib 'taken this course in 1947, the whole history of the transfer of power might have been changed'.[100] Even Sir Fraser Noble was of the view that if only Khan Sahib had realised earlier than he did that his brother's (AGK) extreme position was untenable, he might have led 'a united Frontier more happily with its new role within Pakistan'.[101] But by himself Khan Sahib may have made little difference! For then (viz., 1947), as later in life, he was far from being a political activist and lacked an independent mass base of his own. And it is less than certain if, in 1947, Abdul Ghaffar Khan and his massive Khudai Khidmatgar movement would have bought the Caroe line. In sum, even if the Congress premier had mended his fences with the Muslim League, as Caroe desired, he may not have been able to carry conviction with his own flock!

Khan Sahib's refusal to fall in line with Caroe was only one aspect of the growing rift between the governor and his premier. Their differences had grown from small beginnings from the day Caroe had taken command in Peshawar. Nor were the new governor's encounters with his council of ministers anything but auspicious. And even though powerfully struck by the personality of his chief minister—'he is the most impressive Indian I have ever met'—he viewed his cabinet as no better than a mere 'family affair' which it undoubtedly was. That, however, was not all there was to it: what with his ministry's 'unwarrantable interference' with the courts; their 'most dangerous' plans to abolish the institution of lambardars; unfair use of the Frontier Crimes Regulations by appointing jirgas in settled districts; 'ill-considered and unfair' decisions in petty establishment cases, Caroe had a mouthful of unending complaints against Khan Sahib and his council of ministers.[102]

At one stage, Khan Sahib had threatened to resign bringing Caroe face to face with the prospect of appointing his deputy, Qazi Ataullah, whom

Caroe rated to be a 'very unsatisfactory substitute'. The Qaẓi's 'sharp tongue and bullying manner' were viewed as very damaging to the morale and efficiency of government servants. One may add that it may not have been Khan Sahib who took the lead in interfering with the courts or the judicial processes or with administration in general; Frazer Noble rated the Qazi as 'certainly more blatantly guilty'. While Khan Sahib whose bark was always worse than his bite was indeed 'a friendly and lovable' character, the Qazi, on the other hand, was coarse in the exterior and an 'extremely hardline politician'.[103]

All in all, differences on major administrative policies were further compounded by the governor's alleged bias in favour of the Muslim League. Presently Nehru's visit (October 1946) contributed its own quota of misunderstandings. Nor did Caroe's seemingly well-intentioned efforts to wean Khan Sahib from his Congress loyalties help except in the negative sense of widening his own ever-growing difficulties with his chief minister.

VII

The starkly divergent perceptions and lack of friendly relations between Caroe and his premier were out in the open at two meetings at which Mountbatten was present. The first, in New Delhi, on 18 April; the second, at Peshawar, exactly ten days later. At the New Delhi meeting, Caroe and Khan Sahib apart, both Nehru and Mountbatten were present; at Peshawar, Khan Sahib and his ministers were present, Nehru was not. Of the 18 April meeting, Hodson noted that 'much time was wasted' by Khan Sahib's charge of 'bias and interference' against the governor and the latter's rebuttal: of his ministry's growing reliance upon the army in routine matters; of Khan Sahib's marked political bias in issuing arms licenses to all and sundry; of imposing a virtual press censorship. It was now left to Khan Sahib to offer some explanations.

To start with, Khan Sahib flatly denied the governor's charge that he was arming everybody 'who was likely to vote for him'. He affirmed though that he was issuing permits for firearms 'but only for record purposes'. All the same, he felt that villagers must have something to protect themselves with. To the Viceroy's accusation that Khan Sahib had been holding up some press telegrams, and Caroe's that there had been 'some unwise censorship' by his government, the premier conceded 'only one such case' was within his knowledge and held out the assurance that there would be none in future.[104]

As to Caroe's allegation that the Premier interfered unduly in matters within the purview of magistrates, Khan Sahib countered by accusing the Governor of obstructing him in the discharge of his duties. On Nehru's pointed query as to whether he was 'complaining against being restricted', the premier replied that he was.[105]

Months later, George Cunningham, now reappointed Governor in Peshawar, noted in his diary that during their brief meeting in New Delhi en route to the Frontier on 13 August, Mountbatten had referred to the 18 April encounter between Caroe and Khan Sahib as 'a regular screaming match'.[106]

Two points ought to be noted: one, that apparently with the viceroy's encouragement, this remarkably frank confrontation between the governor and his premier may have been an experiment in blood-letting. Two, that Caroe's reference to his ministry's alleged reliance upon the army 'in routine matters' was a little less than fair. As a matter of fact, curfew had been imposed in Peshawar city for several weeks in April which could hardly be described as a routine matter. The district administration under the leadership of Deputy Commissioner A S B Shah had worked extremely hard to keep the peace. Their liaison with the army was excellent and the police owed a lot to this. The Premier appreciated this even if the Muslim League did not. Remarkable as it may sound, in all these weeks of tension and worse, the army had to open fire only once.[107]

During the governors' conference at New Delhi convened by Mountbatten (14-15 April), Caroe got an opportunity for 'an hour's private conversation' with the governor-general. Among other things, he was told that the Congress regarded him as 'enemy number one', a point that made things difficult for Mountbatten though the latter 'himself did not endorse' this view. Asked whether the governor-general wanted him (Caroe) to resign, Mountbatten said 'not at present' although circumstances might arise in which he 'may be compelled' to ask him (Caroe) to quit. He added that 'in these momentous days' personal considerations were 'a small thing compared to the public weal'.[108] Mountbatten was to refer to this conversation when demanding Caroe's resignation early in June.[109]

Caroe is also said to have taken the opportunity during his sojourn in New Delhi to advise the governor-general that 'a test of public opinion' on the Frontier by means of an election was necessary. Failing which, civil and tribal warfare 'seemed certain'.[110]

Actually, Caroe had rclayed the same advice to the new governor-general through Ismay when the latter visited Peshawar on 1 April. *Inter alia*, the Governor had advocated dismissal of the Khan Sahib ministry, dissolution of the legislature and imposition of Section 93 rule vesting all authority in the Governor as agent of the Viceroy while a fresh poll was being held.[111]

The 18 April meeting, it may be pointed out, was a sequel to an earlier meeting (15 April) at which Nehru, Liaquat Ali Khan and Caroe were present along with the governor-general. Mountbatten had raised the question of elections in the NWFP. Nehru objected, maintaining that the issue had not been taken up either with the NWFP government or the party in power there. It was against this background that Khan Sahib was summoned to New Delhi and a meeting convened (18 April). It was at this meeting, it has been suggested, that Nehru finally conceded the need for a test of public opinion. Nor was Khan Sahib averse to a bout of fresh elections. It was also noted that Caroe was 'quite ready' to let Khan Sahib's ministry stay in office 'until after the elections were over'.[112]

It is interesting to racall that press reports of the 18 April meeting underlined that Caroe 'with his well-known preference for the Muslim League' had suggested dissolution of the legislature, dismissal of the Ministry and ordering of fresh elections. Since 'ordering of fresh elections, following dissolution of the Legislature can only be done by the Governor in his individual judgment or discretion', he was bound to consult the governor-general. The way 'the latter now deals with Frontier developments' will demonstrate whether he has 'a fresh approach' or follows 'the old beaten track' of placating the Muslim League. The *Tribune* indicated that its information was based on the Muslim League mouthpiece, the *Dawn*, which had carried the item 'with the usual characteristic terms and tones of propaganda in support of Caroe's contentions'.[113]

A fortnight later, the *Tribune* commented editorially under the caption 'Sir Olaf Caroe as Mr Jinnah's Lieutenant' and charged that Sir Olaf had now abandoned all 'simulation of impartiality' and appeared 'in his true colours' and come out 'unabashedly' as the Quaid's lieutenant. He had been 'playing that role for a pretty long time'. His 'intrigues' had been set afoot with 'all disgruntled politicians, dissatisfied bureaucrats and reactionary pirs and mullahs and nawabs and even the tribesmen in the pay of British imperialism'. A huge front had thus been established 'against the Khan Sahib Ministry—against Democracy'. Concluding, the paper expressed the hope that Mountbatten would 'refuse to be dragged' into this 'dirty League-Bureaucracy intrigue' and thereby prevent his reputation 'from being wrecked'.[114]

On 2 June the *Tribune* carried a long-winded article, 'Sir Olaf Caroe and the Frontier Government' by Vidya Dhar Mahajan. Essentially, it made three points. One, that the Frontier ministry of Khan Sahib had the 'strong backing of the whole of the Congress organisation' and if Sir Olaf tampered with it an all-India crisis 'cannot only be threatened but also created'. Two, that under the constitution then in force, it was 'not for the Muslim League to demand fresh elections' but for Khan Sahib and his party. And warned the Governor 'to desist from usurping the legitimate right of the Ministry' in ordering new elections.

Finally, the writer conceded that Sir Olaf had 'a lot of influence throughout the Province'; that as agent (to) the governor-general, he had control over the Political Agencies; that in the Frontier, all major posts were reserved for the Indian Political Service. Thus 'fresh elections' under Section 93 rule 'with all his paraphernalia under his control, with the determination of the Governor to bring the Muslim League to power, the results cannot truly reflect the opinion of the electorate'.[115]

To revert to the discussions at the governors' conference at New Delhi, 15-16 April, Caroe appeared optimistic that 'it had at least been understood' that no independent India, 'united or partitioned', could be born that lacked 'a stable international frontier'.[116] Linked to the Gandhi-Jinnah appeal for peace and communal harmony (15 April) and the decision taken at the 18 April meeting in New Delhi, Khan Sahib on return to Peshawar made an official announcement (19 April) for the release of all political prisoners—mostly Muslim League agitators—against whom there were no specific charges of violence. His announcement, however, made no reference to any proposal to hold fresh elections. The viceroy none the less felt free to discuss the issue with the League leader on the clear understanding that the exercise could not be undertaken while the League engaged in 'direct action' against a legally constituted government. In pursuance of the policy he had announced, the Khan Sahib government ordered the release of nearly 5,000 prisoners, then in detention. Most of them, however, refused to leave their prisons, determined they would not yield until their demands had been met.

Not long after the New Delhi meetings, came Mountbatten's two-day visit to the Frontier (28-9 April) which provided him with clinching evidence of how bad the relations were between Caroe and his premier. In planning his visit though, Mountbatten's ostensible objective was to make a personal assessment of the situation on the ground. As Fraser Noble recollected, while Khan Sahib and his colleagues 'fulminated against the governor and all his officers', the governor kept sending 'ominous and despairing' messages to his political bosses in New Delhi. To his own officers and staff, however, Caroe seemed to be 'floundering hopelessly' in face of unfair attacks on his hard-pressed colleagues. Noble recalls that early in March 1947, when he took over as Additional D C, Peshawar, one afternoon there was a telephone call. 'In the most confidential tones and only slightly guarded phrases', Caroe told him that he was 'relying on me to keep a careful eye on what was going on and particularly on what the D C got up to.' Caroe inferred that 'I (Fraser Noble) was to let him personally know if I felt uneasy.' His relations with Caroe being what they were, the latter's message 'seemed to assume an independent rapport' that the governor had done nothing to create. Instinctively, Noble felt that he had been given an instruction on the telephone that should 'only have been hinted at delicately, if at all, in a personal, confidential interview'. In the event, he was left with 'an uneasy feeling' that the governor was 'jittery, or at least more unsure of himself than he should have allowed a more junior officer to infer'.[117] Further, 'everyday the risk of intervention by the Red Shirts as a sort of private pro-Government army seemed to grow, and the evidence was not lacking that the Muslim League was ready for them'.

Even as more and more 'decent' Muslim League members were being arrested, Noble recalled, it was becoming 'an urgent duty' for honourable men to acquire the mark of political martyrdom—the 'badge of imprisonment' in the cause of Pakistan. At the same time, 'the scheming went on—underground, in secret, working steadily towards a deadly climax'.[118]

Coming back to Mountbatten's visit, there was, on his arrival, a huge Muslim League demonstration which appeared to threaten peace. At grave personal risk, the governor-general decided to meet this noisy assembly on the advice of Khan Sahib. 'Go, if you must', Khan Sahib told Mountbatten, 'but it is the governor who has collected them.'[119]

According to Fraser Noble, who was an eye-witness, no word on the demonstration had been passed to the governor-general during the ceremonies of his arrival. But on the way to Government House, Caroe told him about the crowd and the advice he (Caroe) had received from all senior officers, including the military commanders, that the viceroy should agree to see the assembly himself. It has been suggested that the governor as such made no recommendation—'possibly on the ground that it savoured too much of playing the Muslim League game'. All the same, he did explain his fears, 'which everyone shared', that if the viceroy declined to go, 'the demonstration would force their way to Government House to see him'.[120] Later, Noble who had been sent to fetch Khan Sahib records that the viceroy told the Premier 'very briskly' that he had been during the Viceroy's visit could have a disastrous effect on his efforts to procure a peaceful agreement on the transfer of power. Everyone accepted that he had already won unprecedented trust and confidence from all the contending parties, and the thought that that might be lost in the violence of a Peshawar riot appalled me.

About seven in the evening I was so restless that I decided to call on the D.C. Although I arrived without warning, his orderly took me straight to him. He was sitting in his dining room with Sir Firoz Khan Noon. That was the first surprise of many that evening. They had just finished their meal; Shah asked me quietly what I wanted; embarrassed by the presence of Firoz Khan Noon (a former member of the Viceroy's Executive Council,*(1) and a very prominent Punjab politician who was rather on the sidelines of the Muslim League at the time) I stammered out my anxieties about the next day. Calmly, Shah said "That is exactly what we have been discussing, and we don't know what we should do about it." After some discussion, Firoz said that some effort must be made to prevent the crowd assembling at the aerodrome: he seemed to be sure that a demonstration there was intended by the League. But he opted out of any part in pursuing his suggestion, implying that his own influence with the Provincial Muslim League War Council (so it was designated) was so negligible that representation by him would be counterproductive.

So it was left to the D.C. to make a move. To my surprise, he picked up the telephone and asked for a number, explaining to me that it was the number of a phone in a hujra (a meeting place) in the city. After a short conversation, he turned to me and said "Let's go." We drove straight to a place just off the Grand Trunk Road, about half a mile outside the city wall, which he explained was the headquarters of the League's "War Council." Without delay, we were admitted to the main room, where about a dozen men were clearly engaged in a meeting. I had thought that most of the real leaders of the League were in prison; though I knew of the existence of this War Council, I had no idea that it was still functioning so effectively. But the biggest surprise was the presence of Sardar Abdur Rab Nishtar, whom I had known as a minister in Aurangzeb's government in 1943. He was now a League nominee in the Viceroy's Interim Government, and I was shaken to find him engaged in this cabal, which was clearly responsible for arrangements that might threaten the Viceroy's whole mission to India.

Memoirs of Sir Fraser Noble (p. 326).

Nishtar took charge of the discussion at once. Shah explained our anxiety that a demonstration at the aerodrome might become uncontrollable. Nishtar agreed, clearly sharing our anxiety, but asked what was the alternative. The League had already made its dispositions, and parties of men were believed to be already on their way to camp at the aerodrome. In the exchanges which followed it became clear that the **sine qua non** for the League was to set up a situation in which the crowd was assured that the Viceroy personally had seen them and assessed the strength of their numbers. I suggested that this might best be achieved in a relatively confined space, like the Cunningham Garden, which had the further advantage that it was neither in the cantonment nor in the Military environment of the aerodrome, but conveniently near the city from which no doubt many would wish to join the gathering. The aerodrome was several miles away to the west - a long trek across country from the main centre of population. Some members of the War Council emphasised how difficult it would be at such a late hour to alter instructions that had already gone out to various units or groups of League volunteers. They insisted that no change could be made unless they had an assurance that the Viceroy would review the gathering in the Cunningham garden. It was not acceptable to them to say that he would see them from the air as his plane approached the landing ground. When Shah said that in any case he had no means of providing such an assurance that night, Nishtar at once intervened to say that all that was required was a telephone message to Delhi. He knew the Viceroy's working habits, and we could be assured that if the Governor rang Delhi at any time before midnight he would be put through to Lord Mountbatten.

There appeared to be no alternative. It was already nearly eleven o'clock. Shah undertook to ring the hujra with the answer before midnight, to give them time to put out new instructions to their followers. When we left, however, he was very depressed and hesitant about approaching the Governor on this basis. I suggested that in any case, since the proposal would have important implications for the army's arrangements, we should call on Brigadier Cubitt-Smith and seek his support in approaching Caroe. As always, the Brigadier was quick in his appreciation of the situation. He agreed that if the scheme worked, it might provide the best chance of averting a clash of arms. He was very perturbed by the prospect of having to deal with a large crowd at or near the aerodrome. But the matter was one "for the civil power" not the

Memoirs of Sir Fraser Noble (p. 327).

advised to go and 'provided' the chief minister had 'no objection', he 'proposed to go'. Noble records that Khan Sahib was taken aback completely. He was never

particularly good in oral debate, and sputtered, 'Your Excellency must just do whatever you please.' Without hesitation, Mountbatten said, 'Very well, thank you.' Nothing more was said at this stage but later in the day when the Viceroy met the Ministers officially, Khan Sahib remarked that he (Mountbatten) would be aware that it was the Governor who had arranged for this Muslim League demonstration of numbers, and that he had himself cancelled a similar demonstration of Congress supporters in order to avoid the risk of a clash.[121]

At the rally in question, Mountbatten made a powerful impression thereby defusing what everyone knew was an extremely explosive situation. Years later Caroe recaptured the moment:

There he (Mountbatten) stood with magnificent panache, saluting the crowd. There was too much noise for words to be spoken or heard. But the spectacle of the Governor General, to them a regal figure, dressed, they noticed, in a green bushshirt—which, as Muslims, they took as compliment to the Haji's colour affected by pilgrims to Mecca—appealed to those who worship spirit when they see it. Here was manly leadership, not the sort of petulant bravado they had witnessed on Nehru's visit. Cries of *Mountbatten zindabad* could be heard amid the roar of Pakistan. Good humour was restored, honour satisfied, and all went well.[122]

Noble, then joint deputy commissioner at Peshawar, was a witness too:

The crowd in the park was impressive—much more closely packed than when I had seen them. They had spilled over on to the railway. . . . So that the vast majority was below us, the nearest no more than twenty yards away. We were standing only a few yards away from where shots had been fired on the advancing crowd on 10th March, and from the scene of the railway accident involving women demonstration on 14th April. The early morning silence had been replaced by a considerable noise. . . . It was not the angry sound of a mob about to riot, but it was not reassuring either. The Viceroy moved on to the parapet—a low wall hardly more then a foot high—then stood erect. Suddenly, one was aware that the noise was dying away; seconds ticked into a strange silence, then perceptibly the sound increased—a gigantic murmur swelling almost to a roar. One sensed at once that this was not a note of anger, but of amazed approval. The Viceroy must have known at once that he had won the day . . . [Mountbatten's call to 'Get the people nearest to sit down so that others behind can see better.' To broadcast it in Pushtu, Noble and another senior police officer entered the crowd's ranks . . .] the feeling that I got from them all was one of amazement and bewilderment.

28A. Lord Mountbatten's visit to Peshawar

On April 28th in the fortnight between Letters 28 and 29 Mountbatten visited Peshawar, staying with the writer at Government House. He was accompanied by Lady Mountbatten. A crowd of Leaguers, variously estimated at between 50,000 and 100,000 strong, had gathered on the airfield from all over the Province, determined to show the Viceroy the strength of their organisation. Landing of aircraft would have been dangerous, and they were induced with great difficulty to move to the open space by the Fort between Peshawar City and Cantonment. As soon as the Viceroy landed, the writer told him that he must go and see the crowd, or they were likely to storm Government House to see him, with almost certain bloodshed. Mountbatten immediately agreed, provided only that Khansahib also agreed afresh. On arrival at Government House Khan Sahib was asked at once to see the Viceroy and told him in private, 'Go if you must, but it is the Governor who has collected them.' The Viceroy then proceeded to the railway embankment overlooking the crowd, accompanied by Lady Mountbatten, the writer, the G.O.C. and the Inspector General of Police, with one or two other local officers. There he stood with magnificent panache, saluting the crowd. There was too much noise for words to be spoken or heard. But the spectacle of the Governor General, to them a regal figure, dressed, they noted, in a green bush-shirt — which as Muslims they took as a compliment to the Haji's colour affected by pilgrims to Mecca — appealed to men who worship spirit when they see it. Here was manly leadership, not the sort of petulant bravado they had witnessed on Nehru's visit. Cries of Mountbatten zinda bad could be heard amid the roars for Pakistan. Good humour was restored, honour satisfied, and all

Sir Olaf Caroe's Mss (p. 159A).

[margin: bedroom that night]

went well – except that there was an attempt ~~that night~~ to murder the General, into whose ~~house~~ shots were fired. ×

There is perhaps no single act that calls for more courage than that of facing, unarmed and unescorted, an excited and determined crowd of demonstrators. Many of this gathering carried arms, and the small group on the embankment were an easy mark for malcontents or *agents provocateurs*. The cool and debonair bearing of the chief actor on this scene, and perhaps even more the decision to take the risk, changed the course of history. A blood-bath in Peshawar that day would inevitably have led, as in 1930, to tribal incursions and probably to an Afghan war. Plans for an early transfer of power would have gone awry, and Russia lay beyond. The Attlee government could hardly have remained unscathed.

This great crowd had assembled as part of Jinnah's plan to bring the Frontier out of the Congress and into the League camp, as an essential component of his envisaged Pakistan. The writer believes that the evidence of these letters is enough to dispel the figment that he had either the will or the power to organise Frontier politics in this way.

Sir Olaf Caroe's Mss (p. 159B).

They were not noisy or elated, but respectful and a little overawed . . . . It has been said that the Viceroy's green Burma bush-shirt and trousers captured the crowd's approval. It may have helped; all I can say is that the colour of his clothes made no difference to me, but that I was captivated by a demonstration of personal magnetism unique in my experience. . . .[123]

Mountbatten's decision to take the risk, Caroe had little doubt, 'changed the course of history' for bloodshed in Peshawar that day could have 'led to an Afghan war', and 'plans for an early transfer of power would have gone awry'. Should this have happened, the Attlee government 'could hardly have remained unscathed'.[124]

Fraser Noble agrees that 'if something had gone wrong', the effect on Mountbatten's negotiations 'might have been irretrievable'. He has provided more details of the behind-the-scenes drama of the viceroy's visit and the League demostration. Mountbatten had been in touch with Jinnah the evening prior to his visit. Late that evening, he had informed Caroe that he (Mountbatten) had told Jinnah that any League procession would be 'completely contrary' to assurances the viceroy had held out to Khan Sahib. At the same time, Mountbatten had indicated to the Quaid his readiness to meet some League representatives at the Government House. In Peshawar that very evening, Noble and the deputy commissioner had been, off their own bat, in touch with a cabal of League leaders to sort out such details as the venue of the proposed demonstration. Here among others they had accosted Abdur Rab Nishtar, then a member of the Viceroy's Executive Council and of the interim government. Immediately thereafter they had motored to the Government House to keep the governor fully in the picture. 'It is not clear', Noble recorded as to

When the [Viceroy's] telegram reached Caroe. If he had it before we saw him it is strange he should not have said so. [In any case it was clear that Mountbatten] was not altogether taken by surprise by the governor's news that a crowd had gathered and wanted to see him.[125]

Mitchell who as Chief Secretary held a pivotal position and was an eyewitness to Mountbatten's visit, makes some interesting points. To begin with, that 'no words could describe the degree of anxiety and suspense' that preceded the governor-general's arrival. Again, that Khan Sahib 'must have had an exceptional faculty for self-deception' if he thought he enjoyed widespread public support; that the prevalent mood among the vast Pathan conclave did not smack so much of 'fanaticism' as of 'anger and hatred'; that inasmuch as the Pathans 'seldom shoot sitting ducks just for fun', they received Mountbatten and his wife 'rapturously'.[126]

assigned to India when partition arrived. To this end they were also determined that the Viceroy should see the strength and weight of their determination on his arrival. If he did not do so, if he drove from the airfield in a cavalcade of cars straight to Government House, then a hundred thousand Pathans would storm the gates and barbed wire fences of the cantonment and march on from there, One of them said to me that even the machine guns of the very substantial garrison could not kill all of the hundred thousand.

The threat was not empty. The word fanaticism could be applied to the mood of the people, but it would not be wholly fair. There were anger and communal hatred as ingredients in that mood. But above all there truly was an adamant, quite balanced, resolve not to be delivered into the power of the Hindus by their own unrepresentative leaders. Early one morning I met Mehr Chand Khanna out for a walk. (When he joined the Congress Party he had rejected his title of Rai Bahadur.) He looked haggard and ill, and he was flanked by three armed guards. This was a typical example of the party's predicament.

On the morning of the Viceroy's arrival I reached the aerodrome very early. There I met the District Commander, an imperturbable Australian Major General whose intention was to suggest to the Governor that the only course was for the Viceroy to see the people and to be seen by them. This was in fact unnecessary. The Governor had reached the same decision. A few nights before the General's residence, Flagstaff House, which was adjacent to the barbed wire perimetre of the cantonment, had been raked with bullets from a very nasty hazard on the golf course outside the wire. Golf architects never think of such contingencies; but at least he had evidence of what might happen. More potentially disastrous was the fact that on this morning some 8000 men had approached the airfield from a point north of west with the idea of standing more or less where the Viceroy's plane would land. In this way they could not fail to be seen by him. The police had very tactfully

Caroe, for his part, noted that the crowd was part of Jinnah's plan to bring the Frontier out of the Congress into the League camp and as an essential component of the Pakistan he envisaged. To Khan Sahib's charge that it was his doing, the governor noted that it was 'a figment of the imagination' to suggest that he had 'either the will or the power' to organize Frontier politics in this way.[127]

That 'Monday night', Sir Fraser Noble was to recall, some miscreants had fired on the official residence of General Rose McCay, general officer-commanding, Peshawar area. Intelligence reports, Sir Fraser suggests, 'tentatively identified them' as a group of Red Shirts, allegedly henchmen of Qazi Ataullah, the NWFP minister for revenue.[128] Earlier that day, Mountbatten in his meeting with Khan Sahib and his ministers is believed to have raised the issue of a coalition government and insisted upon a popular verdict on the province's future. The premier reportedly took strong exception to the idea of a coalition and stressed that the Frontier Muslim League represented 'only self-interest and a privileged class of Khans' and that he for one would have nothing to do with a coalition government. The premier further charged that the Muslim League had been allowed by officials to break the law. Caroe refuted the allegation, asserting that he knew of 'no single instance where officials were not trying to do their duty'. And yet they were always blamed.[129]

Mountbatten took different positions with the Khan Sahib ministry and a Muslim League deputation that called on him later. He told the former that elections were a must and prior thereto a spell of governor's rule for a couple of months.[130] At the other end, the Muslim League, who demanded the immediate dismissal of the Khan Sahib government and imposition of Section 93 rule followed by fresh elections, was informed that overthrow of an established government by violence would not be allowed. The governor-general advised the League leaders to call off their civil disobedience campaign which had caused so many deaths. Above all, they must trust him for fairplay in the eventual transfer of power.[131]

The above narrative rests squarely on official documentation. Tendulkar's account, based on non-official sources, is slightly varied. He purports to furnish more detailed minutes of the governor-general's meeting with the Congress ministers. Mountbatten, he suggests, started by asserting that the position in the Frontier was one of 'particular difficulty' for him. 'I shall be telling the Muslim League', he continued, 'that I will not yield to violence. I tell you privately that elections are necessary but can make no guarantee to the Muslims that there will by any. Mr Jinnah's promise is that if there is an election, there will be no violence.'[132]

The meeting, it would appear, was marred by allegations and counter-allegations between the governor and his premier, with Mountbatten intervening to say that his 'mandate was impartiality and his problem whether to hold an election before we go or whether law and order are sufficient for the government to hold on'. And suggested, a joint committee of the high commands of the Congress and the Muslim League to advise him on the subject.[133]

An unresolved issue during the viceroy's visit was the dismissal of the Khan Sahib government and promulgation of Section 93 rule. Mitchell's own view was that this course of action 'could do nothing' to restore order largely because 'the authority for the moment' was 'not able' to restore peace. He refers to his request to the commander-in-chief for more troops which was unceremoniously turned down. As to Section 93 rule, he counselled the viceroy that it should not be invoked. Inasmuch as the British government were on the way out, he reasoned, any action against the Congress party in the Frontier would be interpreted 'as a vindictive move', nor would it be of 'any assistance' to the Muslims. Above all, the Congress party and 'its historians' could always say that the Muslim League 'did not succeed' to power on their own merits or even by their own efforts. In the event, the dismissal of the ministry now 'could only provide ammunition' later for enemies of the Muslim League.[134]

Caroe, it has been suggested, tried to persuade the viceroy to promulgate Section 93 rule and order fresh elections. Later, the governor allegedly sent a garbled version of the proceedings to the governor-general while refusing to forward a note of his premier's embodying what the latter viewed as the correct version. This was subsequently sent to New Delhi, independent of the governor.[135]

Jansson has expressed the view that all officials, Indian as well as British, to whom Mountbatten spoke during his visit to Peshawar, were convinced that in order to avoid a catastrophe, fresh elections had to be held as soon as possible. They also believed that it was necessary to proclaim Governor's rule *before* the elections for a period of four to six months—'at a pitch, two months'—or else the ministry would be able to put pressure on the voters.[136]

During Mountbatten's meeting with Khan Sahib and his colleagues, it was suggested that the Frontier Muslim League was run not by Jinnah who evidently had 'no control' over it. ' "Who", I (Mountbatten) asked him (Dr Khan Sahib), falling into his trap, then controls it? He replied "HE the Governor of course and his officials; their one object is to turn my ministry out of power." ' Mountbatten reportedly 'could not repress' his laughter at such a 'fantastic suggestion'.[137] Later, among other things, the Muslim League deputation told the governor-general that they would stop violence and come out of jail only if elections were announced and governor's rule proclaimed.

What exactly was the impact of the Viceroy's visit on the local situation? Fraser Noble has suggested that while the visit 'did not' of course mark the end of the Muslim League's civil disobedience movement, the earlier 'pitch of tension' changed to a 'persistent atmosphere of general unease and anxiety'. Now there was 'an almost routine expectation of trouble' and 'a depressing inability' to overtake arrears of normal administrative and judicial work. In the administration there was, he adds, an all-pervasive 'sense of helplessness and hopelessness' and even though Congress 'persistently' accused British officers of 'manipulating' events, the harsh fact was that 'we had been pushed on to the side lines'.[138]

Jansson has expressed the view that one result of the visit 'must no doubt have been' that in the viceroy's mind the stock of the Muslim League rose and that of the Congress sank.[139] Fraser Noble has suggested that the visit enabled the governor-general 'to grasp the complexities' of the Frontier problem which had—if one were to judge from the record of his meetings in Delhi before his Peshawar sojourn—previously left him 'unusually unsure and hesitant'.[140]

In a 'Personal Report' written immediately after his visit (1 May) the governor-general promised to watch 'this province very carefully.' In a subsequent assessment, composed (25 July) *after* the Referendum had gone in favour of the Muslim League, Mountbatten recorded that the April visit had 'confirmed' him in the view that the Frontier 'would join Pakistan'.[141]

At the governor-general's meeting with tribal leaders at Landi Kotal and later that day (29 April) at the Government House in Peshawar, great resentment was voiced that they (viz., the tribes) had been completely ignored in the British Prime Minister's statement of 20 February 1947. The Afridis also demanded return of the Khyber and other tribal areas and swore that they would not submit to Hindu domination. Noble refers to the Afridi jirga's 'characteristically impressive performance . . . politically subtle but responsible, missing no tricks'.[142] In the event, the Afridis kept their counsel while the Wazirs and the Mahsuds, overt and noisy as ever, pressed hard for Pakistan and demanded the dismissal of the Congress government at Peshawar.[143]

At the close of his barely 26-hour visit to the Frontier, Mountbatten was not a little distressed, and exhausted, with an unending 'stream of officials and delegations'. The senior-most among them, he noted, had felt convinced of 'a great deal of trouble' at the time of transfer of power, and advised the governor-general 'retaining the whole province under Section 93' until the day of British departure. No wonder, Mountbatten informed his political superiors that he proposed, as noticed in an earlier paragraph, 'to watch the province very carefully'.[144]

VIII

Even as relations between Caroe and his premier deteriorated by the day, those between the governor and his political bosses in New Delhi showed no signs of improvement either. On the contrary, they too registered a steady decline.

It may be recalled that on the morrow of his return form the Frontier tour, Nehru had written to Caroe about the 'big hiatus between you as Governor and AGG and the provincial government and those whom they represent'. Adding that with this 'lack of confidence . . . and a desire to pull in different directions', there could be no cooperation.[145] About the same time, as has been noticed earlier, Weightman, Nehru's British Secretary in the External Affairs Department, had expressed the view that Congress were 'gunning for' Caroe and would have him out 'if they can'. Caroe apart, Nehru's visit had upset the highly placed bureaucrats as well as the army top brass: Wavell had talked of Nehru's 'foolish and unrealistic' note on his visit while Auchinleck had felt 'disturbed'. Later, the viceroy felt that Nehru had made amends and commended him for his 'honesty and good feeling'. Wavell's own tour of the Frontier which had followed hot on Nehru's heels was designed to boost the low morale of the services who, regardless of consequences, were planning 'to get out as soon as possible'.[146]

Another virtual storm in a teacup was the constitution of the Tribal Advisory Committee on Tribal and Excluded Areas set up by the Constituent Assembly in New Delhi. The latter, it may be recalled, had convened early in December 1946, despite the Muslim League's virtual boycott and outright denunciation. The Assembly had been quite active in formulating its strategy for the future constitutional setup in the country. Its Tribal Advisory Committee had been charged with responsibility for devising an institutional framework into which tribal areas would fit. To this end, a subcommittee, the North-West Frontier Tribal Areas Subcommittee, had been constituted which scheduled a visit to these areas to meet tribal representatives.

In Peshawar, the news of the subcommittee's proposed visit upset Caroe no end. He told the viceroy that the visit would be disastrous: while 'certain members of the tribes may be ready to negotiate . . . whole jirgas will come down and endanger the peace' of settled districts. He, therefore, appealed to Wavell to do something to dissuade Nehru from 'acting precipitately' even through conceding that his own 'hopes from that quarter were small'.[147]

Weightman who as secretary in the EAD was in the thick of affairs expressed his helplessness: the best he could do was to urge on Nehru 'as dispassionate an appreciation' of the situation as possible, and to restrict the subcommittee 'initially' to a discussion with the Afridis, as the 'key Frontier tribe'.[148] Caroe, deeply distraught, told the viceroy that 'on merits' the right thing for him to do would be to exercise his 'special responsibility' under Section 52 (2) of the Government of India Act 1935, and refuse access to the subcommittee. This, he was apprehensive though, would lead to the resignation of his ministry.[149]

Weightman pointed out that it was 'inevitable' for the subcommittee, charged with submitting a report to the Constituent Assembly within three months, to visit the Frontier within that period. Nor could Nehru, as member incharge EAD, stop the visit on the plea that it would 'endanger' the peace of the border. Equally, Weightman argued, 'it seems to be beating the air' for Caroe to refuse access to a subcommittee appointed under the authority of the Constituent Assembly. That would surely 'precipitate a crisis'.[150]

Wavell counselled tact and patience and gave Caroe clearly to understand that it would be wrong to use his special powers to refuse access to the subcommittee. The risks, he averred, 'will have to be accepted'. Nor should the governor 'attempt to guide' the subcommittee beyond giving such informal advice as they asked for. Weightman, he assured an overwrought Caroe, was in touch with Nehru and would 'try to ensure through him' that the subcommittee took a reasonable stance.[151]

It may be added that in accordance with the Cabinet Mission Plan (para 20), the interim government had appointed a committee to deal with various minorities and such areas that enjoyed a special status. As Member for Home, Sardar Patel was the committee chairman. The parent committee, in turn, had appointed a subcommittee to be in special charge of tribal areas of NWFP; its three members being Abdul Ghaffar Khan, Abdus Samad Khan, a prominent Pakhtun from Baluchistan and Congress Party stalwart, and Mehr Chand Khanna.

Arrayed in political battle, the Muslim League had refused to accept nominations to the subcommittee. This notwithstanding, plans were drawn up for Sardar Patel and the subcommittee to visit the Frontier, including its tribal areas. Rumours about its impending visit had already reached the tribes who viewed it as not dissimilar to Nehru's own earlier sojourn, and as yet another insidious attempt to suborn the Pakhtuns.

Presently, the storm blew over when Wavell informed Caroe that the subcommittee was to remain 'in a state of suspense' until other issues had been sorted out. He noted that Nehru realised the need 'to go carefully' about this.[152]

Hardly had the subcommittee's visit been aborted when another issue cropped up. On 14 March, Nehru, then on a visit to Lahore, received a message from Wavell asking him not to proceed to Peshawar where Khan Sahib had invited him for 'a very brief and private visit'. Wavell underlined that the situation in the province was 'very tense' and there was 'a grave risk' that—'however careful your actions and speeches'—the visit may lead to a serious disturbance of peace in the region.[153]

In deference to Wavell's wishes, Nehru postponed his visit but wondered 'why it should be objected to?' Enraged and in high dudgeon, Nehru posed the all-important question: 'Am I to be prevented from performing my duty and shouldering the responsibility' that went with it 'because someone does not like me' or 'approve' of his going. That someone, and Nehru made no secret about it, was Olaf Caroe. Khan Sahib, he told Wavell, had given him to understand that the governor did not want him (Nehru) to come and that between the Premier and Caroe there had been 'an argument'. Recalling his earlier (October 1946) visit and Caroe's far from helpful role, Nehru made it abundantly clear that he could not 'continue his present responsibilities if I am prevented from doing my work in this way'. 'It was', he told the viceroy, 'an extraordinary position.'[154]

Nehru also took the opportunity to note the growing estrangement between Caroe and the Khan Sahib ministry, pointing out that the Governor's weight was 'usually' on the side opposed to his provincial government. The solution, he counselled Wavell, lay in asking Caroe 'to retire form his present office at an early date'. Nehru also told the viceroy that Khan Sahib 'especially desired my visit and still thinks' he should go. But he had decided not to and alleged that Olaf Caroe had tried 'to prevent my going' to the Frontier.[155]

In his *Journal*, Wavell noted receiving one of Nehru's 'rather intemperate' letters about his (Wavell's) request not to go to Peshawar, to which he had sent 'a soothing reply'.[156] Earlier, the viceroy recorded that

Nehru had 'agreed (not to go) though protestingly' and added that 'I think this will relieve OC's (Olaf Caroe's) mind'.[157] Interestingly enough, Caroe wrote Nehru a line to thank him for not visiting Peshawar: 'an odd matter to be grateful for but he will understand'.[158]

In his reply to Nehru's letter, Wavell put the record straight. Caroe, he revealed, 'did not object' to Nehru's visit. All that he had done, was to point out that troops and police were much too occupied 'to allow of special measures for protection'. All the same, Wavell added, Caroe had agreed to do his best. It was 'on my initiative', the viceroy added, that he (Wavell) had asked Nehru not to go for he was 'apprehensive of your safety'. He did not want the police to be diverted from other duties 'at a critical time'.[159]

In his letter of date to the secretary of state, Wavell wondered whether Nehru's accusations against the governor were not 'stimulated' by the fact that the judicial inquiry against Mahbub Ali Khan had exonerated the political agent, while reflecting adversely on the actions of both Abdul Ghaffar Khan as well as Khan Sahib.[160]

IX

Not long after his angry exchanges with Wavell, Nehru wrote (26 March) to Caroe to inform him of his earlier letter to the former governor-general, and underlined that 'a complete absence of a common outlook' between the two of them persisted. It indeed did between the governor and his council of ministers. Elaborating, Nehru emphasised, that 'in this inherent conflict' Caroe and his chief officers 'seem to function more or less as allies of the opposition than of the Ministry'. He added that reaction to this policy in the tribal areas 'has also been marked'.

He had also been given to understand, Nehru added, that the governor had told Khan Sahib and his colleagues that they 'had made a mistake in aligning themselves with the Congress' and should resign. This, he felt, created 'an impossible position' especially when the province was going through 'a difficult situation'. 'In view of all this', Nehru concluded, 'the only proper course was your resignation' from the governorship. 'The issues before us are too serious for any triflling on our part'.[161]

Even as these messages passed to and fro, there had been change of guard in the viceregal lodge. For towards end-March, Lord Mountbatten had taken over from Lord Wavell. Literally, on the morrow of his assumption of office, the new Viceroy's Chief of Staff, Lord Ismay, had visited Peshawar, to see things for himself. His report was discussed at

Mountbatten's staff meeting on 2 April where the governor-general is reported to have made two points. One, that Nehru was indispensable for a settlement and peaceful transfer of power; two, that he (Mountbatten) would be averse to any 'victimisation' of a British official.[162]

It is interesting to recall that in the course of his visit to Peshawar (1 April), Ismay 'speaking privately' had told Lady Caroe that he thought 'resignation might be best course, for the wells had been poisoned.' Lady Caroe, it would appear, had 'refused to pass on the suggestion and never mentioned it until after' her husband had left India.[163]

On 4 April, Nehru had told Mountbatten about the two letters he had written, to Wavell on 19 March and to Caroe exactly a week later, intimating that these had been to date 'kept secret by me and not put on any official file'.[164] Exactly ten days later, it may be recalled, Caroe had met the governor-general (in the course of the Governors' Conference) and asked him if he (G-G) desired his (Caroe's) resignation. Mountbatten's reply was, 'Not at present' but then the situation might change. Reportedly, he gave Caroe an assurance that he (Mountbatten) shall do nothing 'without sending for you and discussing the question in a friendly and frank manner'. His principal duty, the governor-general added, was to arrange for peaceful transfer of power and he 'cannot allow anything or anybody stand in the way of this being achieved'.[165] Later, in his report to Whitehall, Mountbatten underscored Caroe's 'essential straight-forwardness and desire to handle the very difficult situation in the Frontier in the most impartial and statesmanlike manner. ... But I think that at the moment he is suffering from nerves. ... I do not envy him his job which I should say is the most difficult out here.'[166]

Mountbatten's impression that Caroe was 'suffering from nerves' was exactly the impression Fraser Noble had carried as a junior official at Peshawar. This state of affairs, Sir Fraser records, further undermined the confidence of the officers of the Indian Civil Service and of the Political Service. More so, as they were well aware that 'our subordinate staff', in the provincial civil service, the police and the revenue departments, were 'already aligning' themselves with the politicians whom they recognised as their future masters. The fact was, Noble heavily underlines, that 'normal standards of administration' had now become impossible to sustain. Indeed, from the end of March, 'certainly' in Peshawar, and 'probably in all the districts', very little normal administration was possible.[167]

Nehru wrote to Mountbatten again on 26 April underscoring the point that the Muslim League agitation in the Frontier was designed to force the government's hands on dismissing the ministry and having fresh elections. He roundly deplored 'this business of trying to decide political issues by threats of violence'. The Congress leader expressed the hope that it should be made perfectly clear that 'such activities will not be allowed' to influence events.[168]

In his reply to Nehru's letter four days later, Mountbatten asserted that Khan Sahib was wrong in attributing the present situation in the Frontier to the 'machinations of the Governor and his officials'. There was, the governor-general added, an upsurge of communal feeling against a ministry which was regarded as dominated by the 'essentially Hindu Congress'. Nor were the tribes prepared 'to contemplate absorption into a state which they regarded as likely to be dominated by the Hindus'.[169] Mountbatten's letter enclosed an account of his meeting with the governor and his four ministers (including Khan Sahib) which had taken place at Peshawar on 28 April during his two-day visit.[170] Khan Sahib, it may be recalled, had contradicted these minutes in some significant detail.[171]

In his response of 3 May, Nehru warned the governor-general that in regard to what had transpired at the latter's meeting in Peshawar, he hoped that in view of the broader implications of the issues involved, 'nothing will be taken for granted and if there is any misapprehension' it would be removed 'immediately'.[172]

Two days earlier, in a communication to the governor-general, Nehru had alluded to reports about the reign of terror, murder and arson in D I Khan and the 'deliberate policy' being followed by the Muslim League which had led to the 'most ghastly results in human suffering'. He also indicated that it would appear that during the governor-general's visit the Khan Sahib ministry were 'in the dock and had to defend itself' while 'little if anything at all' was being said about the Muslim League agitation, the results flowing from it and the 'continuing policy' that the League had pursued. He concluded by asserting that while it would be absurd to say that all the trouble in the Frontier was 'due to the machinations of the governor and his officials', he had little doubt that Olaf Caroe and some of his officials, were responsible in many ways for the present situation. He personally thought the governor 'completely unfit' for the post he held, for he 'neither (had) the capacity nor the impartiality' to deal with the situation. This also held true for certain officials in Waziristan. Nehru concluded by asserting that he found it 'increasingly difficult to continue to be incharge of a department which is responsible in some way for the activities of officials who function wrongly and are completely beyond my control'.[173]

Fraser Noble has questioned Nehru's judgement that Caroe lacked in 'capacity' or 'impartiality' to deal with the situation in the province. 'In any normal circumstances', he (Caroe) would indeed have been well-fitted for the post. But circumstances were far from normal. This was largely because the Congress ministry, in the prevailing political climate, no longer enjoyed the respect and confidence of the people. The tribes were 'never backward' in interpreting the political situation. The same was now true of the people in the settled districts and this despite the poor record of the Muslim League when in government.

Caroe, Noble adds, may have lacked judgement and suffered from a loss of nerve. But Nehru 'totally failed' to understand the tribal situation. It was the Political Service, both at the all-India and the provincial level, who were 'remarkably successful' in handling the tribal problem during the difficult World War II years. Any failure on their part at the time would have led to threats to the whole of India from the north-west as well as the north-east.[174]

Nehru's letter more or less brought matters to a head as far as Caroe's continuation at Peshawar was concerned. Two other heavy-weights now joined in the battle against the Frontier governor. One, Badshah Khan who while addressing public meetings in mid-May in Bihar was telling his audience that Caroe had been 'playing a dirty game'. At the tribal jirgas, he pointed out, Caroe professed all friendship for the Pathan people while at the same time urging New Delhi to keep in readiness strong squadrons of bombers to rain death and destruction on the hapless Pathans. Nor was that all. For the governor had told his ministers that there was 'nothing in common' between them and India, and that if they would agree 'to quit the Congress, he would give them all support'.[175]

That was by no means the end of Abdul Ghaffar Khan's anti-Caroe tirade. He stressed that while 400 people had been killed in his province, not a single culprit had been arrested. The governor, he added, must feel ashamed of the kind of administration he was heading. Nor did the Frontier leader camouflage his feelings when he told Mountbatten that he could not trust him (Mountbatten) for all his 'crooked' dealings in the province. For the Muslim League agitation there was 'all Caroe's doing'.[176]

Few, in any, among British administrators, including Fraser Noble, thought that this was not 'typical of the nonsense' which Badshah Khan believed in and propagated.[177]

Just about this time Krishna Menon, always close to Nehru, had written to one of his correspondents (12 May) that Jenkins, the Panjab Governor, was by no means 'the worst of Governors . . . Caroe is hated by our people and is said to be at the bottom of the Frontier mischief'.[178]

A few weeks later, Nehru asked Mountbatten (on 4 June) to hasten the change of governors in the NWFP. There had been, he pointed out, 'progressive deterioration' in the relations between Caroe and his ministry—'a continuous conflict' that was undesirable. Khan Sahib too, he added, had made enquiries on the subject and 'apart from any party or group' there had been 'widespread feeling' in the matter in many circles who had come in contact with the present governor. Besides, he (Nehru) had been suggesting a change even before Mountbatten arrived on the scene and added that any further delay would prove 'harmful'. Nehru recalled that way back in 1930, Caroe, as Deputy Commissioner of Peshawar, had been responsible for 'large-scale shooting and killings of peaceful demonstrators', an event that still evoked 'bitter memories.' He concluded by asking the Viceroy to give 'urgent consideration' to the matter.[179]

Two days prior to Nehru's letter, the Mahatama had gone out of the way to see Mountbatten to convey to him Badshah Khan's message for removing Caroe. In so far as he was observing his weekly day of silence, Gandhi scribbled a few lines for the governor-general on the back of a used cover. Badshah Khan, wrote the Mahatma, was with him at the Bhangi colony (where Gandhi invariably stayed while in Delhi. 'He said "Do ask the Viceroy to remove the Governor. We won't have peace till he is gone." I do not know whether he is right or wrong. He is truthful. If it can be done, Government or you should do it.'[180] Mountbatten noted that the demand for Caroe's removal 'has now been re-endorsed' both by Nehru as well as Khan Sahib.[181]

X

As if to bring matters to a head, the viceroy had asked Khan Sahib for discussions on 5 June, largely in the context of his 3 June plan for the transfer of power. The Premier pleaded that Caroe be replaced before the referendum in the Frontier (envisaged in the 3 June Plan) took place.[182] In the upsoht, on 6 June Mountbatten wrote to Caroe about an officiating governor taking over from him during the proposed referendum. He clarified that lately he had been 'bombarded' again by 'representations from your detractors (whom I need not name) to the effect that there is no hope for peace nor of a fair and orderly referendum, in the NWFP as long as you' hold the reins of office. And though personally he (Mountbatten) had a high opinion of Caroe's 'capacity, integrity and selfless devotion to duty' he felt the time had come to replace him as governor. He was keen that this 'grave step' should not close the door for your 'further employment in India if you were so to desire'. He suggested, therefore, that Caroe proceed on leave 'as soon as' his temporary successor arrived and remain on leave until 15 August. In the event of the Frontier going to Pakistan, Mountbatten added, it may be very well that the Pakistan Government, 'who I believe, share my high opinion of you, would ask for you to be reappointed'.[183]

It would be of interest to note that on 9-10 June, Jinnah was informed about the impending change of governors at Peshawar. This was done at the instance of Ismay who in turn was persuaded by Auchinleck when they met to discuss the replacement of Olaf Caroe by Rob Lockhart. The reasoning was that in its absence, the Quaid may get the impression that Congress had succeeded in liquidating a man of whom he has 'a high opinion'. Jinnah was to be told that during his very first meeting Mountbatten had been persuaded that Caroe's 'health and his nerves rendered him unfit' to continue. The only reason the governor-general had bided his time was lest the Quaid should think that the change had been effected 'under the pressure of Congress'.[184] There is no record of Jinnah registering any protest!

Acknowledging Mountbatten's letter of 6 June, Caroe conceded that the governor-general had made up his mind 'that the charge of partisanship made it wrong' for him (Caroe) to continue. He accepted that judgement with 'deep sorrow' for the change would be regarded in many quarters as a 'surrender to unfair attacks'. The *modus operandi*, he now suggested, was that 'taking the initiative', he (Caroe) would 'go on leave' during the next two months so that 'it should not be said that I had used my authority to influence the course and results' of the referendum. He was not sure if 'it would be right or proper for me to come back if circumstances change and if anybody wants me'. Nor was he clear whether he should go home: 'For if I remain here, it would look as if I were hanging about on an off chance' and it might keep 'propaganda on both sides going'.[185]

Interestingly enough, his own counsel to the contrary notwithstanding, Caroe did hang around on the 'off chance' that Jinnah as well as his (Caroe's) Pakistani friends, would put him back in the saddle at Peshawar. He, therefore, decided to go to Kashmir 'until our staff have packed our things and then go home'.[186]

Oddly though, Caroe's letter of 11 June, which for 'security reasons' was in manuscript, mentioned that if the Frontier did go to Pakistan and he 'were asked to stay on as Governor' he would have grave doubts whether it would be 'right or proper' for him to do so. It would be sad 'if

31 A. Exit.

As indicated in Letter 31 (1) and (2), personal correspondence had passed between the Viceroy and the writer before Letter 32 was penned. See items 2, 3, 4, 5, 7, 8 of Epilogue. The gist of these letters was that the writer, accused by one party as not impartial (though the Viceroy dissociated himself from this charge), was asked to agree to go on leave until the result of the Referendum, to be held in July, was known. It was ×suggested that, if the vote went in favour of the League, he might be recalled to office. The writer himself was not anxious to be sponsored by any party; that apart, he was clear in his own mind that this result was never intended — a view reinforced in a letter from Pug Ismay written a few days later (see item 9 of Epilogue). This shewed that the break was final. Nevertheless he was interested to be at hand, and decided to go to Kashmir to await the outcome. While in Kashmir he was informed that the Referendum had gone overwhelmingly against Congress, but that Jinnah had decided to ask for the relief of Cunningham. Jinnah did not know Cunningham, while he had been a fellow-member of the Central Legislative Assembly with the writer who was Foreign Secretary in Delhi throughout the War.

Later he was told that a reason given for his supersession was that he had had a breakdown in health. ~~This was untrue. He is nevertheless satisfied~~ ×events favoured him in permitting him to haul down his colours when he did. Since 1947 he has paid three visits to Pakistan, and one to India, as a State guest, the last on Nehru's invitation a few months before his death to help in work for Tibetan refugees.

i. This was untrue. He|is nevertheless satisfied (?) ...... that

Sir Olaf Caroe's Mss (p. 179A).

in any way' he were to be identified with one party who had antagonised the other for all time; for 'I say it very firmly and finally (that) I am not a partisan.' If the Muslim League came to power it would be 'in the tradition of being both authoritarian and malicious' and it would have a very difficult time because they were 'not big men.'[187]

Two brief comments may be in order. One, by Caroe himself. Writing years later he recalled that he

> was not anxious to be sponsored by any party; that apart, he was clear in his mind that this result (viz. his recall to office, in Peshawar) was never intended—a view reinforced in a letter from Pug Ismay written a few days later (actually on 12 June). . . . This showed that the break was final. Nevertheless he was interested to be at hand, and decided to go to Kashmir to await the outcome.[188]

In actual fact, the former Governor's return to the Government House *before* 15 August depended upon Mountbatten and Whitehall; *after* that day, upon Jinnah and the Pakistan government. Whitehall and Mountbatten, it should be obvious, were dead set against Caroe resuming office (Listowell had in fact demanded time and again that he be made to resign); much less was Jinnah and his government. Mitchell's observation that Caroe 'himself expected to return if the issue of plebiscite went against the Congress Party'[189]—Fraser Noble 'did not recollect that any of us expected this'[190]—would sound true and is borne out by the former Governor's decision to hang on. His later disavowal of 'not being anxious to be sponsored by any party'—rings hollow and must be rated an afterthought.

On 21 June, the *Tribune* reverted to the subject of 'Pathanistan' and conceded that Sir Olaf's relinquishment of office was 'a step in the right direction'. It asserted that the history of the Frontier Province would have been 'differently written' if Sir Olaf had not been at the helm of affairs for he had been responsible for a lot of 'communal mischief'.

On the other hand, no sooner did the news of Caroe's resignation—or, more accurately, his proceeding on leave—spread, the Muslim League were up in arms. Liaquat Ali Khan, Jinnah's *alter ego* and second in command in the League hierarchy, wrote to Mountbatten to say that removing Caroe without removing the Ministry was 'an extraordinary and dangerous step'. The Nawabzada further alleged that 'abuse of power and patronage' by the Khan Sahib ministry had been serious and his party had made repeated demands for their removal. The accusation that the governor was anti-Congress was, 'as you know, absolutely without foundation'. It followed that the Viceroy's action was 'nothing short of complete surrender' to the Congress which would 'mar all chance of fair and free referendum'.[191]

The League leader's diatribe against Caroe's virtual dismissal did not register any impact on the governor-general, largely it would appear because Mountbatten had taken Jinnah into confidence about the impending change at Peshawar.[192] There is no knowing whether the Quaid in turn had told Liaquat Ali Khan about what he knew before hand. In any case, Liaquat Ali's outburst may well have been a proforma protest with (or without) the Quaid's initiative, or encouragement.

In Whitehall there was strong opposition to any suggestion that Caroe should resume office once he relinquished it. As HMG viewed it, Caroe was 'to ask permission' to lay down his office on the medical consideration that he was overstrained and needed relief from his responsibilities. In the event, for Caroe to resume 'would be taken as implying that we ourselves believe that Caroe is prejudiced in favour of the Muslim League and therefore ought not to be in office during the holding of the referendum'. To achieve this objective, it would have been ideal, secretary of state Listowel reasoned in his minute of 10 June to the prime minister, if Caroe's resignation and Lockhart's appointment had been 'made substantive forthwith'. But aware of the situation on the ground—'now that Caroe had proceeded on leave'—it would no doubt be possible if necessary to induce him to resign while on leave and confirm Lockhart's acting appointment. If however, Listowel concluded, the Pakistan Government 'were to make its recommendation' and in exercise of its rights as Dominion Government, advised the king that Caroe resume or be reappointed, a new situation would arise.[193]

Whitehall's anxiety over the modalities of Caroe's departure was voiced afresh a few days later when the secretary of state told the viceroy that he felt 'very strongly and the Prime Minister agrees with me in this' that it would be most unwise to allow Caroe to resume the governorship. It would imply, Listowel reiterated, that 'we ourselves believe' that Caroe was prejudiced in favour of the Muslim League and 'ought not' to be in office during the referendum.[194] This viewpoint was restated with considerable emphasis in a telegram from Whitehall to Ismay and again in Listowel's minute of 16 June to Attlee. Herein the secretary of state underlined that 'he would have preferred' the matter was handled the way Whitehall wanted it. But since Caroe's letter had already been written and dispatched, Ismay had pressed the urgency of the situation, leaving him (Listowel) 'no alternative to acquiescing' in what Mountbatten had already done. For his part, he still hoped that Caroe would be prepared to tender his resignation while he was on leave and Lockhart confirmed in his acting appointment.[195]

It would appear in retrospect that the matter of replacing Caroe by Lockhart had been taken up as early as May 1947 during Mountbatten's visit to London and informally acquiesced in at the Whitehall end. All the same, as between Mountbatten and Attlee, it was agreed that the matter of replacing Caroe 'should not be pursued for the time being and at any rate until the referendum in the province had been held'. The matter could not be pursued 'to its logical conclusion', Mountbatten told Ismay on 7 May, because of a Congress-inspired 'anti-Caroe agitation' with mounting attacks in the press in Lahore and Delhi and demands for observing 'an anti-Caroe day'. Mountbatten had protested strongly to Nehru who promised 'to do all he could' to stop these attacks.[196]

In a minute dated 12 May, Listowel told the prime minister that Mountbatten had evidently 'quite made up my mind' that he no longer had confidence in Olaf Caroe's competence to hold his charge and had to replace him at a suitable juncture. And even though Caroe was a man of great intellectual capacity 'he was highly strung' and prone to suffer aspersions on his impartiality 'less easily' than a man of more equable temperament. Lockhart, his contemplated replacement, had long experience and 'profound knowledge' of the Frontier and personally the 'temperament required'.[197]

On 12 June, however, on the morrow of Caroe's letter, Mountbatten had, in fact, told the secretary of state that the governor had agreed to go on leave to England and thought this to be the 'best solution for a difficult problem'.[198] To be sure, in the body of his letter of 11 June, Caroe had said: 'on the whole, I think I had better go home' and adduced another reason for doing so: 'my mother has just died, and I have to decide various questions relating to our family home and so on.'[199]

Caroe's change of stance, left Whitehall less than happy and, after a lot of to-ing and fro-ing of urgent messages, the secretary of state confessed on 20 June that he saw the 'advantages' of handling Caroe's resignation on the lines 'finally adopted'. And was glad Mountbatten 'did not contemplate' Caroe resuming as Governor at Peshawar. Unless a recommendation in his favour were made by the Pakistan government.[200]

Meantime on 17 June, Acharya Kriplani, then Congress Party President, wrote to Mountbatten to say that 'there was a complete impasse' in the Frontier administration inasmuch as between the governor and his ministers relations were 'strained to an extreme degree'. He also intimated that Abdul Ghaffar Khan as well as Khan Sahib and his cabinet colleagues had demanded that the Frontier people 'should be allowed to pronounce on the issue of independence', being totally averse to taking part in a referendum which 'must turn purely on the communal issue'. In case the issue cannot be 'between Pakistan and Pathanistan', Kriplani concluded, Badshah Khan would advise his followers to abstain from participating in the referendum.[201]

With the referendrum again in seeming jeopardy, Mountbatten wrote to Nehru to reiterate his earlier position. It was, the governor-general pointed out, 'at your (Nehru's) written request' that the option to the provinces for independence was taken out; that Jinnah who was in favour of Bengal being allowed to vote for independence knew that 'I conceded this point to Congress'; that 'both your position and my position' would be 'completely untenable if either of us went back on this arrangement now'. Besides, Mountbatten added, inasmuch as Olaf Caroe was 'offering to go on leave', Abdul Ghaffar Khan should accept the referendum 'in the right spirit'. He further pleaded with Nehru to use his influence with the press to restrain if from saying that Caroe 'has been sacked'.[202]

In his letter to Mountbatten on the eve of handing over charge, Caroe literally let himself go as for his principal tormentor. Alluding to 'one reflection I ought to make', he emphasised that 'all his troubles started' with Nehru taking over tribal affairs 'under his wing'. Prior thereto, the province was, Caroe stressed, 'going along very nicely'. But bringing these tribes under a Pandit was 'an impossible thing to do'; in the event, 'practically all our frictions and tensions' dated from that time.

Reverting to his own performance, Caroe maintained that 'the most important part' of the governor's work in Peshawar lay 'in keeping the tribes steady'. It was a truism that the tribal situation and the situation within the province 'react to one another continually', and the proper management of both achieved 'tribal steadiness'.

Turning to the new constitution makers, Caroe's advice was in favour of maintaining the status quo: the tribes should not be placed under the provincial government while the authority of the agent to the governor-general. who 'deals locally' with them, must derive from the central government.

A most interesting observation Caroe made may be worth recalling. 'In the long run', he expressed the view, 'I believe HMG will not be able to divorce themselves entirely' from interest 'in the maintenance of this delicate and difficult Frontier'.[203] Perhaps not unknown to him, some of Caroe's compatriots on the North-Eastern Frontier had voiced exactly similar perceptions.[204]

Even when the question of his resignation had not yet cropped up, Caroe had told Mountbatten that, as he saw it, his job was to 'prevent the disintegration' of the NWFP. He was quite clear that the Cabinet Mission Plan had not 'faced up squarely' to this question. And feared that the various forces acting on the North-West Frontier—and unleashed in the wake of the British Prime Minister's statement of 20 February (1947)—'may produce a resultant' that would be highly dangerous and threaten the Frontier's stability. As to the tribes, they did not accept 'even now' that power will be handed over. None the less they were anxious about their position 'and would much rather go on with an orderly balance' which secured them the considerable benefits they enjoyed than to face the chaos which at one time was supposed to suit the Pathan outlook. 'One thing was certain', and it was that they will 'in no sense submit to any control' that could 'even remotely' be represented as exercised by a Hindudominated government.[205]

A word here on the tribal areas *vis-a-vis* the settled districts. The whole subject needs much more detailed analysis than space would permit. Broadly, from a tenable point of view, likely to be held either by the Congress or a Muslim League provincial government, it could not be possible to exclude the provincial government from any role in relations with the tribes. As has been noticed earlier, Sir George Cunningham had a clear perception that the administration of the tribal areas should be integrated with that of the settled districts. More importantly, his views enjoyed a broad measure of support over a wide political spectrum. A major difficulty arose from the fact that the tribes had long standing treaties with the Crown, through the Government of India. In a sense, the terms of the partition or the transfer of power imposed a breach of these treaties, even as the Indian princes were forced to accept a breach of their treaties by the Government of India. It could almost be said in another sense that the separation of tribal territories from the settled districts under the Raj imposed a measure of 'disintegration' on the Frontier *ab initio*.[206]

NOTES

1. For a succinct review of major developments see Tara Chand, *History of the Freedom Movement*, 4, Chapter 2, 'The Cabinet Mission Plan and After', pp. 455-93. Also relevant entries in Parshotam Mehra, *A Dictionary of Modern Indian History, 1707-1947*.
2. Jansson, pp. 163-4; see also ibid., pp. 119, 122.
3. Major Abdur Rahim was a sworn enemy of Iskander Mirza and, 'initially' at any rate, in favour of Aurangzeb Khan. He too fell out with Khan Sahib and left the province in October 1944. For details see Jansson, p. 164.

4. Governor's Report, 9 October 1945, cited in Jansson, p. 154.
5. Rittenberg, p. 341. See also Jansson, pp. 165-6.
6. Jansson, p. 167.
7. Rittenberg, p. 341. The author suggests that there were several quasi-military units who called themselves 'National Guards' yet they had no hierarchy of command, much less any central leadership.
8. Rittenberg discusses the 'reorganisation' of the Frontier Muslim League in the wake of the appointment (April 1946) of a 40-member organising committee which brought about 'transformation' of the Muslim League leadersip. His conclusion: 'despite their considerable efforts', the party 'lacked a sound footing'. For details see Rittenberg, pp. 339-43.
9. The Pir toured the tribal areas in the company of a Muslim League entourage. Rittenberg, p. 341.
10. Jansson, pp.167-8.
11. Cited in Rittenberg, p. 350.
12. The *Daily Telegraph* (London) correspondent in Peshawar cited in Tendulkar, pp. 406-7.
13. Caroe to Wavell, 13 January 1947, *CM*, p. 120.
14. Cited in Tendulkar, p. 407.
15. Wavell's *Journal*, entry for 19 November 1946, pp. 377-8. See also Caroe to Wavell, 23 November 1946, *CM*, p. 97.
16. Jansson, pp. 188-9.
17. George Cunningham agreed fully with Khan Sahib on bringing the tribes eventually under the provincial government at Peshawar. Thus, the following entry in his diary: 'A long talk to Dr Khan Sahib about future arragnements for the tribes. His main points were that they should come under the provincial government . . . in fact much of my own views', *GCD*, 12 September 1945.
18. Caroe to Wavell, 10 April 1946, *CM*, p.12.
19. The Nawab of Hoti for instance resigned from the Muslim League as also from his membership of the provincial legislature. For details, Jansson, p. 178.
20. Jansson, p. 188.
21. In his letter of 10 April to Wavell, Caroe revealed that the Rabi (i.e. spring) crop—mostly wheat and barley—was 'avergae' and that they had been 'pressed from Delhi' to include other items, particularly maize, in the cereal ration. Caroe to Wavell, 10 April 1946, *CM*, pp. 16-17.

    Later, the governor informed the viceroy that the ministry 'have gone back' on their earlier decision to start the extension of rationing to other towns, besides Peshawar. He was convinced that in the conditions prevalent in the province, 'local procurement was definitely more important'. Caroe to Wavell, 23 April 1946, *CM*, p. 18.
22. Fraser Noble, Memoirs, pp. 272-4. Years later, Noble prepared a critical analysis of the scheme and its outcome for the new Economic Development Institute of the World Bank and the International Monetary Fund. Subsequently, a version of this paper was used for the Chicago journal, *Economic Development and Cultural Change* and as a case study in seminars on planning in under-developed areas.
23. Caroe to Wavell, 13 January 1947, *CM*, pp. 118-19.
24. Ibid., p. 120.
25. Caroe to Wavell, 23 January 1947, *CM*, p. 125.
26. Ibid., 13 January 1947, *CM*, pp. 118-19. Caroe called it a 'short ordinance' which

borrowed a single section from its Panjab model dealing with violent speeches and rumours. For the rest, the existing law was deemed adequate to deal with the situation.

27. Among the conditions laid down were a fine of Rs. 75,000 and surrender of 75 rifles and 40 hostages. Caroe reported that by January, just over two-thirds of cash and just under two-thirds of the rifles had been surrendered. Caroe to Wavell, 23 January 1947, *CM*, p. 125
28. Rittenberg, p. 363.
29. Caroe to Wavell, 22 February 1947, *CM*, p. 135.
30. Fraser Noble, Memoirs, pp. 301-2.
31. Caroe to Wavell, 22 February 1947, *CM*, p. 136. Caroe noted that Khan Sahib was 'lucky' to get away with his life and that Mrs Khan Sahib along with the premier's parliamentary secretary 'stuck by him through the worst', ibid., p. 137. See also Fraser Noble, Memoirs, p. 302.
32. Caroe told Wavell that he kept the Sikh woman 'out of the published terms and the news to avoid another Islam Bibi outcry'. Caroe to Wavell, 23 January 1947, *CM*, p. 125.

    Mirza Ali Khan, later famous as the Fakir of Ipi, was a Tori Khel Wazir born about 1890. In 1936 he was Imam of a mosque at Ipi, a hamlet close to the road between Bannu and the lower Tochi valley. He had a humdrum, inconspicuous, quiet religious life. Few knew him; fewer still cared about him.

    Just about then, a Hindu girl, Chand Bibi, wife of a Hindu merchant in Bannu, was abducted—forcibly or otherwise—by a young Waziri who went through a Muslim rite of marriage with her. She was re-christened Islam (Muslim) Bibi. Her husband sued in a Bannu court asking for restoration of conjugal rights and won his case. This led to a loud, explosive, chorus of protest from the tribes amidst a blaze of publicity. Mirza Ali Khan saw his chance and pushed himself to the forefront. Government, he charged, was interfering in religious matters and he for one would have no truck with it.

    The Waziri revolt was to cost the British dear for Ipi was at once brutal and treacherous, took bribes, sheltered outlaws and was not above hiring assassins to deal with his enemies. All through 1936, and the two years following, the Raj was facing a difficult if elusive challenger. Casualties were high and by December 1937 as many as 40,000 British and Indian troops were directly engaged. Nor was that all. For Pakistan inherited the Fakir and his revolt; a Pakistani official in the 1950s described him as 'a vicious old man, twisted with hate and selfishness'. The Fakir who died in 1960 was the subject of an obituary in the *Times* (London) which hailed him as 'a man of principle and saintliness' as well as 'a doughty and honourable opponent'. For details see Arthur Swinson, *North-West Frontier: People and Events, 1939-1947*, London, 1967, pp. 327-32 and J G Elliott, *Frontier 1839-1947: the story of the North-West Frontier of India*, London, 1968, pp. 271-7. See also Caroe to Wavell, 22 February 1947, *CM*, pp. 135-6.
33. Caroe told Wavell that anticipating trouble and delay in the return of the evacuees, he had postponed the byelection in Hazara. Caroe to Wavell, 8 February 1947, *CM*, p. 130.
34. Fraser Noble, Memoirs, p. 299.
35. Caroe to Wavell, 8 February 1947, *CM*, p. 130.
36. Ibid., 22 February 1947, *CM*, p. 135. Also Fraser Noble, Memoirs, pp. 299-300.
37. Nehru to Mountbatten, 3 May 1947, *Selected Works*, Second Series, II, New Delhi,

1985, pp. 326-8. See also n. 168 of this chapter.

In the 1937 elections, the Congress candidate, Amir Mohammed Khan, had defeated the Nawab of Hoti (Independent) by a substantial margin, 3163 to 2,599. In the 1946 elections, the Nawab, now on a Muslim League ticket, had polled 8,354 votes against Mian Shakirullah (Congress) 8,185. Prior to the elctions, the Nawab had been appointed secretary to the provincial League's finance board and had, *inter alia*, paid for the uniforms of Muslim League National Guards apart from handsome donations to the League itself. For details see Jansson, pp. 247, 257.

38. Caroe to Wavell, 22 February 1947, *CM*, p. 135.

Rittenberg has expressed the view that once the polling in the Mardan byelection was over, the 'final restraint' on the Muslim League was lifted. For seven days later the League started its civil disobedience movement on the 'first available pretext'. Rittenberg, pp. 361-2.

39. 'Introduction', *Jinnah Papers*, I,1, pp. xxxii, xl-xli.
40. Caroe to Wavell, 8 March 1947, *CM*, p. 143.
41. 'Fresh Elections on Pakistan Issue: Only solution to NWFP Trouble', *Civil & Military Gazette* (Lahore), 25 March 1947, *Jinnah Papers*, I, 1, Encl. to No. 243.
42. Caroe to Mountbatten, 22 March 1947, *CM*, p. 146.
43. Ibid., p. 147.
44. Fraser Noble, Comments on Draft.
45. Caroe to Mountbatten, 22 March 1947, *CM*, p. 149.
46. Rittenberg, p. 372

Earlier, on 19 March, the Khan Sahib ministry, partly to counter the Muslim League's strong arm tactics, brought in a contingent of 10,000 Khudai Khidmatgars to Peshawar. Sadly, they proved to be only a temporary relief.

For details see Caroe to Wavell, 13 March 1947, *Transfer of Power*, IX, Document 528 and ibid., X, Document 163.

47. Caroe to Mountbatten, 21 April 1947, *CM*, p. 156.
48. In the mid-1950s, the Pir along with Arbab Abdul Ghafoor and Samin Jan joined Abdul Ghaffar Khan to oppose the one-unit West Pakistan scheme. The Muslim League in the Frontier had by then fallen on bad days; it had suffered an open split in late 1948 and wholesale defections in the year following. For details see Jansson, p. 236. Also Rittenberg p. 400, n. 3.
49. The *Tribube*, 2 April, 1947.
50. *Jinnah Papers*, II, Annex III, No. 203. The Annex gives the full text of the report, 'Troops open fire on Peshawar Crowd: Demonstration Before Assembly Chambers: Deputy Commissioner Pleads for Peaceful Means', reproduced from the *Civil & Military Gazette* (Lahore), 14 March 1947.
51. Caroe noted that the Ministry 'with the aid of troops' who had to fire on the protest demonstration, 'managed to carry through the budget session of the legislature while the opposition was behind bars'. Caroe to Mountbatten, 22 March 1947, *CM*, p. 147.
52. Fraser Noble, Memoirs, pp. 308, 311.
53. Ibid., p. 312.
54. In the Peshawar valley, only the Peshawar tehsil was badly affected; Peshawar city witnessed a week of random stabbings, bombings, and scattered incendiarism. Hazara suffered more for the district, predominantly non-Pakhtun, supported the Muslim League. For details see Rittenberg, p. 372.

The *Tribune* (Lahore) dutifully carried official communiques issued in Peshawar all through March retailing major happenings in the town as well as in Hazara. *NMML.*

Also see Fortnightly Report, for the second half of April 1947, Home Political Department, Government of India, *NAI*.

55. Caroe to Mountbatten, 21 April 1947, *CM*, pp. 156-7. See also the *Tribune*, 16-25 April 1947, *NMML* and Caroe's 'note', *CM*, p. 154-A.
56. In contrast to the police, army officers, mostly British, were more stringent in their dealings. For details see Jansson, pp. 195-6.
57. Ibid., p. 197.
58. Jansson, p. 195.
59. Ibid., pp. 196-7.
60. For details see Fraser Noble, Memoirs, pp. 313-18. See also Rittenberg, pp. 380-1.
61. Firoz Khan Noon to M A Jinnah, 30 April 1947, in *Jinnah Papers*, I, 1, No. 367.
62. Fraser Noble, Comments on Draft.
63. Letter to Mrs Mitchell, 6 April 1947, Mitchell Papers, cited in Rittenberg, p. 367, n. 17.
64. Mitchell in a letter to his wife, 16 March 1947, noted that the mob 'turned their anger' against Hindus and Sikhs 'partly because of the very bad communal rioting in neighbouring Punjab and partly because of the army attack of 10 March which was viewed as launched by Congress—a Hindu Party— on the Muslims'. For details see Rittenberg, p. 371.
65. The *Tribune*, 2 April 1947.
66. Rittenberg notes that every Muslim League leader he interviewed stated that the party was 'not the least averse' to the use of violence. Rittenberg, p. 370, n. 24.
67. Ibid., p. 374.
68. For Mountbatten's visit to Peshawar and the tribal areas see pp. 134-46 above.
69. The Gandhi-Jinnah joint appeal was issued under the aegis of the viceroy. The Mahatma commented that his signature had no value because he never believed in violence. But it was significant, he noted, that Jinnah had signed it. For details see Tendulkar, p. 411.
70. The *Tribune*, 11 June 1947.
71. For the full text of the statement, see *Jinnah Papers*, I, 1, Annex to No. 391.
72. In the wake of his and Gandhi's appeal of 15 April, Jinnah is said to have sent 'orders' to the working committee of the Frontier Muslim League to end violence and mentioned this fact to a League delegation that met him at the beginning of May. For details see Rittenberg, p. 375.

    This notwithstanding, Rittenberg noted that 'while violence tailed off, if did not end, nor did the participation of Muslim Leaguers in it', ibid.
73. Rittenberg, p. 376.

    Drawing for most part on press reports, heavily slanted and by no means unexaggerated, in the *Pakistan Times* (Lahore), and a few in the *Morning News* (Dacca), *Star of India* (Calcutta) and the *Dawn* (Delhi), in *Jinnah Papers*, I, 2, Appendix VIII, Nos. 1-161, pp. 326-449, furnishes 'day to day developments' of the League's civil disobedience movement in the NWFP and covers what the editor calls 'the long-drawn struggle' as from 20 February to 2 June 1947.
74. Hodson has charged that Col de la Fargue was 'as wrong in his assessment' of the Congress government's electoral possibilities as 'he was disloyal' in his strictures

on Sir Olaf Caroe. H.V. Hodson, *The Great Divide*, p. 283. Rittenberg wrongly mentions this as p. 285. Rittenberg, p. 381, n. 45.

75. *CM* 2.
76. For the full text of Mitchell's 'Appreciation of Muslim League's situation on 5-4-47', see Durga Das (ed.), *Sardar Patel's Correspondence*, 10 vols, Ahmedabad, 1972-4, vol. 5, item 266, pp. 257-9.

    It is interesting to recall that many years later Sir Olaf told Mitchell that his promotion as chief secretary 'was especially requested by Dr Khan Sahib although it involved the supersession of two of my seniors.' Norval Mitchell, Memoirs, p. 257.
77. The governor's forwarding note which bears the signatures both of Sir Olaf Caroe as well as A N Mitchell and the date '07 April', is found in Durga Das, op. cit., vol. 5, pp. 259-60.
78. Sardar Patel's letter of 12 April refers to his 'discussion' with the governor-general earlier in the day. The Sardar also enclosed the Fortnightly Report for the second half of March (1947) which was 'apparently prepared' on 2 April (1947). For details see n. 76 of this chapter, Durga Das (ed.), pp. 258-9.
79. Norval Mitchell, Memoirs, pp. 257-8.
80. Letter to Mrs Mitchell, 13 April 1947, cited in Rittenberg, p. 382.
81. A prominent Mahsud Malik told Jansson that Abdul Manan, the then Assistant Political Officer, knew all about the plans to attack Tank and other towns. Not only did he do nothing to stop the slaughter but also felt 'very pleased' about the whole affair! Jansson, p. 198.
82. Malik Muhammad Hayat Khan to M A Jinnah, 26 February 1947, *Jinnah Papers,* I, 1, No. 38.
83. Sher Bahadur Khan to M A Jinnah, 21 March 1947, ibid., No. 175.
84. The marakka had served as a backdrop to the Mahsud attack in mid-April, born out of a mix of 'religious zeal and desire for loot', Jansson, p. 197. See also Rittenberg, p. 374.
85. Jansson, p. 198.
86. 'Report by Anonym on Tribes of the NWFP', in *Jinnah Papers*, I, 1, No, 371.
87. Fraser Noble, Comments on Draft.
88. The *Tribune*, 18 June 1947. Jinnah's proposed visit, scheduled for 20 June, never took place.
89. Khurshid to M A Jinnah, 14 June 1947, in *Jinnah Papers*, II, No. 108. The letter originated from 'Khyber House, Peshawar'.
90. Jansson, p. 199.
91. *Jinnah Papers*, II, Annex to No. 299. The statement issued on 30 June was published in the *Pakistan Times,* 1 July 1947.
92. Caroe to Wavell, 8 March 1947, *CM,* pp. 141-2.
93. Caroe's 'long talk' with his ministers was held against the backdrop of the Muslim League's 'Direct Action' campaign which was 'growing in volume'. And the 'alarming developments' in the neighbouring Panjab added to his own strong feeling that the 'flood might conceivably sweep them away'. Ibid.
94. Caroe to Mountbatten, 22 March 1947, *CM*, p. 146.
95. Ibid., 7 April 1947, *CM*, pp. 150-1.
96. Fraser Noble, Memoirs, pp. 304-5.
97. Caroe to Mountbatten, 7 April 1947, *CM*, p. 151.

98. Ibid.
99. Abdul Ghaffar Khan had denounced the Khan Sahib ministry for 'destroying the Pathans by bribing the Punjabis'. He (Khan Sahib) was labelling people honest or dishonest for the 'sake of power.'

    Arrested on 16 June 1956, Badshah Khan was charged with threatening the safety and territorial integrity of Pakistan. And bringing its government into hatred and contempt. Arraigned before the West Pakistan High Court on 3 September (1956), the judgement was delivered on 24 January (1957). AGK was sentenced to one day's imprisonment and the payment of a nominal fine. His 19-page statement before the court is reproduced in Tendulkar, pp. 491-506.
100. 'Note 2' by Caroe, *CM*, p. 154.
101. Fraser Noble, Comments on Draft.
102. For details see pp. 59-63.
103. Fraser Noble, Comments on Draft.
104. Minutes of Viceroy's *Fourth Miscellaneous Meeting*, 18 April 1947, *Transfer of Power,* X, Document 171.
105. Ibid. See also Part B, para 47, in Mountbatten, *Report on the Last Viceroyalty, 22nd March to 15th August 1947*, cited hereafter as *Mountbatten Report.*
106. *GCD*, 12 August 1947.
107. Fraser Noble, *Comments on Draft.*
108. Caroe's 'Note', *CM*, p. 154-A. In the 'Viceroy's Personal Report No. 3', Mountbatten noted that he had warned Caroe that 'I may be confronted with a situation in which it would be difficult to retain him but I will give him every support until such a situation arises.' *Transfer of Power,* X, Document 165.
109. Mountbatten to Caroe, 6 June 1947, *Transfer of Power*, XI, Document 96.
110. Caroe's 'Note', *CM*, p. 154-A.
111. *Mountbatten Report,* Part A, para 87.
112. A draft statement circulated at the meeting had suggested *inter alia* that on return to Peshawar, the governor would announce the holding of elections in the Frontier 'in due course'. Khan Sahib's response: 'he would be prepared for an election at any time' and would not stay in power 'one moment longer' than wanted. Mountbatten revealed that when Liaquat Ali Khan, the League leader, had suggested promulgation of Section 93 rule, Caroe had declared himself 'quite ready' for the present ministry to 'continue in power', until after the elections had been held. For his part, Mountbatten clarified, he would not do anything 'to make matters worse'. Minutes of *Viceroy's Fourth Miscellaneous Meeting*, 18 April 1947; *Transfer of Power*, X, Document 171.
113. The *Tribune*, 19 April 1947.
114. Ibid., 4 May 1947.
115. Ibid., 12 June 1947. For the full text of the article see Appendix 2.
116. Caroe's 'Note 1', *CM*, p. 159.
117. Fraser Noble, Memoirs, pp. 302-3.
118. Ibid., p. 308.
119. 'Lord Mountbatten's Visit to Peshawar', *CM*, p. 159-A. The official version revealed that Khan Sahib agreed that the viceroy 'should show himself to the crowd for a few minutes'. And he (KS) had called off a simultaneous demonstration of Red Shirts for fear it could 'lead to bloodshed' and that Mountbatten 'commended' him for doing so. *Transfer of Power*, X, Document 247.

120. Fraser Noble, Memoirs, p. 329. For more details see Ibid., pp. 325-33.
121. Fraser Noble, 'Recollections of Civil Disobedience Movement: NWFP 1947', *Indo-British Review*, 19, 2, pp. 41-50.
122. 'Mountbatten's Visit', *CM*, pp. 159-A and B.
123. Fraser Noble, Memoirs, p. 331. See also Fraser Noble, 'Recollections', n. 121.
124. *CM*, p. 159-B.
125. Fraser Noble, Memoirs, p. 333.
126. Norval Mitchell, Memoirs, pp. 258-61.
127. See n. 122 of this chapter.
128. Fraser Noble, 'Recollections', *IBR*, 19, 2, pp. 41-50. See also Viceroy's Personal Report No. 5, *Transfer of Power*, X, Document 276.
129. The official version of the meeting does *not* mention any talk of a coalition government; otherwise it broadly agrees with Tendulkar's account. For details see Tendulkar, pp. 413-14.

According to the official version, on the subject of elections, Mountbatten said that his concern was to ascertain 'whether the existing government still had a valid mandate' before power was handed over. He asked the ministers if they agreed: 'Dr Khan Sahib agreed and the others did not demur.' Mountbatten further pointed out that 'he would have to go' into Section 93 rule for two-three months 'to ensure fair elections' and felt sure the Khan Sahib government 'would wish the elections to be fair'. For details 'Meeting of HE with the Governor NWFP and four Ministers on 28th Arpil 1947', *Transfer of Power*, X, Document 259.
130. Ibid.
131. 'Viceroy's Personal Report No. 5', 1 May 1947, *Transfer of Power*, X, Document 276.
132. Tendulkar, p. 413.
133. Ibid., p. 414.
134. Norval Mitchell, Memoirs, pp. 268-9.
135. Tendulkar, p. 414.
136. Jansson, p. 202. See also 'note' by Mountbatten, 29 April 1947, *Transfer of Power*, X, Document 250.
137. *Mountbatten Report*, Part B, para 49. Also *Transfer of Power*, X, Document 276.
138. Fraser Noble, Memoirs, p. 337.
139. Jansson, p. 203.
140. Fraser Noble, 'Recollections', *IBR*, 19, 2, pp. 41-50.
141. 'Viceroy's Personal Report No. 5', *Transfer of Power*, X, Document 276.

In a telegram to the secretary of state on 3 May 1947, Mountbatten expressed the view that the Congress Party had 'a really weak case in the NWFP'. Jansson has argued that the third alternative of inependence for the provinces—which Mountbatten's original plan had envisaged—'does not seem to have been considered' for the referendum. Presumably, he concludes, Mountbatten and his staff 'never thought of this alternative as anything but a formula to bring about partition in the soonest possible way'. For details, Jansson, p. 203, n. 195, and p. 204, n. 197.
142. See n. 140 of this chapter.
143. See n. 141 of this chapter.
144. Ibid.
145. For details see Chapter 2, n. 177. See also Nehru to Caroe, 16 November 1946, *Transfer of Power*, IX, Document 46.

146. *Wavell's Journal,* entries for 4 and 6 November 1946, pp. 372-3.
147. Caroe to Wavell, 8 February 1947, *CM*, p. 132.
148. Weightman to Abell, 15 February 1947, *Transfer of Power*, IX, Document 405.
149. See n. 147.
150. Weightman reasoned that 'it would be a mistake to try to prevent events; they must be left to their course while we do what we can to minimise serious results'. Here 'flat opposition', he added, was not the 'faintest use'. Weightman to Abell, see n. 148 of this chapter.
151. Wavell to Caroe, 19 February 1947, *Transfer of Power*, IX, Document 443.
152. Wavell to Caroe, 4 March 1947. Referred to in n. 2. *Transfer of Power*, IX, Document 433.
153. Nehru to Wavell, 14 March 1947, *Selected Works*, II, item 1, p. 315. Note 2 refers to Wavell's message and its contents.

    Also see, Nehru to Wavell, 19 March 1947, *Transfer of Power*, IX, Document 549.
154. Nehru to Wavell, 19 March 1947, *Selected Works*, II, item 2, pp. 315-17.

    The item also appears in *Trnasfer of Power*, IX, Document 549.
155. A note at the end of Nehru's letter of 19 March to Wavell, *Transfer of Power*, IX, Doc. 549, makes the point that 'no such incident' (viz., relating to Governor Caroe approaching Wavell regarding Nehru's portfolio on tribal affairs) had been traced in India Office Records.
156. Wavell's *Journal*, entry for 19 March 1947, p. 430.
157. Entry for 14 March 1947, p. 428, in ibid.
158. Caroe to Mountbatten, 22 March 1947, *CM*, p. 149.
159. Wavell to Nehru, 19 March 1947, *Transfer of Powers*, IX, Document 550. Wavell revealed that he had himself abandoned his intention of visiting Lahore on an advice from the Panjab Governor for much the same reason—pressure on the police.
160. Wavell to secretary of state, 19 March 1947, *Transfer of Power,* IX, Document 551.
161. For the text, Nehru to Caroe, 26 March 1947, *Selected Works*, II, item 3, pp. 317-18.
162. Governor-General's Staff Meeting, 2 April 1947, *Transfer of Power*, X, Document 7.
163. Caroe's note on 'Lord Ismay's Visit to Peshawar,' *CM*, p. 149-A.
164. Nehru to Mounntbatten, *Selected Works*, II, item 4, p. 319.
165. H V Hodson, *The Great Divide*, p. 284.
166. 'Viceroy's Personal Report No. 3', 17 April 1947, *Transfer of Power*, X, Document 165.
167. Fraser Noble, Comments on Draft. See also his Memoirs, pp. 302-3.
168. Among other things Nehru referred to the elections, held 'a little more than a year ago' when 'identical issues' to those being agitated today were raised. He mentioned specifically the Mardan byelection where the Muslim League had retained its seat 'by a much reduced majority. Indeed they came near to losing it.' Nehru to Mountbatten, 26 April 1947, *Selected Works*, II, item 6, pp. 321-3. See also n. 37 of this chapter.
169. Mountbatten to Nehru, 30 April 1947, *Transfer of Power*, X, Document 259.

    The viceroy confessed to being 'impressed' both by the mass meeting which he saw as well as his conversations with a number of people ragarding the strength of the movement against the Frontier government. The tribes too were agitated and the Afridis threatened to come to an understanding with Afghanistan if 'no satisfactory working arrangements' were possible with the successor government of India.

170. Ibid. Encl. to Document 259.
171. Tendulkar, p. 414.
172. Nehru to Mountbatten, 3 May 1947, *Selected Works*, II, item 8, pp. 326-7.
173. Nehru to Mountbatten, 1 May 1947, *Selected Works*, II, item 7, pp. 324-6.
174. Fraser Noble, Comments on Draft.
175. Tendulkar, pp. 419-20.
176. Ibid.
177. Fraser Noble, Comments on Draft.
178. Menon's letter from Simla to one Chuni Lal Katial. Cited in Durga Das, *India from Curzon to Nehru & After*, revd and enlgd edn, paperback, 1973, pp. 424-6; citation, p. 426.
179. Nehru to Mountbatten, 4 June 1947, *Transfer of Power*, XI, Document 61. For Caroe's version of the 1930 incident see *IOR*, Mss Eur C. 273/5, Transcript of an autobiographical memoir by Sir Olaf Caroe received by BBC. Also see *IOR*, L/P&J/6/2003, File No. 1897 of 1930.
180. Tendulkar, pp. 427-8.

    The official version makes two textual changes: '. . . He is truthful. If it can be done decorously, you should do it'. *Transfer of Power*, XI, Document 24.
181. On 5 June in the course of his interview with Mountbatten, Khan Sahib told the latter that he considered it 'absolutely necessary' that Olaf Caroe be 'replaced' *before* the referendum took place. Record of Interveiw between Mountbatten and Dr Khan Sahib (5 June), *Transfer of Power*, XI, Document 81.
182. Ibid.
183. Mountbatten to Caroe, 6 June 1947, *Transfer of Power*, XI, Document 96.
184. Ismay to Mountbatten, 9 June 1947, *Transfer of Power*, XI, Document 114. See also n. 2, in ibid.
185. Caroe to Mountbatten, 11 June 1947, *Transfer of Power*, XI, Document 142.
186. In 'PS' to his letter of 11 June, referred to in n. 185 above, Sir Olaf wrote 'We might go to Kashmir until our staff has packed our things, then go home. I hope we might be able to travel by air to the U.K.'
187. Caroe to Mountbatten, 11 June 1947, *Transfer of Power*, XI, Document 142.
188. Reproduced as Appendix 3.
189. Norval Mitchell, Memoirs, p. 269.
190. Fraser Noble, Memoirs, p. 343.
191. Liaquat Ali Khan to Mountbatten, 11 June 1947, *Transfer of Power*, XI, Document 143.
192. See page 154.
193. Listowel to Attlee, 11 June 1947, *Transfer of Power*, XI, Document 143.
194. Ibid., 13 June 1947, *Transfer of Power*, XI, Document 182.
195. Sir D Monteath to Ismay, 15 June 1947, Document 211, in Ibid. See also Listowel's Minute to Attlee, 16 June 1947, Document 223 in ibid.
196. Mountbatten to Ismay, 7 May 1947 wherein the governor-general indicated that while 'I have quite made up my mind' he had deferred his decision on Caroe because of the anti-Caroe agitation in the press. Caroe was to be asked to resign failing

which he would 'put his removal down to ill-health,' in *Transfer of Power*, X, Documents 342, 343.

197. Listowel to Attlee, Secretary of State's Minute, 12 May 1947, Document 417, in ibid.
198. Mountbatten to Listowel, 12 June 1947, *Transfer of Power*, XI, Document 161.
199. For Caroe's letter of 11 June 1947, Supra, n. 185.
200. Listowel to Mountbatten, 20 June 1947, *Transfer of Power*, XI, Document 281.
201. J B Kriplani to Mountbatten, 17 June 1947, Document 228 in ibid.
202. Mountbatten to Nehru, 17 June 1947, Document 237, in ibid.
203. Caroe to Mountbatten, 23 June 1947, *Transfer of Power*, XI, Document 310.

    The document was apparently abridged, for the full text of Caroe's letter, *CM*, pp. 180-4, has 5 paragraphs, *not* 3; the document reproduces only a part of para 3. Para 4 dealt with the 'state of dangerous tensions' that existed in Peshawar and Bannu where the Red Shirts had started 'showing off' by carrying large quantities of arms. Para 5 outlined Caroe's immediate plans to go briefly to Pindi and then off to Kashmir. The letter ended with 'My gratitude for all your help and understanding'. For the full text, see Appendix 4.
204. D R Syiemlieh, 'Response of the North-Eastern Hill Tribes of India towards Partition and Independence', *Indo-British Review*, 17, 1-2, September and December 1989, pp. 27-35, outlines the plans to establish a British Crown Colony 'put perhaps under some appropriate department of Whitehall'.
205. Caroe to Mountbatten, 23 March 1947, *CM*, pp. 146-9. Mountbatten took over from Wavell the day Caroe's letter was mailed.
206. Fraser Noble, Comments on Draft.

CHAPTER 4

The Plebiscite (July 1947) and After

AN INTRIGUING aspect of the developing situation in the Frontier even before Caroe left the scene was the decision to hold a plebiscite, or referendum, so as to enable the province make its choice about joining India or Pakistan on the eve of the transfer of power in the subcontinent.

In the neighbouring Panjab, the Khizr Hyat Khan ministry was compelled, under mounting Muslim League pressure, to demit office. There was a growing stridency of the League's direct action campaign in the Frontier itself. The governor had spelt out four lines of action which his government might choose from, one of which was, an 'appeal to the electorate for a fresh mandate'. Caroe was emphatic that the position in the legislature—where the Khan Sahib ministry enjoyed overpowering support—'did not represent' the position in the country. He was also persuaded that in the March 1946 elections, 'the scales were almost equal'. Besides, for the Congress to under-rate their opponents was almost a fatal thing to do.[1]

His fervent advocacy notwithstanding, Caroe's line of reasoning seemed to carry little conviction to his ministers. And he conceded as much:

> They just refused to admit (Caroe noted), that the position is in fact this, in spite of the recent Mardan election, and are determined to cling to power as long as they can. They even said on no account would they agree to another general election before a new constitution had been framed.[2]

On his own though, the governor was certain that his government would be forced into appealing to the electorate again soon enough. In the final count, his strong advice was that while maintaining law with one hand, the Khan Sahib government 'should make overtures through go-betweens' for a settlement with the Muslim League opposition so that all the Pathans could stand together for their proper place in the new India that was emerging.[3]

In his letter of 22 March to the governor-general, Caroe reverted to the subject, referring to the strange position of a Congress government which had now forfeited its hitherto considerable Muslim backing. He argued that the influence of the north-western Panjab to the East and of the tribes to the West—all declaiming against Hindu-Sikh domination—'is, I think certain to squeeze Congress out before long, for Congress is not natural here'. This shift in the balance might have taken place earlier, if the League had had any leaders 'to compare with the Khan brothers'.[4]

Writing to Mountbatten, who had in the meantime taken over as the new Governor-General, Caroe forcefully repudiated the 'new propaganda line' that the governor himself was behind the League movement against the incumbent Khan Sahib government. This, he asserted, was an old canard 'in a new raiment' and was 'equally unture'. He was certain that if if were not 'for what remains of the old prestige and for the presence of troops' on crucial occasions, the Khan Sahib government would have been thrown out much earlier.[5]

At the Governors' Conference in New Delhi, 15-16 April, Caroe is reported to have secured two important concessions:

> The first that Nehru would advise Dr Khan (Sahib) to release his political prisoners, and the second that some method would have to be found of testing opinion of the people of the NWFP with regard to accession to Pakistan. Events were to show that he had correctly divined the means which would enable the dangerous Frontier situation to be held until the time came for the transfer of power.[6]

Here it may be recalled that during the course of the Governors' Conference, a meeting was convened on 15 April at which Nehru, Liaquat Ali Khan, Baldev Singh, Field Marshal Claude Auchinleck and Olaf Caroe were present apart from Mountbatten. Caroe indicated that, on his return to Peshawar, he might announce that a general election would be held in the province. To this Nehru objected though conceding all the same that it would be desirable to obtain the views of the people. 'The idea of a plebiscite', Hodson has suggested, 'can be traced to this occasion.'[7]

Later, in the course of Mountbatten's own visit to the Frontier (28-9 April) and his meeting there with the Khan Sahib council of ministers, Caroe is said to have persuaded the governor-general to promulgate Section 93 rule in the province and, after an interval, order fresh elections. He even 'got a garbled version of the proceedings of the Cabinet meeting' sent to the viceroy and refused to forward the note Khan Sahib had prepared embodying what the latter deemed to be the correct version. Nehru had warned the governor-general that in view of the broader implications of the issues raised, he hoped 'nothing will be taken for granted', and that any apprehensions on the subject 'should be removed immediately'. Nehru went further and told Mountbatten that fresh elections or imposition of Section 93 rule would have 'far-reaching implications', and create 'a very grave situation'.[8]

Badshah Khan's opposition to fresh elections was pronounced. In a press interview at Lahore on 8 May, he 'foreshadowed bloodshed' if elections were ordered because this was being done 'in bad faith'. The motive, it was clear to him, was not so much to elicit public opinion 'but to install' the Muslim League in the ministerial gaddi 'by fair or foul means'. The League agitation in the province, he asserted, was 'primarily confined' to the urban areas and would have stopped by now 'but for the support' of the governor. In desiring fresh elections, the British wanted 'to reward their henchmen—the Muslim Leaguers' and pay back the latter for their past services. It was dishonest, Badshah Khan added, to give a political status to a communal movement whose followers indulged in crime.[9]

Meantime, on 10 May, replying to Nehru's letter of a week earlier, Mountbatten acknowledged that he had indeed received Khan Sahib's amendments to the minutes of his meeting with the Premier and his Cabinet colleagues during his visit to Peshawar on 28 April. However, 'no detailed discussions' of these was called for inasmuch as neither the imposition of Section 93 rule nor holding of fresh elections was now deemed necessary. Instead, Mountbatten continued, he had recommended that 'at a suitable date when the partition of India was clearer', a referendum on the basis of the provincial electoral rolls would be held. Conducted by an organisation under his (viz., viceroy's) control.[10]

It would thus appear that as between 3 and 10 May, Mountbatten's thinking on the Frontier had taken a U-turn: *from* dismissal of the Ministry and holding of fresh elections preceded by a 2-3 month interregnum of governor's rule *to* no elections and no Section 93 rule. What was being advocated in their place was a referendum under the viceroy's aegis: neither under the control of the incumbent Khan Sahib ministry nor yet that of the governor and his civil officers. Regulated in fact, by military officers appointed by the governor-general and responsible to him.

II

Mountbatten's alternative plan for the transfer of power had conceded the Muslim League's fundamental demand for Pakistan. It envisaged that all the provinces had the choice of joining either India or Pakistan or of even becoming independent units; the assumption being that they would group immediately—but were *not* bound to do so. The decision in each case rested with the individual province's legislative assembly. An election in the NWFP *before* the province decided its choice was included in the plan; the tribes were free to conclude new treaties with whomsoever (viz., India versus Pakistan) they chose to.[11]

Caroe's reaction to the Mountbatten plan in the course of the Governors' Conference was measured. His preference still was for some sort of a modified Cabinet Mission Plan—if only to avoid partition. The tribes, he reasoned, cost annually Rs. 25 million to the exchequer; the central subsidy that the Frontier got, added another Rs.10 million. This fact, he underlined, had to be taken fully into account by all parties—especially the Muslim League when pressing ahead its claim for Pakistan.[12]

Barely a fortnight later, on 30 April, Nehru had made it abundantly clear that elections in the Frontier were both unnecessary and dangerous and that Congress would have 'nothing to do with them whatever'.[13] It would also appear that in the alternative, Nehru would only accept a referendum on the issue of whether the NWFP would join Pakistan/ Hindustan. Hence, forcing an election on the Congress under pressure from the Frontier Muslim League's Civil Disobedience movement would mean Congress's refusal to take part in the exercise.[14]

The Congress ministry in the Frontier, Nehru wrote was 'in the dock' and 'on the defensive' during Mountbatten's visit while little was said about the Muslim League agitation. It would be 'absurd' to say that all that happened was due to the 'machinations' of the governor and his officials. None the less, he placed a lot of blame on Caroe who, Nehru declared, had 'neither the capacity nor the impartiality' to head the provincial administration. There were besides 'certain officials' in Waziristan who functioned 'wrongly' and were 'completely beyond my control'.[15]

Meanwhile in response to mounting Muslim League pressure for holding elections, Mountbatten began to be wary. Thus on 2 May he told I I Chundrigar, a prominent League leader, that so long as the Muslim League's Civil Disobedience movement in the Frontier continued, there would 'in no circumstances' be fresh elections. To the contrary, he would 'draft up' fresh troops to contain and 'fight' the movement. Three days later, at a staff meeting, Mountbatten considered Caroe's telegram lending his support to the idea of a referendum.[16] In conveying the suggestion to Ismay in London, Mountbatten revealed that he 'greatly favoured' the referendum plan while at the same time listing three major hurdles in its way. One, the difficulty in finding 'enough outside officials' to conduct it; two, modifications of the existing law through promulgating a 'special ordinance'; and three, a verdict in favour of Pakistan would have to be followed by an election which 'might, though improbably' return Congress to power.[17]

Jinnah's reaction to the referendum plan was not exactly enthusiastic. He noted that people in the Frontier were 'not particularly intelligent'. Therefore, 'unless it were made clear' that an election would follow the referendum, they would 'not be satisfied'.[18] Mountbatten though was in an unenviable position for in his talks with Jinnah and Liaquat Ali Khan on 4 May he had made it clear that any use of the word 'election' would rule out any chance of the viceroy's proposed statement being accepted by Nehru, whose agreement Mountbatten deemed essential for obtaining the clearance of HMG to the referendum proposal. The Quaid, it would appear, had demanded imposition of Section 93 rule and holding of fresh elections.[19]

In the final count, saner counsels appear to have prevailed. For in his long statement of 7 May while confirming that he 'cannot disagree' with the decision of the Frontier League not to call off its agitation, Jinnah did not refer directly to the holding of elections:

> It is quite obvious that the people of the Frontier must be given a chance to express their verdict, and the root cause of popular resentment must be eliminated. There is not the slightest doubt what the verdict will be, and the present ministry cannot possibly thereafter continue.[20]

Earlier, in a 'draft' statement, 'for consideration by M A Jinnah', the Frontier League leader, Abdur Rab Nishtar, had referred to the Mardan byelection which Khan Sahib had 'himself made a test case'. Since he (KS) had failed to adopt 'the constitutional procedure of resigning and seeking fresh election', the Frontier people had been 'driven to' mass civil disobedience.[21]

By 6 May, however, Mountbatten was telling Ismay that he was 'absolutely convinced' that there must be a referendum. More, Caroe 'and all of us', considered it feasible and even Nehru accepted the idea in view of his (Mountbatten's) assurance that 'I do not intend to dissolve the Ministry or go into Section 93.'[22] To all this Ismay's reaction was somewhat guarded. Whitehall was 'very doubtful', he noted, fearing it might imply 'further delay'. For a verdict in favour of Pakistan, would have to be followed by a general election.[23]

On 8 May, in the course of his train journey to Patna, Gandhi wrote to

Mountbatten that a referendum in the Frontier was 'a dangerous thing' and that 'in any case' nothing should 'or can be done' over Khan Sahib's head as Premier.[24] That very day, Mountbatten wrote to Ismay that *after* a decision had been taken in the Panjab, the Frontier will decide, through a referendum, whether or not to join the Indian Union. Additionally, the proposed referendum would have the 'concurrence' of the provincial government but take place 'under the supervision' of the governor-general.[25]

Two days later, however, there was another spanner in the wheels for Nehru wrote to Mountbatten on 10 May of the 'very strong opinion' among his colleagues in the Congress Working Committee, as well as in Khan Sahib's government, about the referendum proposal, for fear it may lead to 'grave consequences' unless the situation was 'much clearer' and 'other final decisions' had been taken. All the same, Nehru was in agreement with the idea that the will of the Frontier people should be consulted *before* a final decision in regard to the province was taken. The 'very important' thing though was 'when this is done and in what context'.[26] Nehru had explained his position at a meeting with the governor-general two days earlier which briefly was: (*a*) that 'an election or referendum, except in the all-India context', would cause trouble; (*b*) that it 'would result' in similar demands from hundreds of places in India; and (*c*) that he (Nehru) was 'intellectually' in favour of a referendum if it could be held 'in a calmer atmosphere'.

Mountbatten countered Nehru's objections by pointing out that: (*a*) the fact that there was 'a divergence of opinion' between Caroe and Khan Sahib, made a referendum all the more necessary; (*b*) the longer the present situation was allowed to drag on, the worse inter-communal feelings would become; (*c*) the referendum would 'quickly' settle matters, 'one way or the other'. Hence, both Nehru and Mountbatten agreed, the latter noted, that 'the only disagreement was not whether to hold a referendum but when'.[27]

For his part, Caroe conceded that fresh elections in the province would entail a measure of risk but this was to be preferred to the existing impasse or stalemate. 'It is noteworthy', Jansson underlines, 'that Caroe did not propose to dismiss the Khan Sahib ministry and impose governor's rule *before* the elections.' This stance, he underlines, ran counter to the advice of many of his officials. Caroe instead intended to dissolve the assembly and at the same time ask the ministers to remain in office during the election.[28]

Here it may be recalled that in the first week of May, Mountbatten had despatched Ismay to London with his draft plan for the transfer of power. It included *inter alia*, his proposal for the dismissal of the Congress ministry in the Frontier prior to the holding of a fresh poll. 'On a hunch', but in the strictest confidence, Mountbatten had revealed the plan to Nehru during the latter's brief halt at Simla as the governor-general's guest. Congress reaction in general, and Nehru's in particular, was 'so violent' that Mountbatten had the plan redrafted. While under the original plan, the provinces had the right to determine their future, that freedom, was now taken away. Initially, for instance, the Frontier could opt out, it if so chose, outside of India or Pakistan. The redrafted plan sealed the fate of the Frontier outside the orbit of Pakistan—as it did of a 'sovereign, united Bengal'.[29]

III

In the plan of 3 June, in the NWFP, as in Sylhet, a referendum was provided for; to be held to decide whether or not the province (or the district) would join India or Pakistan. At the Congress Working Committee meeting on 3 June, both Patel as well as C Rajagopalachari 'strongly favoured' having a referendum in the NWFP. Finally, when the Committee accepted this position, Khan Abdul Ghaffar Khan declared that the Congress party had deserted the Pathans and 'thrown us to the wolves'. He affirmed that the Khudai Khidmatgars would not agree to a referendum for the issue had been decided at the March 1946 elections. 'Now as India has disowned us', he declared, 'why should we have a referendum on Hindustan or Pakistan? Let it be Pakistan or Pathanistan'.[30]

Badshah Khan's disillusionment with his erstwhile Congress colleagues is brought out vividly in Tendulkar's study. '*Toba*', '*Toba*' (God forbid! God forbid!) were his words as he emerged from the conclave. Later, the Khan noted that the Sardar, who along with 'CR' had supported the referendum plan, told him that he (i.e. Badshah Khan) was 'worrying over nothing'. The Maulana, sitting next to him, advised: 'you should join the Muslim League'. The Mahatma alone appears to have held out firmly for him, being of the clear view that if the Frontier and the Khudai Khidmatgars 'were oppressed', he 'would not hesitate' to advise the Indian government 'to treat it as a casus belli' against the Pakistani regime.[31]

On 4 June while Nehru asked Mountbatten to hasten the change of governors in the NWFP,[32] Caroe informed Mountbatten that he had been

ELEPHANT DOES NOT FORGET

While addressing a press conference Khan Abdul Ghaffar Khan remarked. For anybody even to imagine that we could be dominated by any outsider is beyond my comprehension. Pathans will be masters in their own land.

The *Tribune*, Lahore, 10 June 1947.

given to understand that in terms of para 4 of the 3 June plan, the Khudai Khidmatgars 'will decline' to take part in the referendum; that they envisaged a constituent assembly with a large number of members that would place them 'in a stronger position' to make a 'good bargain' with Pakistan.[33] Earlier, the governor had warned the viceroy that an attempt may be made to interpret the terms of the 3 June announcement as allowing the province the option of such a 'separate' constituent assembly.[34] Caroe was also somewhat dubious about Mountbatten's ability to secure his ministry's cooperation 'in putting the referendum through'.[35]

The following day, Mountbatten invited Khan Sahib for discussions in New Delhi and informed him that a third choice, viz., of independence, had been refused to all the provinces 'on Congress insistence'. He was less than sure how a province of 3 million people 'could stand by itself' with 'any reasonable' chance of success. Proforma he asserted that the fact that western Panjab would stretch between the NWFP and the rest of Hindustan 'in no way made it impossible' for the Frontier to join Hindustan. In reply, all that Khan Sahib would say was that his province would never join Pakistan. The Premier indicated that it was absolutely necessary that Caroe should be replaced *before* the referendum took place, for a new governor would make an immense difference. He also reiterated his earlier assurance that he will 'do my best' to cooperate in running the referendum. Mountbatten noted that the Khan Sahib commitment was made 'quite sincerely'.[36]

That very day Caroe threw another spanner in the works. For in a telegram to the governor-general, he noted that the provincial chief secretary 'and other officials' held that 'a peaceful referendum' was far more likely if the three issues—of Hindustan, Pakistan or Pathanistan—'could be put before the electors'. It was true, Caroe had little doubt, that it was 'impossible' that the Muslim League would agree and that a third choice 'might upset' the large measure of agreement between the principal parties on an all-India basis and that the reality of the case was that the Frontier 'could never stand alone'. The above notwithstanding, the governor underlined that the case for Pathanistan 'should be fully weighed'. 'Too many of its advocates', he pleaded, 'are sincere' and even some of those aligned with Jinnah were 'not without sympathy' for this idea.[37]

It is interesting to note that at his press conference on 4 June, when asked if the people of the Frontier were 'free to select the issue on which they will vote in the referendum', Mountbatten's reply was far from straight or direct. 'Yes', he said, 'if they can get the high commands of the two parties to agree to it.' If not, he added, we stick to what was agreed upon originally.[38]

The Muslim League agitation in the Frontier was formally called off on 5 June with the party jubilant on its undoubted victory.[39] That same evening, Jinnah in his broadcast from All-India Radio outlined the two alternatives which the people of the Frontier Province had about joining the Pakistan or the Hindustan Constituent Assembly. He asked the Provincial Muslim League 'to withdraw the movement of peaceful Civil Disobedience' which they 'had perforce to resort to' and expressed his 'appreciation' of the sufferings and sacrifices made 'by all classes' of Muslims and 'particularly the great part the women of the Frontier' played in the 'fight for civil liberties'. Furthermore, he added, 'I call upon all the leaders of the Muslim League and the Muslims generally to organise our people to face this referendum with hope and courage.'

He felt 'confident' that the people 'will give their verdict by a solid vote' to join the Pakistan Constituent Assembly.

Understandably, the Quaid's broadcast evoked widespread protest. In a letter to Mountbatten, Patel, who as Member for Information & Broadcasting apart from Home, held charge of AIR accused Jinnah of committing 'a sacrilege' by making 'a political, partisan and propagandist' broadcast, and justifying a movement that had brought 'so much blood and destruction of property' in its wake. In asking the Frontier to vote according to the League persuasion, not only had Jinnah taken 'undue advantage of the courtesy and consideration' shown to him but turned AIR 'into a Muslim League platform', thereby being 'grossly unfair' to the Frontier ministry.

Khan Sahib was most unhappy too and called into question the Quaid's 'conception of civil liberties'. The Muslim League movement which Jinnah had eulogised had started 'very definitely on a communal basis' and was responsible for 'brutal murders on a large scale', continuing violence and occasionally arson. There had been destruction of public records too, Khan Sahib added, while 'riots and mutinies' in jails had resulted 'in death and injury'.[40] All in all, Jinnah's broadcast, caused no end of dismay among Congress leaders, requiring the governor-general to 'jolly them out of their gloom'.[41]

In a personal report to London, Mountbatten noted that he had to turn down a Congress request for allowing a third choice in the proposed referendum 'unless the Muslim League leadership agreed to it', which, Nehru admitted, 'was out of the question'. Mountbatten had taken the opportunity to remind Nehru that it was at 'his insistence' that he

(Mountbatten) had 'renounced' the choice of independence in the case of Bengal as well as other provinces to avoid, what Nehru feared, would lead to 'Balkanisation'. It was a surprise to him that Nehru should have been a party to such a measure (viz., a third choice), more so as he (Nehru) admitted that the Frontier 'could not stand on its own'. In any case, the province would 'eventually' have to join with one side or the other.[42]

IV

As may be evident, there was a sharp divergence of opinion between Gandhi in general and Nehru in particular on the question of the Frontier's participation in the proposed referendum. Briefly, the Congress High Command were of the view that the only way for the Pathans to save their autonomy was to fight the referendum with all their might and win it, or else, the battle of the NWFP, as a part of India or even as an independent entity, was lost.[43]

Gandhi, powerfully influenced by Badshah Khan, was strongly persuaded to the contrary. There was, as yet, he had concluded, no peace in the Frontier and there could be no referendum unless strife had 'completely abated'. Nor did the Pathans—or millions of others for that matter—have a fair picture of the Pakistan scheme. Hence, 'it would be unfair . . . to choose between Hindustan and Pakistan without knowing what each is'. In sum, Gandhi's exhortation to Nehru was: 'Would it be wrong if you insisted that referendum would be wrong without the presentation of the picture of Pakistan?'[44]

In a last minute bid to retrieve the situation, Gandhi met Mountbatten on 6 June to request that the latter should meet Jinnah and persuade him to spell out to the Pathans how the Frontier would fit into his proposed Pakistan. Should the Pathans react in a positive manner, there would be no need for a referendum. For Badshah Khan and his colleagues in the Khudai Khidmatgar movement were convinced that holding one would spell disaster for his people and 'lead to permanent feuds'. Hence, their anxiety to go to almost any length, consistent with honour, to avoid it. In the final count, the Khan would be prepared to advise his brother to resign and ask the viceroy to place the province under Section 93 rule.[45]

Understandably, there were sharp differences among the Congress high command too. Thus, on the evening of 6 June, the day the Mahatma met Mountbatten to ask him to intercede with Jinnah, Sardar Patel complained to Gandhi that Nehru was 'largely responsible' for the present situation in the Frontier, and also that Badshah Khan's influence was on the wane.

Gandhi stoutly repudiated the latter suggestion and maintained that the Frontier leader had 'more steadiness today than ever before'. Besides, Khan Sahib and his colleagues would be nowhere without him and that it was Badshah Khan alone that 'counts' so far as the Congress influence in the Frontier was concerned.[46]

Nehru's own assessment of the situation as regards the referendum in the Frontier was spelt out in a lengthy memorandum, 'Note on the situation in the NWFP'. To start with, there was a narration of events leading to the present ground reality. Nehru recalled that initially the question of fresh elections and imposition of Section 93 rule in the Frontier was strongly objected to by the Congress and given up; that the Muslim League agitation in the province had in many ways been encouraged by the British and Indian officials; that the governor and his officials 'have not only not cooperated' with the provincial government but have, actually, 'sometimes obstructed its work'.

The question of a referendum came up, Nehru continued, 'not exactly on the Pakistan issue'. When the proposal for the secession of western Panjab came up for scrutiny, it was thought advisable to have a referendum in the Frontier to determine to which constituent assembly—that of India or Pakistan—it desired to belong. The proposal was not meant just for the Frontier province; it was part of a larger plan that provided for a referendum in Baluchistan as well as Sylhet.

Further Nehru argued that having a referendum in the Frontier depended on 'certain previous decisions'—relating to the Panjab as well as Bengal. And as both the provinces were likely to decide in favour of secession, the question was more or less settled with the British government as well as the viceroy 'definitely committed' to hold a referendum. Nehru added that 'some of us are also more or less committed' too. Nor could the viceroy wriggle out of it. The referendum, therefore, was well-nigh 'a settled fact'. As regards a third choice, the viceroy 'can only agree, if the parties agree'. Besides, it may also induce 'an element of confusion in the voting'.

For the Congress to keep out of the referendum would mean 'accepting the Muslim League domination in the NWFP—in effect a surrender to the Muslim League agitation'. This, it was clear to Nehru, would be a wrong decision, for

> To fight democratically and to be defeated does not weaken us for long and we can renew the struggle in other ways later. But to give up without a struggle means a certain lack of integrity through fear of consequences .... To give up the battle when the final decisions are being taken, will result in deep psychological injury to our people.

Mountbatten's stake, Nehru underlined, was high because he was 'definitely committed' to the course of action mentioned earlier and therefore 'cannot get out of it without grave injury to his own prestige and impartiality'. In the circumstances, Mountbatten would 'probably prefer to resign'.[47]

On 8 June, Badshah Khan wrote to inform Gandhi that he and all his 'important workers' were of the considered view that they could not agree to the holding of the proposed referendum. For, in the conditions prevailing in the province, it could only lead to 'serious violence'.[48] On receipt of Nehru's note on the subject, retailed in the preceding paragraphs, another meeting was convened on 11 June; the invitees included members of the Provincial Congress Committee (PCC), the Congress Legislative Party (CLP) in the Frontier legislature; and the 'commanders' of the Khudai Khidmatgars. The conclave deliberated for almost four hours and the consensus that emerged was that they 'should not take part' in the referendum unless the issue was amended 'on the basis of Pakistan or free Pathan state'.[49]

Nehru and the Congress were in a dilemma, for Badshah Khan was not exactly persuaded by the arguments that had been so cogently marshalled. His own difference in approach notwithstanding, Nehru conceded that 'more that any other person' the Frontier leader understood the thinking of his people and hence his views were of 'great importance'. He also saw the logic of the Frontier being 'completely isolated' from India, should Panjab opt out to join Pakistan. In the event, he would have the Congress affirm that the NWFP would 'enjoy the fullest freedom and such help' as India could afford, if its people decided to come into its fold. This would imply, Nehru argued, that the Frontier people's vote for the present constituent assembly would mean 'a vote for self-determination and freedom'.[50]

To allay any fears about the independent Pathan state that he envisaged, Badshah Khan mounted a determined bid to come to an understanding with the League supremo. To this end, he met Jinnah in New Delhi on 30 May and later on 18 June. At the earlier meeting, apart from AGK, two Muslim League stalwarts, Abdul Qaiyum Khan and Samin Jan, were present. In fact, the meeting had been arranged through them. They had sought 'instructions' from the Quaid who indicated that he would meet the two and 'If Abdul Ghaffar Khan wants meet me and if you approve', he (Jinnah) would 'meet you all' in New Delhi.[51]

Caroe had much hoped that all this might be a prelude to a Congress-League coalition in the Frontier. 'Local indications are', he wrote, 'that negotiations have been proceeding in Peshawar possibly for coalition with

Ahmed in the *Hindustan Times*, 10 June 1947.

Abdul Qaiyum (and) Samin Jan holding office'. He had been urging on his Ministry a 'genuine coalition' for a long time and felt sure it would 'go far to steady' the situation in the province. Not surprisingly though, Caroe concluded, the main body of League workers 'apparently distrust' this development and had sent three representatives to Delhi 'to contact Jinnah'.[52] Sadly, the end-result of New Delhi parleys was disappointing and, not only for Sir Olaf.

It would be of interest to note that press reports suggested that the Frontier League leadership reneged on its initial commitment to support the demand for an independent sovereign Pathan state. To start with, the League leaders while in detention had told one of the mediators of their three demands:

(*a*) a share in the Khan Sahib ministry;

(*b*) removing 'a fear complex' of Hindu domination;

(*c*) in return for (*a*) and (*b*) above, a commitment to 'an independent Frontier State'.

While Badshah Khan was able to persuade the Congress High Command to accept the above stipulations, the paroled League leaders who had accompanied Badshah Khan to New Delhi were not able to carry conviction with Jinnah. In the event, they backed out of their commitment.[53]

Earlier, in a letter to Jinnah datelined 'Central Jail, Peshawar, 14 May, 1947', Abdul Qaiyum had referred to some intermediaries meeting him on behalf of AGK and intimated that the latter was prepared to accept Pakistan. 'But this is from his lips and not from his heart.' AGK's object was 'to bribe us with the offer of two seats in the cabinet' and to win us over 'in this manner. . . . His idea seems to be to keep his party intact (and) enter into some sort of coalition with us, while accepting Pakistan in name only.'[54]

For the second meeting there was some manoeuvering. Initially, Jinnah had refused to invite Badshah Khan to his residence nor would he meet him alone at the viceroy's house where Gandhi too was present. At the meeting itself at Jinnah's house, Badshah Khan told the League leader that the Pathans were 'quite agreeable' to join Pakistan provided it was on honourable terms. To start with, he pressed for the right 'to opt out' if, after independence, Pakistan decided to stay under British tutelage. Again, all matters concerning the tribal people should be settled by the Pathans themselves 'without the interference or domination' of the non-Pathans. For obvious reasons, the Quaid would not commit; no wonder, Badshah Khan drew a blank.[55]

Even as the Frontier leader maintained that he had approached Jinnah 'as a Muslim for maintaining unity among the Muslims' and because of his earnest desire to have peace in the Frontier, the League leader, it was obvious, could not resist the temptation of humiliating a political adversary. He viewed the Khan's overtures as born out of his weakness, for he (Jinnah) was shrewd enough to see that he was in a winning position and would not yield ground. He certainly would not like to oblige his principal political antagonist in the Frontier by giving him back the power 'he (AGK) was on the point of losing'.[56] This was more than evident in the virulent attack mounted on Badshah Khan in the columns of the League's mouthpiece, the *Dawn*. Badshah Khan's dignified rejoinder that he wanted 'a peaceful and honourable way' out did not register, nor yet his contention that the 'tone and manner as well as the contents' of the newspaper's assault on him were not conducive to a peaceful approach.[57]

To demonstrate his own transparent honesty, the Frontier leader sent Jinnah a copy of the resolution adopted by members of the Frontier PCC as well as the Congress Parliamentary Party in the provincial assembly, the Khudai Khidmatgars and the Zalme Pakhtuns at their combined meeting held at Bannu on 21 June. It visualised 'a free Pathan state of all the Pakhtuns. . . . The constitution of the state . . . framed on the basis of Islamic conception of democracy, equality and social justice.' It appealed to 'all the Pathans to unite for the attainment of this cherished goal and not to submit to any non-Pakhtun domination'.[58]

A week later, the final decision of Frontier Congress not to take part in the ensuing referendum was conveyed to the governor-general. The choice offered, it reiterated, revolved not so much on the question of Pakistan or Pathanistan but on a 'purely communal issue.'[59] In the sequel, Jinnah charged that both Gandhi and Abdul Ghaffar Khan supported the idea of Pathanistan which was 'a direct breach' of the Congress acceptance of the 3 June plan. Reacting sharply to the boycott resolution, Jinnah called the Pathanistan demand as both 'insidious and spurious . . . a new stunt invented to mislead' the people of the NWFP. The 'new volte-face', as he termed it, on the part of the Congress in the Frontier was 'a piece of pure political chicanery and a manoeuvre intended to prop up the Khan clique in power'. He charged Gandhi with giving the new move his 'apostolic blessings'.[60]

A vicious campaign was mounted at the same time alleging that the Khan brothers had despatched an emissary to Kabul to demand a revision of the Durand Line. Khan Sahib stoutly repudiated the canard, and wrote to Nehru to affirm that he and his government had 'never thought of joining' Afghanistan. Much less did they know of the Kabul government approaching New Delhi on the subject. Or, for that matter a Congress emissary approaching Kabul.[61]

Sadly though 'doubts persisted and even Fraser Noble would have us believe that emissaries 'were sent by the Ministers to Kabul' where the active interest taken in the whole affair by the Afghan government 'called into question the notion that Pathanistan would or could be independent'. Mountbatten, he affirms, 'firmly scotched the proposal'.[62]

Nehru's position was set out in his letters. To Khan Sahib, he was at once brief and to the point: 'we cannot admit Afghanistan's right to any part of India'. To Badshah Khan, he was more specific: 'It would be unfortunate if the Afghan government was encouraged in its foolish adventures because of anything you said or did.' And recalled the Pakhtun leader telling him that he 'strongly disapproved' of the Pushtu-speaking areas of India joining Afghanistan. 'What you wanted you told me', Nehru affirmed, 'was for a free Pathanistan to be created in the sense of having full autonomy within its own area and then joining hands with the rest of India for defence, external affairs and such like matters'.[63]

Quite clearly, AGK was far from betraying Pathan much less the impending Pakistan's interests. Equally plain is the Afghan stance which demanded that 'the population of the former Afghan territories annexed by Great Britain during the past century be afforded an opportunity either to re-join Afghanistan or to form a separate state enjoying complete independence'. Later, an Afghan newspaper, the daily *Anis,* denounced the referendum as 'wrong, both from the point of justice and democracy'. Individuals in a referendum, it argued, should be given 'a free choice to exercise their votes' and in so far as this was being denied, the referendum was 'not legal'. Afghanistan had, therefore, no choice but 'not to recognise it'.[64]

Mountbatten made a point of emphasising that Art 2 of the Durand Agreement bound Kabul 'to refrain from interference in territories lying beyond the Durand Line' on the Indian side. While Whitehall was equally emphatic that the area in question formed an integral part of India under the Anglo-Afghan Treaty of 1921. And that the future rested with the Government of Pakistan which would be the 'successor to all applicable treaty rights and obligations'.[65]

As if this were not plain enough, at a cabinet meeting on 4 July Nehru stated that India had 'repudiated' Afghanistan's 'irredentist claim' and

I had the task of signing the passport of one of the junior ministers to enable him to visit Kabul at very

Memoirs of Norval Mitchell (p. 265).

short notice; and there could not be a shred of doubt that the visit, combined with all else that was going on, was concerned with Pakhtunistan. Yet only a matter of days earlier the Congress government had been indissolubly wedded to the idea of union with India when partition was brought about. The Viceroy made it clear to them within hours of his arrival that there must be a reference to the electorate to determine this. They knew what the result of that would be, however angry they might be over my confidential assessment which was "blown" in Delhi. One might expect a reluctant acquiescence. Instead, this time in a matter of hours, not days, they voluntarily adopted an objective which in effect repudiated everything for which they had stood for nearly twenty years. The turning of the coats seemed contemptible. But these were by no means contemptible men. Dr. Khan Sahib in particular was in my view a noble man. My own conclusion is that there were two motive forces. One was a feeling that they had been democratically and constitutionally elected and must therefore hold on to office as trustees of their constituents. The second was an absolute hatred for the Muslim League leader, Mohammad Ali Jinnah. Dr. Khan Sahib once said to me in private conversation that Jinnah was "a horribly vindictive man". There were admirable Muslim leaders in the Punjab who would hold the same view, as Jinnah declared war on them for not supporting his pure Islamic doctrine for the theocratic state of Pakistan. One of them retired to England because he quite simply feared some form of impeachment followed by execution. The tide was running against the Congress in the N.W.F.P., however, and in 1947 Pakhtunistan was a meaningless word.

Pakistan was the vibrant word. One generalization which can never be shown to be invalid is the statement that Pathans are very strong individualists. Their revolt against union with India, which meant sujection to an overwhelming Hindu majority, was balanced by their revolt against anything which might involve subjection to Afghanistan. And so the plebiscite went overwhelmingly in favour of Pakistan. Of those who voted about 98% were in favour. This was not,

*All efforts to identify the junior minister in question have been futile.

Memoirs of Norval Mitchell (p. 265).

pointed out that the issue regarding an independent Pathan state was a matter essentially for the Government of India and that the Afghan government had no *locus standi* in the matter.[66]

V

For fear matters got mixed up, Gandhi clarified that to dub Pathanistan as a so-called 'new cry' was a deliberate attempt at distortion by its adversaries. For Badshah Khan had long had 'Pathan independence in internal matters' on his mind. Nor did the Frontier leader want an 'additional state'. 'For his part', the Mahatma did not understand the 'objection' to this yearning after Pathan autonomy, 'unless the object is to humiliate the Pathans and tame them into subjection.'[67]

In actual fact, the Mahatma's support to the cause of Pathanistan became pronounced with every passing day. Thus at his prayer meeting on 19 June he called it 'a solid movement' that had come to stay and advised both the Congress and the Muslim League 'to honour' the Pathan sentiment with the Pathans having their own constitution 'for internal affairs and administration'. It would, Gandhi added, 'promote Pathan solidarity, avoid internal conflict, retain Pathan culture and Pathan language'. Later, it would 'better enable' to let the Pathans federate 'unitedly' with Pakistan—or the Union of India.[68]

Whatever, its detractors might say, the fact is that the shift of Frontier Congress to Pathanisatan, was 'neither abrupt nor clear-cut'. Vaguely it had been there for a period of time; and occurred 'incrementally rather than in one great leap'. As its critics saw it however, the Congress, up against the Muslim League agitation gathering ever greater momentum, had re-packaged its demand for autonomy under the new, more militant banner of Pathanistan to give it greater popular appeal and improve the party's political image.[69]

It is possible, Mitchell argues, that the idea of Pakhtunistan originated in the minds of the Afghan government. There might be great benefit to them as they fished in the troubled waters of the Frontier and its murky politics. Russia too would no doubt encourage this. He reveals that the Afghan Minister in Rome (Abdul Hamid) on his way to Kabul delivered a harangue (at Jamrud) in favour of Pakhtunistan and hostile to the British in India. In the turmoil of the time, this incident did not attract much attention, but it did draw from the Government of India, 'at Caroe's instance', a very sharp protest to the Afghan government.

There is however, Mitchell contends, 'no certainty' as to where the

TREE PLANTING

Ahmed, in the *Hindustan Times*, 20 June 1947.

concept originated. It may well be, and the possibility was one favoured by Sir Olaf Caroe himself, that Khan Sahib and his brother, AGK, felt that they had been betrayed by Nehru's agreement that a vote should be taken at all and 'fell back on a fanciful idea of some sort of Pakhtun independence' as reason for refusing to take part in a vote. However, that may be, 'it was probably not in the minds' of the Khan brothers that Pakhtunistan should include any portion of Afghanistan. Nevertheless the concept was adopted by the Congress government of the province.

Yet only a matter of days earlier, the Congress government had been 'indissolubly wedded' to the idea of union with India when partition was brought about—'in a matter of hours, not days'. They now voluntarily adopted an objective which in effect repudiated everything for which they had stood for nearly twenty years. The 'turning of the coats seemed complete'. But these were 'by no means contemptible' men. Khan Sahib in particular was 'in my view a noble man'. Mitchell's own conclusion is that there were two motive forces. One, a feeling that they had been democratically and constitutionally elected and must therefore hold on to office as trustees of their constituents. The second, 'an absolute hatred' for the Muslim League leader, Mohammad Ali Jinnah. Khan Sahib once told Mitchell in private conversation that Jinnah was 'a horribly vindictive man'. There were admirable Muslim leaders in the Panjab, he adds, who would hold the same view, as Jinnah 'declared war on them' for not supporting his pure Islamic doctrine for the theocratic state of Pakistan. One of them, Mitchell reveals, retired to England because he quite simply feared some form of impeachment followed by execution. 'All the same, the tide was running against' the Congress in the NWFP, and in 1947, Pakhtunistan was 'a meaningless word'.[70]

As a matter of fact, in his letter of 22 May to Sir John Colville, Caroe made a mention of the 'new propaganda line' of the Frontier Congress—for a 'Pathan national province under a coalition if possible and making its own alliances as may suit it'. The change, he averred, had probably come too late but 'to my mind it is a strength, and not a weakness'. In any case, he concluded, the appeal 'is a far more constructive one than that of Islam in danger'.[71] It may be of interest to note that the editor of *Jinnah's Papers* has found it 'indeed ironical' that the Khan Sahib ministry 'should have found it hard' to get on with Caroe 'who was sympathetic towards their nationalistic aspirations'. At the same time, he underlines that the 'propagation' of this Pathanistan alternative to Pakistan was 'another threat' to the 'ideological foundations' of the Pakistan ideal.[72]

Writing years later, Caroe noted that this projection may well have been the 'origin of the Pakhtun theme, Khan brothers' style'. The Afghan theme, he recalled, 'was played on a different chord, that of Afghan irredentism'. The Khan brothers, he clarified, thought 'more in terms of Pathan autonomy within a united India'.[73]

For the concession it had wrested on the referendum issue, the League had paid no mean price either. For one, it had said good bye to constitutional methods; for another, it had thrown the province into turmoil and perpetrated naked communal violence. It even encouraged unrest in tribal territory. But as the League leadership viewed it, the stakes were high and the party left with little or no choice. For without a frontal assault on the well-entrenched position of the Congress, the Raj may not have acceded to the League's wishes on the future alignment of the Frontier.

On 17 June, the Quaid had announced the constitution of a 4-member committee 'to supervise and control' the Muslim League organisation in the Frontier and 'to make arrangements' for the referendum. The committee was to remain 'in close contact and touch' with the Quaid and was to be 'guided' by him 'in making all the arrangements that will be necessary' for the League to participate 'effectively' in the referendum. The committee members included I I Chundrigar, Ghazanfar Ali Khan, the Pir Sahib of Manki Sharif, and Syed Wajid Ali.[74]

Caroe reported to Mountbatten about 'mounting tension' in Peshawar and other parts of the province as the referendum neared. Thus on 20 June a League demonstration of about 5,000 men including 550 of their National Guards, brought matters to a head. Armed with 'about 200 rifles and guns, 1 tommy gun, sten gun, numerous pistols, revolvers and other weapons' they chased and fired at a small group of Red Shirts. Fortunately there were no casualties. The Congress flag was torn up, and later, a Leaguer was stabbed 'allegedly by Red Shirts'.[75]

This incident was followed the next day by some Red Shirts planning to attack a Muslim League office. And it was, only the chief minister's 'personal intervention on the spot' that saved an ugly situation.[76]

Meanwhile the way the referendum was being organised filled Badshah Khan with dismay and disgust. Writing to the Mahatma on 12 July, he mentioned the presence in the Frontier of a large number of Panjabis who openly incited people to violence and threatened to put to death the top leadership of the Khudai Khidmatgars, holding out the threat of a 'Nuremberg trial' for all the 'traitors'.[77] There were complaints from the other side too. On 4 July, Mountbatten had written to the Mahatma on reports about the Red Shirts 'persuading' people not to vote. And feared that this was 'likely' to lead to the very violence they were all anxious to avoid.[78]

Responding to the allegation, Gandhi wrote back to the governor-general that Badshah Khan and his followers were 'undoubtedly' telling the voters that it was 'wrong' for them to take part in the voting. But conceded that there should be no demonstrations during the days polling was scheduled and no approach to voters during the voting time. Mountbatten for his part asked the Mahatma to 'go a little further' and deprecate any agitation before the polling days that may lead directly or indirectly to disturbances.

Reacting to the viceroy's plea, Gandhi wrote to Badshah Khan on 5 July that 'in the present state of tension and misrepresentation' there should be 'no demonstration' against the Muslim League while the Khudai Khidmatgars might keep their counsel and not vote one way or another.[79]

Badshah Khan's unequivoval reaction to the governor-general's charge was that while he had been going around asking people 'to remain absolutely non-violent', the Muslim League took out daily processions raising highly objectionable slogans. He revealed that he had been personally hooted down and alleged that there was an 'organised conspiracy' between the Muslim Leaguers and the officers incharge of the referendum.[80] As one closely associated with organising the referendum, Fraser Noble has stoutly denied that there was any 'such organised conspiracy'.[81]

VI

The referendum in the Frontier started on 6 July and was completed by 17 July which was the date when the holy month of fasting, Ramadan, was expected to start. Beginning with the four districts of Peshawar, Mardan, Kohat and Bannu, it covered the remaining two districts of Hazara and D I Khan a few days later. Final results were announced on 20 July.

In the 'almost peaceful conditions' in which, Mountbatten claimed, the referendum took place, the final tally was:

Valid votes cast for Pakistan	:	289,244
Valid votes cast for India	:	2,874
Majority (for Pakistan)	:	286,370
Percentage of valid votes to the total electorate entitled to vote	:	50.99
Valid votes cast in the last elections (held February-March 1946)	:	375,989
Total electorate entitled to vote in the referendum+	:	572,798
Votes for Pakistan:		50.49 of the total.[82]

Note: +Out of this only 84,781 were Hindus and Sikhs.

Not unexpectedly, the Khudai Khidmatgars cried themselves hoarse about large-scale rigging. Badshah Khan charged that the military took 'a large number of people' to the polling booths and even 'fraudulent registration' of voters was resorted to. He drew pointed attention to an army unit in Bannu whose commander confessed to taking his men three times to the polling booth to cast their votes in favour of Pakistan. The Frontier leader also revealed that the vote of the president of the Provincial Congress Committee was impersonated.[83]

Contemporary observers noted that coercion was freely resorted to by the Leaguers for what they deemed to be a vote against 'Kafiristan'; that the votes of the dead as well as those who either boycotted the poll or were out of station, were all polled in favour of Pakistan. According to some estimates, about 25-30 per cent of bogus votes were cast in the referendum. It has been computed that if a conservative 15-17 per cent of the bogus votes were discounted from the total polled and then compared with the number registered in a normal election (65.6 per cent in 1946), the 'precarious nature of the League's victory' would be evident. It should not be forgotten either that in the final analysis, a little less than 10 per cent of the total population of the NWFP determined the fate of the province.[84]

It has been suggested that much of what has been retailed in the preceding paragraphs was 'biased Congress propaganda' which did by no means correspond with the conduct of the referendum, much less its outcome. Sir Fraser Noble contends that the latter, in any case, was 'quite clear', despite the Congress boycott.[85]

An insider, Sir Fraser had a ringside view of the conduct of the referendum and had been designated as Civil Aide to the Referendum Commissioner, Brigadier John Booth. Earlier, Booth had been Commander of the Wana Brigade in South Waziristan. The commissioner was to be helped by a number of military officers with a good knowledge of the Pushtu language and experience of the Frontier; they had been brought back from their service with units then deployed outside the province or in its tribal areas.

At the viceroy's staff meeting on 8 June it was argued that since the referendum was to be held 'in consultation' with the provincial government, a reference to Khan Sahib about the choice and deployment of these officers was called for. The suggestion that Khan Sahib's request for change 'might be refused' on the ground that 'there would be no time to do so' was over-ruled. The premier was to adduce 'exact reasons' for any objections that he raised but was to be told that these 'would be subject to be over-ruled' by the viceroy. Accordingly, a list of officers to be deployed was shown to Khan Sahib for his approval. He was asked if he had any objections and if so the exact reasons thereof. It would appear that Khan Sahib's approval was forthcoming and no objections were raised.

Noble's own appointment came in the wake of Booth's quick realisation that he, and his military staff, would be seriously handicapped by their lack of knowledge of civil administration, constitutional law, electoral procedure and such other sundry but important matters that they would have to deal with. 'Untainted apparently by suspicion of partiality for either side', Noble's was a happy choice in that he was acceptable both to Khan Sahib as well as the League leader, Abdul Qaiyum Khan.

In the Frontier, the weeks following the 3 June announcement had been relatively quiet, the province virtually 'exhausted' after a long bout of civil disorder and worse, but now 'almost at peace with itself'. The Muslim League, it would appear, awaited the referendum with a measure of quiet confidence; the Congress, at a loose end, unsure what to do. There were rumours galore: about a campaign to form an independent Pathan state; of some sort of a coalition between the Khan brothers and the Frontier Muslim League.

Local help needed by Brigadier Booth, Referendum Commissioner, Noble recalled, was easy to provide. What was more difficult were the answers to the legal and constitutional conundrums that the referendum posed. To start with, the Government of India Act 1935 was 'not helpful' about the validity of the referendum. As a matter of fact, in his anxiety not to offend against the constitution by dismissing the ministry and calling for a general election, Mountbatten had really 'invented' a method of achieving the same effective result which was 'so novel and so persuasively orchestrated' that nobody questioned his power to drive ahead.

This left the provincial ministry in a spot. It argued for instance that if civil disturbances broke out during the period of the referendum, it had the constitutional authority to suspend or postpone voting. The referendum commissioner claimed that such authority must vest in him. For where-ever the 1935 Act provided that the judgement or discretion of the governor became operative, it would now be for him (viz., R C) to take a decision. All this, Noble argued, made 'good practical sense' and reflected the viceroy's instructions but it 'stretched the constitutional powers far beyond' what the Act provided.

Booth as well as Noble had jointly worked out the referendum poster. It briefly spelt out the details of the 3 June plan which had been accepted both by the Congress as well as the Muslim League. Below the text was a map which showed, in red, details of the provinces which were included in India; in green, those which had elected to join Pakistan. Areas which still had to decide between the two, were shown in white. The poster then posed in simple terms the issue for the voters and heavily underlined that there was no other alternative issue for them to decide. At the end, the procedure to express the individual voter's choice, or preference, through the ballot paper was spelt out.

Lockhart had held consultations with Mountbatten on various legal and constitutional issues. For instance what was he to do if the Khan Sahib ministry forbade its officials, who were responsible to the provincial government, to play an active part in the arrangements? 'Sensibly', Noble records, the viceroy did nothing 'or as little as possible'.

'There were rumours', Noble recalls, that the Red Shirt mafia were 'threatening to make things difficult' for some officials of the provincial government. Happily, the officials 'generally observed' the Khan Sahib government's exhortation to stay out of the whole affair. In the result, threats that the polling stations would be picketed came to nought largely because during the campaign leading to the referendum, the League mustered 'very large numbers' at its rallies. The Congress ministry's official line was to decry the referendum and deplore the communally-inspired partition of India.

The ticklish issue of carrying firearms was easily sorted out. Ordinarily, most Pathans carry their guns but in fact these had 'little influence' and provoked 'less violence' as the polling progressed. There was a firing incident somewhere in the Charsadda subdivision; happily, it proved to be an isolated affair.

Accompanied by Booth, Noble toured around the province but saw 'little to disturb' him except some evidence in Hazara where more votes were being cast than the number on the electoral rolls would justify. That apart, the special officers deputed were, on the whole, 'efficient and alert'. Besides, at each polling station, the Congress as well as the League was entitled to have three agents present at the clerk's table to challenge any bogus voter or check anyone from voting more than once. Inasmuch as 'very few challenges' were made under the procedure laid down, the vague 'generalised complaints of malpractices' with which the Congress subsequently challenged the result of the referendum do not wash.[86]

Both Maulana Azad as well as Sardar Patel believed that the referendum results were 'a definite indication' of the waning influence of the Khan brothers. Azad further charged that the two-some were tight-fisted in the use of party funds as well as the graces of hospitality which largely accounted for their unpopularity.[87] Badshah Khan's biographer has stoutly repudiated either insinuation. The Pathan tradition, Tendulkar has suggested, is so repugnant to not sharing all one had with one's guest that Azad's charge sounds 'incorrect both in fact and in inference'. As to the parsimonious use of party funds, the Khudai Khidmatgars', he has pointed out, was far from being a purely political organisation; its social and economic planks rested squarely on people's active involvement. Therefore, generous use of party funds was neither important nor perhaps that relevant.[88] Azad's own objectivity has been questioned. Thus, it has been suggested that in the midst of the fast-thinning ranks of nationalist Muslims, he rated the Khan brothers' influence as a challenge to his own supremacy among the Congress high command. In sharp contrast, Noble has averred that these senior Congress politicians (viz., Azad and Patel) made 'much shrewder judgements' of the whole episode of the referendum than did Abdul Ghaffar Khan.[89]

The changing scenario in regard to the Pathanistan issue as between the 3 June plan and the aftermath of the referendum may be gauged from the tone and temper of editorial comments in the *Tribune* on the subject. Much of it was repetitive but a lot reflected the tumultuous political scene in the Frontier province as well as the rest of the country. A few excerpts from these leading articles may thus help to place the Pakhtun issue in a proper perspective.

To start with, in the wake of the 3 June plan, the paper wrote under the heading, 'Frontier Referendum':

> The fact is that British Imperialism wants a strong Pakistan as a buffer between itself and communism, which it cannot have without the Frontier forming its integral part. It is confident that now when minds on the Frontier are unhinged and passions are running high, the majority of the Pathans will not vote for the marriage of their province with Pakistan. The professed British aversion to the Balkanisation of India is nothing but hypocrisy.[90]

A week later with some major Indian princely states planning to declare their independence, the *Tribune* reverted to the subject under the caption 'Pathanistan and Balkanisation of India':

> If the ultimate emergence of States like Hyderabad and Travancore as sovereign states will not mean the Balkanisation of India, what else will it mean? . . . If Kashmir can become an independent state, why cannot the Frontier Province become an independent Pathanistan. The limiting of the Pathans' choice to Pakistan and Hindustan is a glaring injustice to the Pushto speaking people.[91]

On 21 June, the paper was to come back to the subject—'Pathanistan'—and trotted forth much the same argument:

Therefore the plea of Balkanisation cannot hold water. A grave wrong has been done to the brave Pathans. Reason, logic and consistency demand that this wrong must be righted and the Pathans must be allowed to give their verdict on the issue whether they want to join Pakistan or Hindustan or set up a new State of their own free from the dominance of Hindus and non-Pathan Muslims.[92]

Four days later, the *Tribune* reverted to the theme, 'Pathans' Demand Must Be Conceded', and recalled Khan Sahib's comment that those who were opposed to the Pathan demand were 'till yesterday in conspiracy with' their British patrons

and who ruthlessly obstructed the patriotric Khudai Khidmatgars in their efforts to win freedom. . . . If the Muslim League leaders really believed in self-determination—in the right of the Pathans to settle their political future according to their own desire—they would have unhesitatingly agreed to the raising of the issue of Pathanistan. After all, culturally and linguistically the Pathans are quite different from the Punjabi or Sindhi or Bengali Mussulmans. Why should not they be allowed to safeguard their culture, their language, their customs and their traditions?[93]

With the Khudai Khidmatgars deciding to boycott the referendum, the paper changed its tune though not its rhetoric. It now accepted the fact that the Muslim League

may have a walk-over. But that does not mean the end of the Pathan independence movement. The Khudai Khidmatgars are in the saddle in the province. They can easily carry the fight into the League camp. Ultimately the Pathan independence struggle will be crowned with success and a truly sovereign Pathan State will come into existence upsetting the feudal-capitalist-imperialist apple-cart.[94]

By mid-July there had been some more rumblings of the storm with Afghanistan taking a keen interest in the Pakhtun question and pledging its strong support to their right for self-determination. The *Tribune's* thinking would appear broadly to reflect the views on the subject held at the highest levels of government:

We are strongly opposed to the Frontier Province's joining Afghanistan. We are indeed inclined to think that the Afghan Government has not claimed that the Frontier Province or any part thereof should go to it. Such a claim would obviously by preposterous. But as a close neighbour of the Frontier Province Afghanistan may be interested in its becoming an independent Pathan State. It will be sheer mischief to represent a legitimate Afghan desire as something inspired by the

Soviet Union. . . . As regards the Frontier Province's right to become sovereign, it is clear that in this age of self-determination it cannot be denied to it. Pakistan is itself a child of Self Determination. How can it say to the Frontier Province, 'Thou shall not freely exercise thy will'?[95]

A little over a week later, the *Tribune* took up the call of the Speaker of the Frontier Assembly, Allah Nawaz Khan appealing to Mountbatten, Nehru and Jinnah to pay 'prompt attention' to the Pathanistan issue which had 'deeply attracted' the imagination of Pathan mind'. The paper expressed the hope that Jinnah who 'is a firm believer in the principle of self-determination' would not stand in the way of the Pathans 'taking advantage of it and declaring themselves independent'.

More, as a contiguous country 'even the independent Pathanistan will be linked up with Pakistan. Let Mr Jinnah allow the Pathans to run their affairs as an independent nation and let us all—Pathanistan, Pakistan, India—march together to the common goal of permanent peace and unbounded prosperity.'[96]

VII

The result of the referendum, Mitchell noted, brought a measure of political peace. As a matter of fact, even the announcement of the holding of the referendum ground the Muslim League agitation to a halt. It had filled the provincial jails with 'respectable and respected' Muslims who had committed purely technical offences in order to embarrass the government.[97]

The few weeks intervening between the declaration of the result of the referendum (20 July) and the proclamation of Pakistan (14 August) were packed with events. Even as the referendum was in progress, Lockhart composed a long letter for the governor-general under the broad rubric, 'The post-Referendum Problems in the NWFP' which touched on such subjects as reactions to a coalition government; future policy of each party; arms and the private armies; government under Section 93; and the Tribes. He informed Mountbatten on 9 July that Khan Sahib had given him to understand that 'he would not rule out the possibility' of some of his colleagues joining a coalition ministry with the Muslim League on the ground that Pakistan was 'temporarily inevitable'. On the other hand, Lockhart reported that the Muslim League perception was that 'on no account' should the Khan Sahib ministry continue in office after the referendum because they would 'squander' the provincial finances apart from stirring up trouble through the Fakir of Ipi and 'generally create chaos'. He outlined three courses open to him including the formation of a coalition ministry, 'of which I do not altogether despair, but am not very sanguine'. The other two were the dismissal of the Khan Sahib ministry with its necessary concomitant of government under Section 93 and the imposition of martial law. He ended by saying that he was by 'no means without hope that there will be a constitutional change of Ministry'.[98] Fraser Noble has made a slightly different emphasis. Its rout in the referendum vote notwithstanding, the Congress, he has suggested, was 'still playing a powerful part' and was determined 'to find a way to still higher stakes'. Its attempt to introduce the Pathanistan issue was 'in itself understandable' but 'what precisely the objective was, or the working definition of the slogan', remained 'most obscure'.[99]

At a meeting Mountbatten convened with Liaquat Ali Khan and Jinnah in New Delhi on 29 July, Lockhart was present. He told his interlocutors that, to start with, Khan Sahib had given him to understand that if there were 30 per cent vote for Pakistan, he would resign. Later the Premier complained about the conduct of the referendum and averred that its results would 'not be a fundamental issue'. More, he would not resign 'because he had a majority' in the legislature and enjoyed the support of a majority of the electorate. A coalition was deemed impracticable both by the Khan Sahib ministry as well as the Muslim League. As to the imposition of Section 93 rule, Lockhart affirmed that it would, as of date, be 'the least offensive' to either party. But on 15 August there would be no one to carry on the government.[100]

For his part, Mountbatten let it be known that he was 'violently opposed' to Section 93 rule: 'It would be interpreted by the public as the last act of the British to induce direct rule.' On inquiry, Lockhart stated, that there was 'little chance' of the members of the legislature changing sides or swapping loyalties. Jinnah's considered view was that the legislature 'should not be summoned' and that Section 93 rule should be avoided. While the referendum, he averred, meant a 'thumping vote of no confidence' in the present ministry, Khan Sahib was acting in a manner which confirmed the Quaid's view 'that he (Khan Sahib) was unfit to be a prime minister'.

Lockhart assured the meeting that the Khan Sahib ministry, if allowed to continue, could not do a great deal of harm. Financially, 'there was no more to spend'; all the same, there may, however, be interference in the posting of officials. To stall this, Mountbatten expressed the view that a 'standstill order' may be enforced holding over all postings. While Liaquat

Ali Khan thought that a new ministry should be formed 'as soon as possible', the Quaid, edgy as ever, feared that every day that passed made the situation 'more dangerous'. He had heard of trouble being stirred up in the tribal areas and even of 'terrorisation'.[101] Independent of him, HMG too had a spate of reports from Kabul of 'collusion' between the Afghan government and the Congress Party and of a renewed campaign for an independent Pathanistan.[102]

On 8 August, Mountbatten retailed to Whitehall the tentative programme that had been worked out for NWFP. Briefly, Lockhart was to dismiss the Khan Sahib ministry on the afternoon of 11 August or the following morning while Cunningham was to take over on the evening of the 12th or the morning after. Immediately thereafter, the new governor was to invite the leader of the Muslim League to form a government. At the same time, Lockhart was to arrange for 'military precautions' to prevent 'trouble' by the Red Shirts over the dismissal of the Khan Sahib ministry and its replacement by the Muslim League.[103]

In his personal report of date (viz., 8 August), Mountbatten referred to Jinnah and Liaquat Ali Khan 'getting very worried' over the NWFP. He reiterated that Lockhart was to dismiss the Khan Sahib ministry while Cunninghman was to swear in the Muslim League ministry 'in accordance with Jinnah's instructions and in anticipation of the transfer of power' on 15 August. Adding that Jinnah did not like this delay 'but finally shrugged his shoulders' and said, 'I am in your hands in this matter'.[104]

From Whitehall, on 8 August, the secretary of state telegraphed Mountbatten to say that Liaquat Ali Khan's 'unsupported assertion' about Khan Sahib's 'intentions' to proclaim Pathanistan should be accepted with 'a pinch of salt': 'He (LAK) is very interested party' whereas 'you in India and we in Parliament' would 'have to justify our action'. Listowel made it abundantly clear that he was 'still not sure that action by you before 15th August is the wisest course'.[105]

On 9 August, Lockhart reported from Peshawar that 'general situation' remained 'much as it was' when he saw Mountbatten a week earlier. 'Pathanistan' was being vigorously advocated 'and the idea is, I think, proving attractive' to many Pathans. 'Rumours and reports' about the Fakir of Ipi, Lockhart added, 'flow in daily' and there was no doubt that Congress 'are in touch with him'. Meantime, Khan Sahib 'still adheres' to his intention not to resign. Lockhart added that he would, according to Mountbatten's instructions, try to persuade Khan Sahib even though he feared there was 'little chance of my success'. The governor added that Khan Sahib had told him that he would cooperate and accept Pakistan if

Jinnah 'would agree to full Provincial Autonomy'. Added to his (Jinnah's) placing no prohibition 'on political party programmes'—if advocated and executed 'constitutionally'.

All this while, it should be obvious, the Muslim League were keen that the Khan Sahib ministry must quit office *before* 15 August. Lockhart and 'the officials I have consulted' were clear, however, that this course of action should be taken by the new Pakistan government. After all, he argued, the latter had brought about this situation by its insistence on *not* dissolving the legislature. And in so far as Khan Sahib commanded a majority there, he had refused to resign.[106] It has been suggested that in the aftermath of the referendum, Khan Sahib seemed to be 'coming to terms with reality', so that should Mountbatten, and Lockhart, have decided to dismiss his ministry, he would have accepted the position and preferred to fight an election on a new platform that accepted the need to come to terms with Pakistan.[107] As it happened, Whitehall had stoutly resisted any move to dismiss the Khan Sahib ministry.

On 10 August, Mountbatten informed Liaquat Ali Khan that the secretary of state for India had instructed him to the effect that either of the following courses suggested by the Pakistan Executive Council: (*a*) that the NWFP ministry be asked to resign by the governor, and if it refused, be dismissed; (*b*) that if (*a*) were considered unconstitutional, the governor be asked to go into Section 93 'so that the new governor could appoint a new ministry' on 15 August, would, 'in the present circumstance be unconstitutional'. He would, thus, find it 'impossible' to accept the advice tendered. As to what action Sir George Cunningham was to take on 15 August, may be discussed with him 'when he comes through Karachi'.[108]

A word on Cunningham's appointment. Writing to India Office on 4 July, the former governor noted 'with much regret', that his answer to Jinnah's offer of appointment on 2 July must be in the negative. Later, it would appear, Cunningham had a change of heart and after personal consultations with India Office and Ismay (just about back in England) accepted the offer on or about 11 July. At India Office on 8 August, Mitchell tell us, Cunningham was 'horrified' at the suggestion that the Frontier ministry should be dismissed:

> Dismissal of the Ministry while they still had a majority in the Assembly, without even offering them the choice of dissolution, would simply be unconstitutional. On the practical side, dismissal would embitter local feelings to the extent of provoking violence.

He was replaced by Lieutenant General Sir Rob M.M. Lockhart. He presided with firmness and tact over the chaotic situation which prevailed in the province until the return of Sir George Cunningham on the 13th August 1947. By that time I was no longer in India, but the story of the invocation or otherwise of Section 93 may be completed.

It was Mr. Jinnah who had stated in the proper quarters that he would like to have British Governors for all the provinces of Pakistan, of which he announced that he wished to be Governor-General. In particular, he was anxious to get Cunningham for the North West Frontier Province. Cunningham, actuated by an austere sense of duty, accepted the appointment; and was confronted with the problem on 8th August in the India office. He was "horrified" at the suggestion.* Such a word from someone so confident and strong is startling, but it is in his own diary. Dismissal of the ~~Congress~~ Ministry while they still had a majority in the Assembly, without even offering them the choice of dissolution, would simply be unconstitutional. On the practical side, dismissal would embitter local feelings to the extent of provoking violence. The India office shared his views. It was intimated to the Viceroy that the matter should be left for action to the Pakistan Government after 15 August, the date fixed for the actual achievement of independence. Of course Jinnah did what everyone knew he would do.*

* Caroe was very casually treated in all this. The first that he knew came in a letter from the Viceroy dated 15th July. He might have received it in Kashmir two or three days later. Cunningham received the offer of the post on 4th July. He wrote in his diary on 12th August:- "I was surprised to learn (in Delhi) that it was only last week or so that Olaf Caroe had been told that he would not be coming back to Peshawar. He surely ought to have been told as soon as they had decided to ask me, which is now five weeks ago." Cunningham was not told all the ~~details~~ DATES**, but his main criticism was justified.

* that the Frontier ministry should be dismissed.

** Dates

Memoirs of Norval Mitchell (p. 270).

Happily for him, Mitchell recorded, Whitehall 'shared his views'.[109]

It may be noted that India Office regarded Cunningham's acceptance of Jinnah's offer as 'saintly' for it was 'actuated by an austere sense of duty'. The Quaid's 'haggling' over his salary and other emoluments was a subject of comment and it was noted that the terms finally offered Cunningham were 'not very generous'.[110]

On 11 August, Lockhart informed Mountbatten that he had seen Khan Sahib at 'normal routine interview' that morning and referred to rumours, and press reports, that he (Khan Sahib) proposed to declare Pathanistan on 15 August. In reply, Khan Sahib 'assured me' that the rumours were 'nonsense' and that there was 'no question of this or any other unconstitutional action'. In view of this assurance, Lockhart added, 'I gave no warning nor did I refer to resignation.'[111]

Meanwhile Cunningham had arrived in Karachi on the afternoon of 11 August and conferred with Jinnah who expressed the hope that the Khan Sahib ministry could be dismissed before 15 August. In reply, the governor-designate 'made it clear pretty quickly' that he 'would not do this'. When he arrived in New Delhi on 12, the viceroy informed Cunningham at the airport itself that since 'hard political decisions had to be taken', the governor-designate 'might continue on his journey', go to Peshawar 'at once' and travel that very afternoon. Cunningham, however, had other thoughts. 'A few hours', he reasoned, 'could not make any difference'. Besides, there 'might be an advantage in not appearing to be hurried'. He, therefore, stayed overnight in New Delhi and had an opportunity to confer with the governor-general.[112]

Cunningham arrived in Peshawar on the morning of 13 August and took over as governor the same evening. Almost immediately, he reported to Mountbatten that he had 'no doubt' Jinnah 'will order' the dismissal of the Khan Sahib ministry between 16-18 August and added that he was 'not particularly gloomy as to the course of events thereafter'.[113]

The new governor had a long talks with Khan Sahib on the evening of 13 August and 'told him pretty frankly' of his consultations with Jinnah in Karachi two days earlier. Cunningham had told the Quaid that 'I had to satisfy my own conscience as to any action that I took myself' and needed a day or two to assess the situation. 'I repeated to Khan Sahib', Cunningham wrote, 'what I had said to Jinnah: that the only grounds on which I considered I could feel justified in dismissing him would be: (a) if he (Khan Sahib) insisted on declaring that Pathanistan was to be an independent unit; or (b) if he could not satisfy me that he meant generally to cooperate with the constitution'. In turn, Jinnah had decided 'to wait until 15 August' before Cunningham sent in his 'final views'.

'As long as he remains minister', Cunningham felt assured, Khan Sahib 'will do nothing injurious' to the Pakistan constitution. Besides, the premier had 'no intention' of making any declaration about an independent Pathanistan. The new governor added that should he dismiss the Khan Sahib ministry, the premier and his colleagues 'will accept that decision and not give trouble'.[114]

The Quaid, it would appear, was not easily persuaded. Mountbatten, however, noted that Cunningham 'entirely shared my view' that to dismiss the Khan Sahib ministry would at once be 'unconstitutional and a foolish move'. But it was 'with great difficulty' that Cunningham was able to bring Jinnah around to his line of reasoning, insisting he (Cunningham) would try his hand with Khan Sahib to obtain a satisfactory settlement instead of resorting to such drastic action.[115]

Cunningham expressed the view that he thought it better 'at this stage' not to give his premier any indication of what he was about. Khan Sahib, he added, was 'in a very friendly frame of mind' and promised that he and the other ministers 'would go to the flag hoisting ceremony' on 15 August. For himself, the premier promised, he would 'pull down his present Congress flag and probably fly nothing in its place'. Of the Muslim League leader, Abdul Qaiyum Khan whom he was to swear in as Premier a week later, Cunningham remarked, that he 'seems to have acquired more sense of responsibility' than he was showing 18 months earlier. 'He spoke', the governor concluded, 'without any bluster' and he (Cunningham) was 'generally' quite favourably impressed.[116]

Khan Sahib and his colleagues were reportedly planning to attend the Pakistani flag hoisting ceremony (scheduled for 15 August) but decided not to, in the light of intelligence reports that the mob will 'pull off' the flag from the ministers' cars. Khan Sahib gave the governor to understand that 'if this once happened' (viz., pulling off the flags from the ministers' cars) he for one could not answer for the acts of his followers. Cunningham's assessment was slightly different. The ministers calculated, he argued, that if they attended the ceremony and were dismissed almost immediately thereafter, their followers would laugh at them. For it would seem that while the Khan Sahib ministry had extended its hand of friendship to the new regime, the latter rudely spurned it.[117]

Cunningham for his part had hoped that Khan Sahib and his ministerial colleagues would resign of their own, thereby avoiding the necessity of dismissal. Khan Sahib, it appeared to him, 'would clearly have preferred' to do this but he was 'evidently overruled' by Mehr Chand Khanna and

Qazi Ataullah who wanted to make it appear that Jinnah had taken 'a false step'.[118]

In the final count, after the necessary amendments to the Pakistan constitution had been effected, Jinnah directed Cunningham that should the Khan Sahib ministry fail to resign, it may be sacked. Faced with this course of action on 23 August, the premier and his colleagues refused to oblige and were summarily dismissed that afternoon.[119]

NOTES

1. Caroe to Wavell, 8 March 1947, *CM*, pp. 141-3.
2. Loc. cit.
3. Loc. cit.
4. Caroe to Mountbatten, 22 March 1947, *CM*, p. 146.
5. Ibid., 7 April 1947, *CM*, pp. 151-2.
6. Ronald Wingate, *Lord Ismay*, London, 1970, p. 152.
7. Hodson, *The Great Divide*, pp. 284-5.
8. Nehru to Mountbatten, 3 May 1947, *Selected Works*, Second Series, II, item 8, pp. 326-8.
9. Tendulkar, pp. 417-8.
10. Mountbatten to Nehru, 10 May 1947, *Transfer of Power*, X, Document 384.
11. For the 'Plan Balkan', Documents 147, 279 and 279 read with *Transfer of Power*, X, Document 260, Appendix C.
12. Governors' Conference, first day (15 April), *Transfer of Power*, X, Document 158. See also Jansson, p. 200.
13. Eric Mevielle to Mountbatten, 30 April 1947, *Transfer of Power*, X, Document 257.
14. Mountbatten to Listowel, 1 May 1947, *Transfer of Power*, X, Document 275.
15. Nehru to Mountbatten, 1 May 1947, *Selected Works*, II, Item 7, pp. 324-6.
16. Viceroy's Special Staff Meeting, 5 May 1947, *Transfer of Power*, X, Document 314.
17. Mountbatten to Ismay, 5 May 1947, Document 317, ibid.
18. Eric Mevielle to Mountbatten, 5 May 1947, Document 322, ibid. See also Mountbatten to Ismay, 6 May 1947, Document 327, ibid.
19. Mountbatten to Jinnah, 5 May 1947, No. 386 in *Jinnah Papers*, I, 1. An 'undated May 1947' draft 'by M.A. Jinnah on the situation in the NWFP' mentioned among other things that 'the only honourable course' for Khan Sahib and his co-ministers was to resign and seek re-election. For the text, ibid., Annexure II to No. 386.
20. For the text, see Annex to No 391, in ibid. Jinnah had sent a copy of the statement to Mountbatten. Jinnah to Mountbatten, 7 May 1947, No. 391 in ibid.
21. For the text, Annex IV to No 386, ibid. The statement was dated 6 May 1947.
22. Mountbatten to Isamy, 6 May 1947, *Transfer of Power*, X, Document 328.
23. Ismay to Mountbatten, 6 May 1947, Document 330, in ibid.
24. Gandhi to Mountbatten, 8 May 1947, Document 348, in ibid.
25. Mountbatten to Ismay, 8 May 1947, Document 358, in ibid. For more details, see Tendulkar, p. 417.
26. Nehru to Mountbatten, 10 May 1947, *Transfer of Power*, X, Document 385.

27. Minutes of Viceroy's 10th Miscellaneous Meeting, 8 May 1947, *Transfer of Power*, X, Document 350 .
28. Governors' Conference, 15 April 1947, *Transfer of Power*, X, Document 158. Also Minutes of Viceroy's Third Miscellaneous Meeting, 16 April 1947, Document 162, ibid.
    See also Jansson, p. 201.
29. Tendulkar, p. 421. See also Jansson, pp. 205-6.
30. Tendulkar, p. 424.
31. Tendulkar, pp. 424-5.
32. See Chapter 3 above.
33. Caroe to Mountbatten, 4 June 1947, *Transfer of Power*, XI, Document 65.
34. Caroe's telegrams of 27 and 30 May 1947 referred to in n. 4 in ibid.
35. See Chapter 3 above.
36. 'Record of Interview with Dr. Khan Sahib', *Transfer of Power*, XI, Document 81.
37. Caroe to Mountbatten, 5 June 1947, Document 83 in ibid.
38. The *Statesman*, 5 June 1947; see also *Transfer of Power*, XI, Document 83, n. 2.
39. Caroe to Mountbatten, 5 June 1947, Document 85 in ibid. The governor underlined that jubilation among the Muslim League camp meant that a state of 'depression' marked the feeling among the minorities.
40. Patel to Mountbatten, 3 June 1947, Annex I to No. 4, *JPs*, II. Also Khan Sahib to Mountbatten, Annex II to No. 4, ibid. The text of Jinnah's broadcast is in No. 4, ibid.
41. Viceroy's Personal Report, No. 8, 5 June 1947, *Transfer of Power*, XI, Document 91, para 15.
42. Loc. cit.
43. Tendulkar, p. 428.
44. Gandhi to Nehru, 9 June 1947, cited in Tendulkar, p. 432.
45. Ismay to Mountbatten, 7 June 1947, *Transfer of Power*, XI, Document 99.

    It would appear that all that transpired at Gandhi's meeting with Mountbatten was reduced to writing by Ismay in the form of an annexure to Proc 99 entitled 'Mr Gandhi's suggestions to HE the Viceroy'. Here apart from NWFP, Bihar and the UP (Panjab?), 'Cooperation between Mr. Jinnah and the Congress leaders' and 'Agreement between HMG and the two Indian dominions' were the subjects mentioned.

    After spelling out his line on the NWFP: 'Mr. Gandhi emphasised' that he had not discussed the above with his colleagues and therefore 'it should not be mentioned to anyone at this stage'.

    See also Tendulkar, pp. 428-9.Tendulkar does not mention the Mahatma's request to Ismay that the matter be kept a secret.
46. Tendulkar, p. 429.
47. For the full text of Nehru's 'Note on the situation in the NWFP', see *Selected Works*, III, item 1, pp. 273-9. For a summary of Nehru's note, see Tendulkar, pp. 429-32.
48. Tendulkar, p. 433.
49. Ibid, pp. 433-4.
50. For the full text of Nehru's 'The Approach to the Referendum', a note of 13 June 1947, see *Selected Works*, III, item 3, pp. 279-80.
51. Samin Jan and Abdul Qaiyum Khan to M A Jinnah, 26 May 1947, No. 485 in *Jinnah Papers*, I, 1.

Also M A Jinnah to Samin Jan and Abdul Qaiyum Khan, 27 May 1947, No. 488 in ibid.

52. Caroe to Mountbatten, 31 May 1947, *Transfer of Power*, XI, Document 14.
53. The *Tribune*, 14 June 1947.
54. Abdul Qaiyum to M.A. Jinnah, 14 May 1947, No. 422 in *JPs.*, I,1.
55. For details, Eric Mevielle to Mountbatten, 18 June 1947, *Transfer of Power*, XI, Document 253.

    See also No. 163 and Annex III to No. 299 in *Jinnah Papers*, II. Also Appendix X. 3 in ibid.

    See also *Transfer of Power,* XI, Document 321. For the full text of Badshah Khan's statement of 24 June in which he refers to his talks with Jinnah, see Tendulkar, pp. 439-40.
56. Jansson, p. 214.
57. Badshah Khan's letter to Jinnah, 19 June 1947, refers to the attack on him in the *Dawn*. For the text, Tendulkar, pp. 438-9.
58. In a lengthy statement issued on 24 June 1947, at Peshawar, AGK concluded by saying how he wished 'even at this eleventh hour' Jinnah had recognised the 'justice of our position and refrained from dividing Pathans from Pathans'. For the texts of the resolution and AGK's statement, see Tendulkar, pp. 439-41. Also Annex II to No. 299, *Jinnah Papers*, II.
59. Tendulkar, pp. 441-2. This was in the form of a letter from Acharya Kriplani to Mountbatten.
60. Revised draft of a press statement by M A Jinnah, No. 299 in *Jinnah Papers*, II. The statement, dated 28 June, was published in the *Pakistan Times* on 1 July 1947.
61. Extracts from Khan Sahib's letter are reproduced in Tendulkar, p. 443.

    See also India (Department of External Affairs and Commonwealth Relations) to Secretary of State, 29 June 1947, *Transfer of Power*, XI, Document 395. The Indian communication gave a detailed assessment of the Afghan campaign and charged that it constituted an 'unwarranted attempt to interfere' in New Delhi's internal affairs.
62. Fraser Noble, Memoirs, p. 342.
63. Nehru to Khan Sahib and Nehru to Badshah Khan, both 30 June 1947, items 8, 9 in *Selected Works*, III, pp. 286-7 and 287-91.
64. Secretary of State for India to HM Minister at Kabul, 16 June 1947, *Transfer of Power*, XI, Document 212. See also the *Tribune*, 24 July 1947.
65. Governor-General to Secretary of State, 29 June 1947, *Jinnah Papers*, II, No. 310. See also Listowel to Mountbatten, 5 July 1947, *Transfer of Power*, XI, Document 517.
66. For details see *Selected Works*, III, items 8, 9, 10, pp. 286-92.
67. For Gandhi's speech at his prayer meeting on 30 June see Tendulkar, pp. 443-4. See also item 9, *Selected Works*, III, pp. 287-91.
68. The *Tribune*, 20 June 1947.
69. Rittenberg, pp. 385-6.
70. Norval Mitchell, Memoirs, pp. 264-6.
71. Caroe to Sir John Colville, 22 May 1947, *CM*, p. 168.

    With Mountbatten away to London for consultations, Colville was officiating as governor-general.

72. Introduction, p. xvii, *Jinnah Papers*, II. See also 'Introduction', p. xxxiii, ibid., I.
73. Note 3, *CM*, p. 171A.
74. For the text of Jinnah's statement see Appendix V. 14 in *Jinnah Papers*, II. The statement appeared in the *Pakistan Times*, 18 June 1947.
75. Olaf Caroe to Mountbatten, telegram, 21 June 1947, Appendix V. 16, *Jinnah Papers*, II.
76. Olaf Caroe to Mountbatten, telegram, 22 June 1947, Appendix V. 17, ibid.
77. Tendulkar, pp. 445-6, gives the text of Badshah Khan's letter to Gandhi.
78. Mountbatten to Gandhi, 4 July 1947, *Transfer of Power*, XI, Document 496.
79. For the Gandhi-Mountbatten exchanges, Tendulkar, pp. 444-5.
80. Badshah Khan to Gandhi, 12 July 1947, Tendulkar, pp. 445-6. *Inter alia*, Badshah Khan revealed that threats had been held out to the leaders of the Khudai Khidmatgars to the effect that they 'should be done away with'.
81. Fraser Noble, Comments on Draft.
82. Mountbatten to Listowel, 20 July 1947, *Transfer of Power*, XI, Document 187.
83. For Badshah Khan's version, see Tendulkar, pp. 446-7.
84. For a detailed analysis of the results see Gupta, pp. 199-200. 'The ridiculous part of the whole episode', the author concludes, 'was not the tall League claim, but the poor numerical strength behind the decision of the referendum'.
85. Fraser Noble, Comments on Draft.
86. For further details, Fraser Noble, Memoirs, pp. 341-5.
87. Abul Kalam Azad, *Indian Wins Freedom*, p. 170, has charged that the Khan brothers would not offer biscuits to their Pathan visitors and that their tight-fistedness in the use of party funds was 'notorious'.
88. Tendulkar, p. 448.
89. Fraser Noble, Comments on Draft.
90. 'Frontier Referendum', the *Tribune*, 7 June 1947.
91. 'Pathanistan and Balkanisation of India,' the *Tribune*, 15 June 1947.
92. 'Pathanistan', ibid., 21 June 1947.
93. 'Pathans' Demand Must be Conceded', the *Tribune*, 25 June 1947.
94. 'Pathanistan', ibid., 7 July 1947.
95. 'Pathanistan Problem', the *Tribune*, 27 July 1947.
96. 'Pathans' Demand,' ibid., 7 August 1947.
97. Mitchell, Memoirs, p. 267.
98. Lockhart to Mountbatten, 9 July 1947, *Transfer of Power*, XII, Document 45.
99. Fraser Noble, Memoirs, p. 345.
100. 'Minutes of the Viceroy's twenty-third miscellaneous meeting', 29 July 1947, *Transfer of Power*, XII, Document 278.
101. Loc. cit.
102. HM's Minister at Kabul to India, 2 August 1947; Lockhart to Mountbatten, 9 August 1947; Mountbatten to Listowel, 16 August 1947, in *Transfer of Power*, XII, Documents 321, 394 and 488.
103. Mountbatten to Listowel, 8 August 1947, *Transfer of Power*, XII, Document 374.
104. Viceroy's Personal Report No. 16, 8 August 1947, *Transfer of Power*, XII, Document 385.
105. Listowel to Mountbatten, 8 August 1947, *Transfer of Power*, XII, Document 387.
106. Lockhart to Mountbatten, 9 August 1947, *Transfer of Power*, XII, Document 394.
107. Fraser Noble, Memoirs, p. 345.

108. Mountbatten to Liaquat Ali Khan, 10 August 1947, *Transfer of Power,* XII, Document 407.
109. Norval Mitchell, Memoirs, p. 267.
110. For details, see Cunningham Collection, *IOR*, Mss Eur D 670/9. See also Mitchell, pp. 128-30.
111. Lockhart to Mountbatten, 11 August 1947, *Transfer of Power*, XII, Document 433.
112. Mitchell, p. 131.
113. Cunningham to Mountbatten, 14 August 1947, *Transfer of Power*, XII, Document 481.
114. Loc. cit. The letter mentions Cunningham's 'brief note' on his talks 'so far'; the 'note' itself taking the form of an enclosure. For details, *Transfer of Power*, XII, encl. to Document 481.
115. Viceroy's Personal Report No. 17, 16 August 1947, *Transfer of Power*, XII, Document 489.
116. The interview with Khan Sahib took place on the thirteenth evening, immediately after Cunningham was sworn in; with Abdul Qaiyum, on the morning of the fourteenth. Both were 'recorded' on 14 August.
117. *GCD*, 15 August 1947.
118. Ibid., 23 August 1947.
119. Cunningham to Jinnah, 8 September 1947, *IOR*, Cunningham Collection, Mss Eur D 670/23. This was the new Frontier governor's first fortnightly report to Pakistan's governor-general.

CHAPTER 5

The Dramatis Personae

As THE DRAMA unfolds, Sir Olaf Caroe doubtless emerges as the principal actor for his role in the chain of developments that led to the transfer of power in the NWFP. Supporting roles are played by the Khan brothers, especially the elder, Dr Khan Sahib, as well as Nehru and Mountbatten. At a farther remove are the Muslim League and its cohorts with their solid base in the predominantly non-Pakhtun Hazara district. They queered the pitch for the Congress and its ministry, allegedly in an unholy collusion with Sir Olaf. Sir George Cunningham whom Caroe succeeded as the provincial Governor and who, in turn, succeeded him, barring a few weeks' interregnum under General Rob Lockhart, had only peripheral, though by no means unimportant, roles to play.

Sir Olaf Caroe. In opposing Nehru's 'ill-starred visit' to the tribal areas in October 1946, was Sir Olaf acting under extraneous pressures? And in so far as Nehru had refused to heed his advice, vowed to make things a little less than easy for the new member of the governor-general's council? Or, did he, as an honest civil servant, sound a timely warning to his political superior who, for his own good reasons, was constrained not to take notice of it? In retrospect, Caroe was to view Nehru's foray as the 'most important event—fatal to the Congress and to the unity of India', insisting that 'nothing falls into place lacking an appreciation of that event'.

Some of the questions Nehru's visit raised are singularly pertinent. Was Caroe not directly or indirectly responsible for permission to the fire-eating Muslim League propagandist, the Pir of Manki, to tour the tribal areas a week or so ahead of Nehru's visit? Or, for the behaviour of the Political Agents in the tribal agencies on Nehru's itinerary which had left a lot to be desired? And especially of Mahbub Ali Khan, incharge of the Malakand Agency, whose gross neglect of his elementary duty—to escort his visitors safely through his territorial beat—culminated in physical assaults on Nehru and the Khan brothers that may well have proved fatal.

Caroe's explanation that Nehru's one-sided views had to be countered by the Pir of Manki's does not really wash. For one, the tribes were not innocent babes in the wood to be taken in that easily; by and large, they had a mind of their own. But with the Pir sowing the wind, Caroe could no doubt have anticipated the whirlwind Nehru had to reap. As for the political agents, they may well have taken their cue from the known stance of their chief at Peshawar. Nor does Mahbub Ali's later judicial exoneration take away the charge against him of dereliction of duty.

Nehru, on second thoughts, did not press his allegedly 'hot-heated accusations' against the other officials. To be sure, he was characteristically magnanimous and asserted that he was 'not prepared to accuse any officers (excepting one)' whose conduct during his tour he rated to be 'thoroughly discreditable'. But for Mahbub Ali Khan, Nehru had no desire that 'any particular individuals should be held responsible' for any incident. He stoutly denied having levelled any 'general charges' against the officers of the Indian Political Service.

Another facet of Caroe's tenure—and this long before Nehru appeared on the scene—was his singularly unhappy relationship with the provincial premier and his ministerial colleagues whom he accused of interference in judicial processes and wrong-headed administrative policies. A bad beginning that became worse with every passing day. Governor-General Wavell confided in his journal, that Caroe was 'very much on edge' and 'highly strung'. 'He takes things', Wavell continued, 'too hardly and seriously'. Also Caroe and Khan Sahib were 'essentially different types' who were 'not likely to get on well together'.

Wavell had not based his strong views against Mahbub Ali's conduct on mere hearsay. For even though he had not visited Malakand as such, the governor-general had motored by the Malakand pass to Chakdharra at the junction of the Dir and Swat valleys. At the pass, he had looked 'at the scene of the assault on Nehru' and his party and drawn his own independent conclusion that Mahbub Ali's conduct was 'inexcusable'.[1]

It is interesting to note that in August 1947, Khan Sahib confided in Cunningham how bad he had felt in his dealings with Sir Olaf. 'Personally', Cunningham noted, the premier was 'extremely friendly, though he was rather bitter about Olaf'. Khan Sahib divulged that his ministry had for some time 'been inclined to resign' and 'indeed very probably' have done so 'about April (1947)'. But the fact that Caroe 'would obviously have been too glad to get rid of them', made Khan Sahib and his colleagues stay put. 'This', Cunningham noted, 'was illuminating'.[2]

Further complications arose from Caroe's unsolicited advice to his

Premier, Khan Sahib, that to tide over a deteriorating law and order situation in the province where the Muslim League was on the warpath, the latter should loosen his apron strings with the Congress, get rid of his solitary Hindu minister and induct members of the Muslim League into his council of ministers. This was sometime in February-March 1947. Unable to bring the Khan around, the governor swung to the other extreme of recommending the dismissal of his ministry, followed by a spell of governor's rule and holding of fresh elections. His plea was that the party in power had forfeited its popular mandate.

As Caroe saw it, the Khan Sahib ministry, linked to the Congress, and Hindustan, was opposed to Jinnah and the partition advocated by the Quaid. Did it, Caroe wondered, still have, in the developing situation in the first quarter of 1947, the mandate to keep the Pathans out of Pakistan? Nehru held that having been democratically elected at the February 1946 polls, Khan Sahib's position was unassailable; Jinnah, and the League on the other hand believed that the unrest in the province proved otherwise. Nor could the ominous silence of the tribes who had, in October 1946, clearly demonstrated their rejection of Nehru and of Hindustan, be misinterpreted.

The governor's early advice was: a fresh election, preceded by dismissal of the ministry and promulgation of Section 93 rule. Later, Caroe was no doubt made to realise that it was hard to establish a legal case for sacking the ministry while Nehru and his colleagues, under pressure from Mountbatten, were adamant that there could be no election under the duress of the League's civil disobedience and disorder. But with 3 June plan, the right of the Frontier people to make their own choice was conceded. Equally, there could be no question now of Section 93 rule under a governor whose impartiality his ministry challenged implacably.

All this while, the growing rift between the Khan Sahib Ministry and Caroe widened. All that the governor recommended—dismissal of the ministry, promulgation of Section 93 rule, holding of fresh elections—was music to the ears of the Muslim League, and by definition, anathema to the Congress. What better proof was required that the governor was colluding with the Muslim League and sabotaging the incumbent Congress ministry? No wonder, Khan Sahib told the visiting governor-general in April 1947 that the real leader of the Muslim League in the province was not Jinnah 'but His Excellency the Governor', who, he alleged, had stage-managed the massive demonstration Mountbatten had to face, both to impress his visitor as well as browbeat his ministers. The allegation has been dismissed as 'laughable' for quite clearly Caroe had nothing to do either with the demonstration or the arrangements of the local Muslim

League's 'War Council'. The important point though is not that it was 'laughable' but that Caroe's detractors were powerfully persuaded to the contrary.

Caroe's alleged partisanship and his bitter, even hostile, references to Abdul Ghaffar Khan, Nehru and other Congress leaders are evident in his private papers and official reports; as also the support he, overtly, and his officials, covertly, gave to the provincial Muslim League. Mountbatten's official biographer, Philip Zeigler has maintained that Caroe's 'deep knowldege and affection for all things Muslim was reflected' in his attitude towards his ministers and the opposition 'however much be strained to be impartial'.[3] At the same time it is necessary to underline here that anyone else in Caroe's position may not have behaved differently, for as his relations with his political boss in New Delhi deteriorated in the aftermath of the latter's October visit (and the aborted March 1947 sojourn), Weightman, Nehru's British Foreign Secretary in the External Affairs Department, noted on 6 November that Congress are 'gunning for' Olaf Caroe and 'will have him out if they can'. Hence, the combined assault of the Khudai Khidmatgars and the provincial ministry nearer home in Peshawar as well as Nehru and the top Congress hierarchy in New Delhi meant, as Caroe must have viewed it, the blighting of his brilliant service career. Not yet 55, the unmistakable demand now was for his head—on a platter as it were. Badly beleaguered and exposed to strains of an unprecedented character, it is not unlikely that Caroe may have wittingly, or unwittingly, leaned over to the other side. A contemporary observer has stoutly contested this formulation; Sir Fraser Noble holds that Caroe 'may have lost his judgement' but he did *not* 'lean over to the other side' Sadly for Sir Olaf, Khan Sahib and his ministerial colleagues and the entire Congress outfit in the Frontier, and beyond, were strongly convinced that he did.

As to the blighting of his service career, it may be of interest to note that on return home in August 1947, Sir Olaf sounded out the Foreign Office if he could be useful but 'received no encouragement whatever'. Again, the usual privilege of an interview with the king 'was not accorded, at least to myself'. In short, he ruefully concluded, 'all my efforts to secure employment failed'.

Caroe long nursed a grouse that a clear understanding that he would go back to Peshawar, if the Congress lost the referendum, was not honoured. That he was, in fact, a victim of 'sharp practice' and received 'unworthy treatment'. In a personal letter to Sir Olaf written in September 1968, Mitchell confessed that not until he had read Sir George

Cunningham's diaries did he know 'how badly' Caroe had been treated. And recalled 'a mention of the fact' that Mountbatten's conduct in all this was 'unpardonable'.[4]

Archival records also bear out the fact, as has been noticed, that it was the India Office in London who had insisted that Caroe was not to go back to Peshawar while the Raj lasted. For Caroe to resume, Whitehall had argued, 'would be taken as implying that we ourselves believe that Caroe is in favour of the Muslim League and therefore ought not to be in office'. Should Pakistan, however, as a dominion government, advise the king that Caroe 'resume or be reappointed', the situation would be different. Jinnah did not do so, thus, leaving Mountbatten little choice, presuming that the latter wanted to honour the commitment.

Caroe was, Mitchell notes in his Memoirs, 'very casually' treated in all this. The first that he knew came in a letter from the viceroy dated 15 July. He might have received it in Kashmir two or three days later. Cunningham received the offer to resume on 4 July. He wrote in his diary on 12 August: 'was surprised to learn (in Delhi) that it was only last week or so that Olaf Caroe had been told that he would not be coming to Peshawar. He surely ought to have been told as soon as they had decided to ask me, which is now five weeks ago.' Mitchell noted that Cunningham was not told all the dates 'but his main criticism was justified'.[5]

It is interesting to note that Zeigler would have us believe that Caroe held nothing against the governor-general who sacked him. Even though his dismissal 'caused him lasting distress', Caroe's bitterness was transitory for 'any grievance he might have had' against Mountbatten 'quickly passed'. And reproduces a statement with Caroe affirming that to him 'personally, then and later, Mountbatten behaved with honour and dignity, and an attitude that I can only describe as royal'.[6] His first official encounter with Mountbatten (April 1947) resulted in what Zeigler calls 'a somewhat over-emotional condition' for he describes the Viceroy to his wife as the 'Leader of my prayers' whom he 'could follow to the death'.[7]

A logical outcome of Sir Olaf's alleged solicitude for the Muslim League would have been his restoration at Peshawar. On the eve, if not the morrow, of the transfer of power. Somehow this happy ending to an otherwise stormy interlude never came to pass for Jinnah asked for the re-induction of George Cunningham, *not* the re-installation of Olaf Caroe.

The Quaid's behaviour and choice continued to rattle Caroe no end even long after the dust had settled down on the traumatic events of 1947. Thus, more than two decades later, sometimes in the third week of September 1968, the former governor wrote to Iskander Mirza as well as

From Lord Ismay, Wormington Grange, Broadway, to the writer's wife, 2nd April 1955

My dear Kitty,

Thank you so much for telling me about Olaf's return to the land we loved. It has made me so happy, because it proves that the Pakistan Government, quite apart from wanting the history of Pathans written by the man who could do it best, are anxious to make amends to one who was sacrificed on the altar of political expediency. What a nightmare it was to see the things we gave our life to - broken. But perhaps it was all for the best? England was no longer interested in India, and successive British Governments had played their hand very badly.

Anyway I like to think of Olaf at the ~~hand~~ head of the ~~tiller~~ table in G.H. Peshawar. That is exactly as it should be.

I am home on a short Easter holiday. We return to Paris tomorrow. We are having a pretty rough time there in the way of insoluble problems: and I shall be glad when I am allowed to retire.

Love from us both,

Yours ever,

Pug

Sir Olaf Caroe's Mss. (Appendix).

Norval Mitchell posing more or less the same question. Jinnah did not know Sir George Cunningham and had known Sir Olaf pretty closely as a member of the governor-general's top civil advisers, being Foreign Secretary and incharge of the conduct of New Delhi's foreign affairs during all the years of World War II. The Quaid himself being then leader of the increasingly important Muslim League Party in the Central Legislative Assembly where, thanks to the Congress committing political harakiri, Jinnah's star shone ever brighter. Caroe asked Mirza who, in 1947, was 'in touch with affairs', why Jinnah had asked for Cunningham's 'return' to the province and not opted for Caroe?

Sir Olaf was posing more or less the same question to Norval Mitchell then engaged in writing a biography of Sir George Cunningham: why was he treated the shabby way he was, by the former governor-general. The two answers were, by and large, on similar lines. After a better acquaintance with Cunningham's diaries, Mitchell thought Mountbatten's conduct in all this was 'unpardonable'.

Mirza too sounded the same note. Mountbatten, 'no friend' of Caroe's, was 'guided more by Nehru than by anybody else.' The Muslim League too had ratted on Caroe. 'I told the late Liaquat Ali Khan', Mirza confessed, 'of your great qualities and urged . . . that you should go back as Governor'. Also the Muslim League was 'honour bound' to insist on Caroe's reinduction as Governor at Peshawar. Sadly though, Mirza added: 'But believe me there was no honour then or later.'

It may be of interest to recall that Caroe's health and more especially the mental strains to which he was exposed, were so patently obvious to every visitor to the Government House in Peshawar—Wavell, Ismay, Mountbatten. It also finds frequent mention in a number of official communications. Mirza noted that 'even before you went to Kashmir (June 1947), stories were going round that you had a nervous breakdown and required rest'.[8] Mirza apart, another friend it appears had pleaded for Caroe. Thus, in a letter to Jinnah, Major Sahibzada Mohammad Khurshid, then Political Agent in the Khyber, intimated that he proposed to write 'a brief note' on the future of the Tribal Areas of both the NWFP and Baluchistan which he would give to Caroe who 'unlike some of his countrymen is, in my opinion, straight, sympathetic, fair-minded and a good friend'.[9]

In the light of the League's debt to him, as Iskander Mirza put it, Jinnah's final decision in turning down Caroe's choice for governorship at Peshawar, sounds not a little harsh. On the face of it, it tantamounts to an almost complete turn around on the part of the Quaid and such advisors as he may have deigned to consult. While there is no clue in terms of any concrete or conclusive evidence, a guess or two may be hazarded. Firstly, Sir Olaf was useful to the Muslim League precisely in the degree and to the extent he had become anathema to the Congress. He represented in his person the principal target of attack by the Khan Sahib ministry in the province as well as Nehru from his high pedestal in New Delhi. Not to mention the entire Congress component of the interim government and the party machine, both in and outside the Frontier.

A measure of the Congress Party's gross misunderstanding of Caroe's alleged pro-League bias may be gauged from the fact that Jinnah and his cohorts did not trust him either. Thus, the editor of *Jinnah Papers* makes no secret of what he views as Caroe's subversive role, maintaining that Abdul Ghaffar Khan and the Congress Ministry in the NWFP had 'at the instance of Governor Sir Olaf Caroe . . . mounted a counter-attack on the League'. Their weapon: 'a threat of provincial independence and their method a propaganda campaign for the Pathan state, a Pathan national Province'. This appeal

> to ethnicity to forge political union, Caroe contended, was a 'far more constructive one than that of Islam in danger' and was in fact suggested by Caroe himself . . . . The propaganda of this Pathanistan alternative to Pakistan was another threat to the ideological foundations of the Pakistan ideal.[10]

The editor's charge would appear to be valid for there is no denying that Caroe had indeed lauded this move for an independent Pathan entity and been mounting pressure on Khan Sahib and his colleagues that they come out openly for it. And long before they actually did. Would it perhaps be nearer the truth to say that Caroe suffered from a split personality. His head, for all that the leadership of the Frontier Congress, and AGK, stood for; his heart though for the Muslim League and its ragtag of cronies whom he had often reviled and described as that 'miserable crew'. Did he perhaps do it out of spite for the Congress—and Nehru, his *bete noire*—who had little liking for him and trusted him even less?

No wonder that when his long-awaited resignation was announced, the *Tribune* commented that it was 'a step in the right direction'. And reiterated its oft-repeated view that the history of the NWFP would have been 'differently written' if Sir Olaf had not been at the helm of affairs. For 'much communal mischief' had taken place when he held office.[11] Khan Sahib too was to charge Sir Olaf with having acted 'as a partisan' against the Congress in every way. He recalled that to start with, Caroe 'much tried to frighten' his Ministry to resign 'by staging a Muslim League show'; when this failed, he raised the question of Section 93 rule in the province. And leaked out all information to the League before his government received it, thereby enabling that party to carry on its violent agitation. Even 'the imposition of this referendum' was the 'doing' of Sir Olaf for he had 'deliberately misled' all officials both in Peshawar as well as New Delhi.[12]

The Governor mouthed wittingly or otherwise, all that the League wanted in the province: dismissal of the Khan Sahib ministry, Governor's rule *ad interim*, a fresh appeal to the electorate. To the extent the Congress Party tom-tomed his recall, the League equally vociferously insisted that he be kept where he was. This is amply borne out by Liaquat Ali Khan's loud and angry outburst when Mountbatten finally relieved Caroe of his post. The moment however a referendum was decided upon—and once the Congress party had accepted it in Syhlet, it could not deny it to the electorate in the NWFP—and won, there was no need to pay debts, assuming that such had been incurred.

Additionally, it needs hardly to be emphasised that Khan Sahib and his Ministry had, on the morrow of the referendum, become for all to see, politically impotent. If also anachronistic, redundant, even irrelevant. There was now no need for a Caroe to keep them on the leash as it were. Cunningham had a saner, sounder reputation. He had the healing touch. Could he not, Jinnah may well have argued, be more useful. Cunningham could persuade a recalcitrant Khan Sahib to see the light; in any case, he was free from the anti-Khan Sahib taint with which Caroe was so thickly tarred. Hence, the decision to recall him and let Caroe into the limbo of oblivion. Surely, the latter had played his part in bringing the realisation of Pakistan nearer; but once that had been achieved, he was no longer needed.

Mirza had noted that on the eve of the transfer of power in New Delhi, Caroe had been painted by one and all as 'pretty ill—and exhausted', a suggestion Sir Olaf was stoutly to repudiate later. That he 'had a breakdown in health', he affirmed, 'was untrue'. None the less it is more than likely that this bit of information about the state of his health had permeated to the top echelons among the League leadership. Hence the latter's decision not to employ one who was known to be ill. The decision must no doubt have come as a rude shock to Caroe but not altogether unjustified from the point of view of Pakistan's rulers.

Caroe had maintained that Pakhtunistan was not 'really a new Congress policy evolved during the Viceroy's visit (April 1947)'. And that Khan Sahib's government did not 'ever contemplate' a Pakhtunistan 'embracing the Pathans of Afghanistan'. His 'own belief' was that 'betrayed' by

Nehru's agreement to a vote being taken, the Khan brothers 'fell back on a fanciful support for some sort of Pathan independence' as a reason for boycotting the referendum. As for himself, he had pressed for a fresh election: 'the idea of a referendum was hatched in New Delhi and was *not* mine' (emphasis added). He never discovered whose it was: 'The probability is that it was easier to obtain Nehru's agreement to a referendum than to an election, when my Provincial Government still had a majority in the Legislature'.[14]

To be fair to him, Caroe's solution of the Frontier imbroglio bore not so much a pro-Pakistani, as a pro-Pathan imprint. As he visualised it, the Pathans of the settled districts, in conjunction with the tribes outside, may yet constitute a viable political entity which, with some vague institutional support from Whitehall, need not have fallen into the Indian, much less the Pakistani lap. It may be recalled that on the eve of the transfer of power some such plan was seriously debated in so far as the two parts of Bengal, and the north-east frontier areas, were concerned.

That Caroe's scheme was not altogether illusory is evident from the fact that some time in June 1947, Khan Sahib and the entire Khudai Khidmatgar outfit in the Frontier owned it up, albeit in a slightly modified form. By then, however, it was a little too late. The sweep of the Pakistan tide was by now so irresistible that all counsels of reason or moderation were at severe discount.

This should also perhaps explain Caroe's assessment that the Congress in the Frontier was so 'unnatural'; a variant no doubt on the theme of Ismay's 'bastard situation'. The harsh truth was that in the sharp political and communal polarisation in the province in the wake of the Hazara and D I Khan riots, the Congress found itself at a loose end. Later, the fact that the party's stand on the issue of a referendum was so ambivalent and even confused only goes to show how the leadership itself had lost its nerve and was incapable either of giving a fight or taking a coherent stand. The boycott decision itself was an admission of political bankruptcy. Then, as to some even now, Caroe's verdict may have sounded harsh, but was perhaps not that unfair.

Sir Olaf more than once gave eloquent expression to the view that in handing over charge of tribal affairs to Nehru, Wavell made a grave error of judgment. It was, he confessed later, the beginning of all his subsequent troubles. Repeatedly he had counselled New Delhi that the charge be revoked. Later, Mountbatten was to express much the same view with the difference that while a reversal of gears was impossible, the matter should have at the very outset been scrutinised with greater care. On inquiry, however, he was told that any attempt to separate the external affairs department from the charge of tribal matters would have led to difficulties and even a breakdown of the arrangements for the induction into office of the interim government.[15]

In a detailed personal note 'From 1947 On' written long after the heat and dust had settled down on his traumatic tenure, Caroe heavily underlined the point that it was his handling of tribal affairs during 1946-7 that alone ensured a peaceful transition in the Frontier. 'If there had been tribal disorder', the transfer of power may have 'proved impossible'. Again, but for the test of opinion in the referendum there may have been '(a) civil war in the province, (b) tribal invasions as in 1930, (c) probably an Afghan invasion, (d) a failure to carry through the transfer of power in 1947, and possibly even in 1948 or later'.

Caroe was convinced in his own mind of the important role he had played in a smooth transfer of power in the Frontier. Apart from heavily underlining this in his letter of resignation and in the personal note alluded to in the preceding paragraph he rarely lost an opportunity to lay stress on it. Patting his own back apart, he was no less keen that such compliments should come from others. This is amply borne out by Norval Mitchell's assurance that he would have a hard look at his draft of Sir George Cunningham's biography

> and try to make it quite clear (and I am most sincere in this) with what fortitude and distinction you bore the burden of those almost intolerable years.[16]

Mitchell kept his word. And in his slender volume on George Cunningham, wrote of Caroe the following: 'His period of office was marked by an extraordinary degree of fortitude and distinction during a period of political and civil convulsion such that many might think that earth's foundations had fled.' This, Mitchell recorded many years later in his memoirs, 'was and remains my personal view of his achievement'.

Earlier in an exchange of mutual back scratching with Mountbatten in 1950, the former governor-general wrote to Caroe to say that 'of all the Governors of India you (Caroe) had the most difficult job and the most thankless task', and complimented him for the 'magnificent way' in which he had behaved in the 'difficult circumstances' in which Mountbatten had been placed. More specifically 'if you had not behaved as a very great gentleman and made it easy for me by allowing a temporary *locum tenens* to come during the Referendum, I would never have got it through'.[17]

That Caroe's fears of the tribal situation were not altogether imaginary is borne out by some harsh ground realities. The serious troubles in Hazara, in February, followed by unprecedented disturbances in D I Khan and Tank, in mid-April, had been responsible, as in the neighbouring districts of the Panjab, for large-scale destruction of property and massive loss of life and limb. The whole of northern India was on the verge of civil war. Caroe's greatest worry may well have been that if the troops had to use their fire power freely against Muslims in the settled districts, the tribes would rise in mass revolt. Fortunately, they kept their counsel, and their heads. The Fakir of Ipi seemed uncertain what he should proclaim: his enemy had always been the British! When he kept his cool, tribal voices, influenced no doubt by the Pir of Manki, hinted that he, i.e. Ipi, had been in the pay of the Congress Party all along! The Afridis decided to stand back to drive a hard bargain *after* the Partition; confident that the Hindus were no longer in the reckoning. Their lead influenced other tribes; some vague consultations followed, though no united front emerged. From the perspective of mid-April 1947, however, all this was still uncertain. Hence, the governor's fears of the tribal dimension of the problem may not have been unjustified.

Stoutly repudiating the charge that he was a partisan, Caroe had maintained that 'had he really been' one, Khan Sahib and Iskander Mirza may not have arranged his visit to the Frontier as a state guest in 1956.

Mountbatten disbelieved entirely the accusation that Caroe was a 'League propagandist'. So does the Swedish scholar Jansson who is convinced that Caroe's views and aims 'were basically contrary to what he has been accused of: he was not in favour of Pakistan; he was opposed to partition . . . he preferred the Khan brothers to the Muslim League leaders'.[18]

In 1946, Caroe had not only bemoaned the passing away of tribal affairs, and therefore vital problems of the Frontier, to Congress (read Hindu) control but also the handing over of the defence portfolio to a non-Muslim which had compounded the initial error. In retrospect, it may seem a curious way of looking at things, typical of the thinking of top British bureaucrats on the eve of the transfer of power. It tied up with another fond hope that Caroe and his friends entertained, namely that HMG would have a role to play in the future political setup of the Frontier in general, and its tribal areas in particular. That events outpaced him was neither his fault nor yet his failing, for Olaf Caroe's tragedy was not that of an individual; a whole system, an entire structure had given way.

Dr Khan Sahib's role during this entire span of two years though seemingly pivotal remains somewhat shadowy. Few, including Olaf Caroe, questioned his outstanding human qualities: his fresh, boyish charm; his fearless, manly courage; his steadfast adherence to political loyalties and affiliations. What has been held against him was his alleged lack of administrative capacity; a singular absence, as Wavell put it, of the 'necessary force of character or wisdom to run a province'.

On his interview with Khan Sahib (14 November 1946), the viceroy noted that the premier's 'whole theme was that the governor and the British officials were not supporting him and the government'. His accusations though, Wavell recorded, 'were completely vague, he did not name anyone'. Mountbatten too took note of Dr Khan Sahib's incessant complaints against his officials; so had George Cunningham. In retrospect, it is necessary to recall that Congress ministers—and not in the Frontier alone—were anathema to the upper echelons of the Raj's bureaucracy. Again, under the Government of India Act 1935, the higher public services which were the special responsibility of the provincial governor could have been anything but friendly to the Congress ministers, much less cooperated with them.

Sir George Cunningham clearly felt that Khan Sahib was not only extremely honest but also understood properly the problems of the tribes and the difficulties they could create for any government in the NWFP, whether British or Indian. By 1945, it would appear, he was in favour of 'withdrawal', under agreement—being always conscious that the tribes had special rights under treaty with the British government. Had Cunningham not retired in early 1946, he and Khan Sahib would have cooperated sensibly in working towards what eventually transpired in relations between the tribes and the government of Pakistan. But by that time, Khan Sahib's position had become very difficult and it was not made easier by the pressures from Abdul Ghaffar Khan and, of course, Pandit Nehru. Ideally, by 1946, certainly, by 1947, Khan Sahib would have been working towards some sort of a viable arrangement, a *modus vivendi* with the Muslim League. The latter, however, was *not* in good shape in the Frontier, and as men like Liaquat Ali Khan and Firoz Khan Noon understood, badly in need of reform.

One of Jinnah's correspondents lambasted Khan Sahib for 'stooping to low and mean tactics' in accusing the Quaid of arguing well 'in the imperialist corrupt code where justice is done to the poor man'. He forgets, she alleged, his 'right-hand hand (*sic*)', Mehr Chand Khanna, 'who had lived under the corrupt Mahasabhaite code' and was now the 'brain' of the Frontier Congress. She charged that Khanna had 'drowned the Pathans under his own dictation (*sic*)'. 'It's a pity', she lamented, that the Pathans 'should be so losing their balance under the fast approaching avalanche of the League's strength'.[19]

Jinnah and his correspondent apart, nobody ever doubted Khan Sahib's integrity; it was, George Cunningham noted, the source of his remarkable political stature. He was 'uniquely incorruptible', though his judgement may have been swayed by personal prejudices and pressures. 'A bluff agreeable man, he could reveal' flashes of Pathan temper; a much firmer, stronger character than the suave, deferential and equally friendly, Aurangzeb Khan, his Muslim League predecessor. But Khan Sahib did not strike one 'as being either sharp or particularly intelligent'. He certainly 'could not match in debate' the lawyers who were so prolific in Frontier politics: Qazi Ataullah or Abdul Qaiyum or even Aurangzeb Khan or Sardar Bahadur, the Haripur lawyer whose brother General Ayub was to become the President of Pakistan.

Khan Sahib was very allergic to any cohabitation with the Frontier Muslim League either on the eve, or even the morrow of the formation of Pakistan. That he had spurned such suggestions under Olaf Caroe has been noted earlier. Here it is instructive to recall that a little after a week of his return to Peshawar, George Cunningham recorded that while 'many of the more thinking members' of the Muslim League 'would still like a coalition' with the Congress, Khan Sahib was 'adamant against serving' with any League ministers.

His later years though would suggest a propensity to wheeling-dealing at the cost of political principles and life-long political loyalties. Thus, as early as October 1954, Khan Sahib had mended his fences with Pakistan's rulers to emerge as a minister in Chaudhari Mohammed Ali's cabinet. Later, in close conjunction with Iskander Mirza who was to take over as Governor-General, Khan Sahib lent his support to the one-unit West Pakistan scheme under which he was to be its Chief Minister for a little over two years (April 1955–July 1957). He also launched his short-lived Republican party. Abdul Ghaffar Khan and people of his persuasion were vehemently opposed to the new political configuration as being grossly unfair to the Frontier. For his pains, Badshah Khan was prosecuted and placed behind bars by the Khan Sahib government!

Another facet of Khan Sahib's place in the scheme of things is to recall that, in sharp contrast to his younger brother, he does not appear to have played any significant role in the Khudai Khidmatgar movement. It is doubtful if outside of legislative politics, he had or cultivated much of a rapport with the masses. Cunningham alluded to his proforma allegiance to the Red Shirts while a secret Pakistani document in the 1950s would appear to suggest that his political clout, such as it was, derived exclusively from Badshah Khan: 'If the two brothers stay together, they will have a united strength. If they are separated, Khan Abdul Ghaffar Khan will retain his position, whereas Dr Khan Sahib will pass into eclipse because individually he has no position'.[20] This is borne out by Gandhi's own assessment as early as June 1947. Informed by the Sardar who was then Member for Home (and thereby privy to all intelligence) that in his considered view, Badshah Khan's influence in Frontier 'was on the wane', Gandhi retorted that he had 'no such impression' and that there was 'in fact more steadiness' in his position than ever before. He also felt that Khan Sahib and his colleagues 'would be nowhere' without the Badshah, for 'he (Badshah Khan) alone counts so far as the Congress influence is concerned'.

George Cunningham's obituary note on Khan Sahib makes for a glowing tribute. He was, the former governor noted, 'prominent' among his fellows, and 'upright, straightforward and warm-hearted'. He was 'incorruptible' and worked above all 'for the good of his people' and would brook no 'disturbance to law and order'.[21]

Cunningham thought that Khan Sahib took to politics 'rather unwillingly' and never coveted office 'for office's sake'. Above all, he would be remembered for 'his courtesy, good humour and integrity'.

Olaf Caroe recorded that Khan Sahib often spoke to him of the compulsion under which his affection for George Cunningham placed him in difficult days. 'On a light note when trouble arose, the Governor would invite his Wazir to a game of bridge, and smooth out roughness, by losing the hand'.[22]

A charge against Khan Sahib that needs to be taken seriously was his, and his younger brother's, inability to adjust to a fast-changing scenario. Thus, in the mounting communal polarisation in the Frontier in the months following the Hazara riots, the Muslim League propagandists in general, and the Pir of Manki in particular, had mounted a vicious campaign to paint the two brothers as betrayers of their faith, and their heritage, to the Hindus. To give it substance they pointed to the two-some allowing their children to marry outside Islam: Khan Sahib's daughter, Mariam, to an Indian Christian boy; AGK's son, Ghani, to a Parsi lady. This, in the eyes of the true believers, was blasphemy. To the 'explosive' Khan Sahib, the charge was so patently ridiculous and unreal, that he swore as it were to refuse to parley or have anything to do with those who made it. He, thus, remained strangely 'blind and obdurate' in a developing situation 'that called for insight and imagination'.

The same would seem to hold true for AGK. Closely aligned to the Mahatma and his mystique, he yet failed to appreciate that the latter's influence counted for little among the Congress high command in the crucial decisions leading to the Partition. The fact was that when it came to the crunch, the Mahatma, their lip sympathy notwithstanding, had been more than once disowned by his own flock. On independence day, Gandhi found himself not so much at the heart, and hub, of things as cast out on a limb as it were: he was in far away Calcutta healing the wounds of communal fracas! The harsh truth is that it was not Badshah Khan alone (or his Khudai Khidmatgars) who was 'thrown to the wolves'. So indeed was his political and ideological mentor!

Abdul Ghaffar Khan's part in this brief interregnum though indirect was by no means unimportant. Then, as later in life, Badshah Khan did not measure up to the stereotype of a politician, for, not unlike the Mahatma—and the sobriquet of Frontier Gandhi was neither ill-deserved nor yet inappropriate—his politics were suffused with a singularly unalloyed dedication to the cause of honesty and truth as he perceived them. All through life, he remained powerfully convinced that the real solution to the Frontier's problems lay not in ganging up with the rag-tag of time-servers who constituted the provincial Muslim League—a course of action Jinnah had strongly urged on him both prior to and even more forcefully after Pakistan's birth—but in standing up for the rights of the Pathans to carve out their own independent identity. This was by no means outside the territorial domain of Pakistan.

Badshah Khan's assessment of Caroe's role in subverting the authority of the provincial government was no different from that of Khan Sahib or Nehru's for that matter. He too added his own powerful voice for the Governor's recall.

One of Jinnah's correspondents accused the Frontier Gandhi of organising the 'Zalme Pakhtun', the 'armed army of the province, whereas in the same breath he talks of non-violence'.[23] Echoing her, it may be noted that the editor of *Jinnah's Papers* has described the 'ZP' as 'a militant organisation raised by Abdul Ghaffar Khan to counter' the Muslim League in the province.[24] Badshah Khan, it must be remembered had made it abundantly clear that the 'ZP' which had been founded *not* by him but his son Ghani had 'no connection' with his own Khudai Khidmatgars. Even though it was a 'direct reaction' to the violent movement then being pursued by the Muslim League in the Frontier, the object of the outfit was 'to defend and not to offend'. The 'ZP' volunteers believed in violence, wore deep red uniforms and carried firearms.[25]

Later it was Abdul Ghaffar Khan who forcefully pleaded that Pakhtunistan offered an ideal solution to the problems of the Frontier. Sadly, in the frenetic activity and the breathless pace of events in the few months preceding the partition, the demand came with a certain unseemly haste, and was, to start with at any rate, vaguely defined. Understandably, this lack of clarity was seized upon by its detractors who charged that it implied an indirect if devious way of demanding accession to India. Here it is necessary to underline that Badshah Khan refused to kowtow to the compulsions which Nehru faced *vis-a-vis* the holding of a referendum and, despite the latter's forceful advocacy that he take part in it, opted for a boycott. Any participation, Badshah Khan ruled, would be tantamount to a betrayal of all that he and his Khudai Khidmatgars stood for: the circumstances leading to it and the issues raised were 'essentially communal in their nature'. The irony was the greater in that long dubbed as Hindus and Hindu agents, 'now when we have refused to join Hindustan, we are forced to fight the referendum on the issue of Pakistan versus Hindustan.'

A political analyst has underscored the point that Nehru's views on the referendum, based on Mountbatten's advice, would have led to the 'political isolation and virtual liquidation' of the Khudai Khidmatgars among the Pathans. Sensing this fatal conspiracy against them, Badshah Khan 'refused to swallow the bait'.[26]

A recent biographer has charged that both Badshah Khan (as well as Abul Kalam Azad) were 'neither consulted nor informed' before the Congress rejected the Cabinet Mission plan for a united India and accepted the partition which had a 'direct bearing' on the future of the Pathans.[27] Such a 'disgraceful treatment' of two topmost nationalist leaders exposed Congress 'pretensions' of representing the Muslims of India. In so far as he held Congress responsible for 'throwing him to the wolves' and 'not intimidating' Pakistan over the issue of Pathanistan—Badshah Khan too was guilty of 'lacking enough courage' to stand up to Gandhi and Nehru, of 'suppressing his conscience' when he should have been 'outspoken' and of 'becoming eloquent' when it was too late.

Again, the work in question would have us believe that Congress emissaries approached the Afghan government 'to extend active support' to the Khan brothers' campaign for 'the independent state of Pakhtunistan' and that there was 'a sinister design' to secure Kashmir 'as part of border (broader?) strategy' covering Kashmir and the NWFP. In other words, Kashmir was to be used as 'a backdoor' to reach the Congress-dominated

NWFP. 'Had Badshah Khan publicly denounced these secret contacts' between Kabul and the Congress, 'he would have proved his bona fides'. Sadly though the contacts 'bacame more intimate and sinister in the days to come', while the Khan kept his counsel.

On a closer scrutiny both charges fail. Badshah Khan was fully in the picture both in regard to the Cabinet Mission and the Congress Party's decision to accept the partition which, for the record, he opposed. More, as has been noticed earlier, there appear to have been no Congress emissaries to Kabul.[28]

Those who have accused Abdul Ghaffar Khan of betraying Pakistan's interests or being less then loyal to the new nation do him grave injustice and are, in fact, grossly unfair. His movement, they have charged, was secessionist and would have led to Pakistan's dismemberment. The harsh truth is that Badshah Khan's was a 'modern' nationalist movement with its own ideology inextricably linked to a reform programme for the Pakhtun people, as distinct from the Pakhtun movement in the tribal areas which was 'only a matter of the same traditional tribal divisions and groupings as before and the same old political horse trading which now appeared in yet another form'.[29] Badshah Khan's Pakhtunistan, it should be obvious, did not constitute a threat to the integrity of Pakistan for it envisaged no extraterritorial loyalties. It received significance only because it was exploited by others.

The fact is that those who supported the Khan brothers' cause, and there were not a few, were mystified by their sudden, and not easily explained shift to the cause of Pakhtunistan. All out of the blue, it appeared, Badshah Khan and his men who had sworn their honour by a united India for almost a quarter century now adopted a cause that repudiated it without qualification. Men of honour appeared to be 'turncoats'. The Quaid denounced the new demand as both 'insidious and spurious . . . a new stunt invented to mislead the people'.[30] Sadly, for Pakhtunistan, few had the inclination, much less the patience, to assess it on its merits. Time had almost run out and the atmosphere far too surcharged for any cool consideration. No wonder, there were few takers for the new idea. In the context of June-July 1947, Mitchell thought the slogan was 'meaningless'.[31]

It is interesting to recall an entry in Cunningham's diary inscribed shortly after his meeting (15 February 1939) with Abdul Ghaffar Khan (who had, for the first time since 1931, met a British official): 'My rough impression . . . on this short acquaintance, is that his chief object is generally the social and economic improvement of the Pathan; that he is not bitter against the individual British officer, though he dislikes our system of government—not unlike the South Irish.'

The tragedy of Abdul Ghaffar Khan's life (d. 1988), and Caroe's brief interregnum of 15 odd months marks a watershed of sorts in his long and eventful span of almost a century, lay in that he was far ahead of his times. The British had no use for him—in the privacy of his confidential reports, Caroe referred to him as 'that idiot Abdul Ghaffar Khan'—nor did Jinnah and his successors. No wonder for long spells—longer even than of his Raj gaolers—they kept him behind bars without even the fig leaf of a trial. And on the morrow of the birth of the new state banned the Khudai Khidmatgar movement and hounded its individual members in a shameless vendetta that knows few parallels in political persecution. The end-result was there for all to see—an alienated Frontier whose proud Pathans have added their mite to Pakistan's myriad other problems. If only the 'idiot' had been respected and understood and listened to!

Nehru's multifaceted personality with all its charm and vitality suffered from some crippling flaws. One such was his emotional attachment to men and situations which defied all cool-headed, rational analyses. A case in point was the hangover of decades of empty rhetoric fed on imaginary scenarios about the tribes of the NWFP. They conjured up a romantic vision of brave men whom the Raj had grievously wronged, and who were only too keen to hug and embrace its political legatees. No wonder that on the morrow of his assumption of office, and against the better judgement of his colleagues including Azad, the Sardar and the Mahatma—and in the face of the not-so-dishonest advice of the local functionary—Nehru launched on his luckless tour.

In extenuation though, it is only fair to underline that the bombing of the Shabi Khel in Waziristan in retaliation for the abduction of the political agent and his party (June 1946)—almost synchronised with the swearing in of Nehru's government. His detractors in general, and the Muslim League in particular, blamed him squarely for this barbaric act of aerial bombardment. The first news, it would appear, was relayed to him by Badshah Khan who, as well as his own officials in New Delhi, now suggested that Nehru undertake a tour of the tribal areas to familiarise himself with the ground realities and judge things for himself. It is hard to imagine anyone in similar circumstances reacting differently.

Sadly for him, his hopes—that the tribes, enthused by the threshold of independence to which he beckoned, were but waiting for his words of wisdom—were rudely belied. Preceding his visit, the fire-eating Pir of Manki had no doubt sown the wind and raised the ante but clearly this time round his tour was limited to the Afridi strongholds in the Peshawar area while hostility to Nehru appeared fairly widespread, including among others, the Wazirs and the Mahsuds. Nor was Sir Olaf exactly friendly. All in all, it was clear that the tribes were far from responsive to the pep talk Nehru and the Khan brothers gave them. To be fair to them, the Raj's political intrigues and manoeuvrings apart, the tribes were less than sure of Nehru's own *bona fides*. The fact that he was a non-Muslim also did not go well with them. All told, a bad situation had been made worse for him as no doubt for the already beleaguered Khan Sahib and his ministerial colleagues. Nor was there to be any retrieval in the months to come. Nehru's first visit to the Frontier, after assumption of office, was to prove his last.

His strong advocacy of the Frontier Congress taking part in the referendum needs a word by way of explanation. Boycott, Nehru was convinced, was 'not an easy weapon' because 'to fight democratically and be defeated', did not weaken a movement for long. But 'to give up without a struggle' meant a 'certain lack of integrity through fear of consequences'. On the more pragmatic level, since the Congress had committed itself to the 'fullest freedom and help' to the Frontier people—a vote for India 'would mean a vote for self-determination and freedom; it would recognise the urges for Pathanistan and yet afford an opportunity to participate in the referendum'.

Besides, there was a good prospect of winning—Mountbatten and Caroe had rated the chances to be 50 : 50; Khan Sahib, we are told, was convinced of carrying the day. But even if we lost by a small margin, Nehru argued, 'We would have struck a big blow at Pakistan'. Sadly, in the Frontier at any rate, there were few takers for his line of reasoning. Outside, even Gandhi was not convinced. He posed Nehru the all-important question: 'Would it be wrong if you insisted that referendum would be wrong without the presentation of the picture of Pakistan?' With Jinnah refusing to oblige and Nehru in a 'no win' situation, Gandhi's plaintive cry appears to have elicited no response!

Mountbatten's part in the Frontier drama is at best peripheral. His was a difficult, seemingly impossible task to reconcile diametrically opposite positions. Caroe was not far wrong in suggesting that his ministry's popular base had fast eroded. It indeed had. But its dismissal, imposition of Section 93 rule and holding of fresh elections did not offer the panacea the governor visualised. Nor was this course of action, with its dubious legal and constitutional validity, without grave risk to the peace of the province. The compromise finally wrought was far from satisfactory. But given a situation where all initiative was fast slipping away, the referendum was perhaps the only way out. Put differently, Mountbatten accepted the core of Caroe's policy—of testing the political waters afresh—and made the Congress toe his line by getting rid of Caroe. A measure of the governorgeneral's success may be gauged from the fact that his approach to the Frontier won the complete confidence of Nehru who in his 'Note on the Situation in the NWFP' of 8 June 1947, talked unabashedly of the viceroy's 'sincerity and bona fides and his desire to do the right thing' and 'go ahead in the right direction'. In striking contrast was Badshah Khan who hated John Bull for the latter's allegedly diabolic designs against his beloved Pathans and told the viceroy as much in an interview given in May 1947: 'How to trust you when I see your crooked dealings in the Frontier Province?'

It should also perhaps bear mention that the third choice demanded by the Frontier Gandhi and his cohorts did not offer a viable alternative. Jinnah's refusal to reconsider the question apart, it would have opened a Pandora's box—in Bengal no less than in Assam. Clearly, Nehru and his colleagues could not have it both ways—eat their cake and have it too. The Khan brothers' later charge that the Congress threw them to the wolves was legitimate and, on the face of it, perfectly valid. Sadly, for the party leadership, in the political configurations of June-July 1947, there was hardly any choice. Or, was there?

NOTES

1. *Wavell's Journal,* entry for 13 November 1946, p. 377.
2. *GCD,* 15 August 1947.
3. Philip Zeigler, *Mountbatten: The Official Biography,* Fontana, Paperback, 1988, p. 376.
4. Mitchell to Caroe, 23 September 1968. For the text see Appendix 5.
5. Norval Mitchell, Memoirs, p. 270.
6. Zeigler ascribes this to Caroe's unpublished memoir, Zeigler, *Mountbatten,* p. 377. The Caroe Mss, in the author's possession, makes no such mention!
7. Caroe's letter to his wife, 20 April 1947, cited in ibid, p. 376.
8. For details see Iskander Mirza to Caroe, 26 September 1968, Appendix 5, pp. 321-3.
9. 'Private' letter to M.A. Jinnah, 14 June 1947, *Jinnah Papers,* II, No. 108.
10. *Jinnah Papers,* I,1, Introduction, p. xxxiii,
11. The *Tribune,* 21 June 1947.

12. Ibid., 9 July 1947.
13. *CM*, p. 179A.
14. Caroe's 'Note on Norval Mitchell's draft on N.W. Frontier Events in 1946-47', p. 4. Elsewhere Caroe noted that the decision on the referendum 'may not have been unconnected with the concurrent determination to have a change' of governor. *CM*, p. 166A.
15. Mountbatten Report, Part A, para 88.
16. Mitchell to Caroe, 23 September 1968. For the text, see Appendix 5.
17. Mountbatten to Caroe, 30 June 1950. (Caroe's letter of 29 June is referred to but not reproduced.) Listed at No. 16 in the Epilogue to *CM* ('A Price for Freedom').
18. Jansson, p. 215.
19. Mrs K L Rallia Ram to M A Jinnah, 10 May 1947, in *Jinnah Papers*, I, 1, No. 403.
20. Cited in Tendulkar, p. 511.
21. Norval Mitchell, *George Cunningham*, pp. 159-60.
22. Ibid., p. 163.
23. Mrs K L Rallia Ram to M A Jinnah, 12 May 1947, *Jinnah Papers*, I, 1, No. 411.
24. Ibid., n. 4.
25. Tendulkar, p. 418.
26. Baren Ray, 'Pakhtun National Movement and Transfer of Power in India', in Amit Kumar Gupta (ed.) *Myth and Reality: The Struggle for Freedom in India,* New Delhi, 1987, pp. 225-65.
27. M S Korejo, *The Frontier Gandhi: His Place in History,* Karachi, 1994.
28. For more details see Parshotam Mehra, 'He is reviled even after death' (a review of Korejo's book), the *Tribune*, 12 May 1996.
29. Jansson, p. 238
30. Revised Draft of the Press statement by M A Jinnah, 28 June 1947, *Jinnah Papers*, II, No. 299.
31. Mitchell, Memoirs, p. 266.

APPENDIX 1

The Frontier Muslim League

IN THE FRONTIER drama of 1945-7 the Muslim League in the province had an important, even crucial, role to play. The starting point no doubt was the Muslim League Ministry of Aurangzeb Khan (1943-5), which was notorious for its corruption and lost much popular support by the way it handled commodity scarcities and rising prices, both endemic in the closing years of World War II. A ramshackle minority government kept in office by its unethical detention of some Congress MLAs, its choice of Aurangzeb Khan as Premier was a little less than happy. Fraser describes him as an ineffectual man: 'mild in manner, bulky in physique and—I think—extremely lazy'. Aurangzeb would appear to have been caught unawares, failed to build on the opportunity and broaden his own support base in the party which, under his stewardship, remained largely divided and leaderless.

Besides, most of Aurangzeb's henchmen were non-descript characters. Another minister, Sardar Bahadur was a shifty lawyer whose personality did not match up to that of his military brother, General Ayub Khan. The only exception seemed to be Abdur Rab Nishtar; he was intelligent and sharp, and displayed foresight.

As has been noticed earlier, the Muslim League as a party had sprung from the ranks of the big landowners; the Congress, by contrast, represented the underdog, the landless labourers and the social have-nots. To that extent, it found it much easier to mount demonstrations against the alleged oppression, and corruption, of the Aurangzeb ministry.

Inasmuch as the League's political power base lay with the landowing classes, the latter were now only too eager to recover as it were the 'losses' sustained during the earlier Congress regime (1937-9). Sadly for him, the Aurangzeb ministry not only defended but indeed insisted on control of commodity prices and rationing of civil supplies. It doubly offended the landlords by choosing price levels which were low and would discourage procurement. At the same time, it enforced compulsory purchase of foodgrains. The Congress which should have normally defended controls—for the latter protected the landless and the poor and guaranteed them against starvation—strongly opposed these measures. With singular shortsightedness they accused the Muslim League government of wanting controls simply as an instrument of power which it would administer in a manner to suit its own political gains. Later, when in power, the Khan Sahib ministry (1945-7) was in the dock for much that it had earlier alleged against the Aurangzeb Khan outfit.

A major preoccupation of the Muslim League ministry was the party factional feuds. These were so deep-rooted that a rival 'Progressive Muslim League' had emerged in Peshawar, a fact that certainly did not help the party's general standing. It may be recalled that George Cunningham treated his Muslim League premier with a measure of disdain, if not outright contempt, all too evident from the pages of his diary; later, Olaf Caroe was to refer to the Frontier Muslim League leadership as 'that miserable crew'.

In the February 1946 elections, despite Jinnah's loud, and unambiguous, call that 'Every vote in favour of Muslim League candidates means Pakistan; every vote against the Muslim League means Hindu Raj', the League fared badly despite hordes of its student workers from the Panjab and Aligarh who tom-tommed the League slogan. The reason for its electoral debacle was not far to seek; it lay in the fact that the mass of Pathan voters appeared convinced that the Khudai Khidmatgars were neither anti-Muslim nor yet tools of the Hindus. No wonder the League's tactics of using 'gundi', factional rivalries, and 'piri-muridi', the *guru-sishya* ties, yielded little in electoral gains. The Congress garnered solid rural support, captured 19 of the 36 seats reserved for Muslims, thereby exposing the League to be a party of towns and the non-Pathan Hazara district.

A Congress victory at the hustings notwithstanding, Cunningham had warned the viceroy that 'it would be dangerous to deduce' that the Pathans as such 'will be quite happy in a united India without safeguards'.

The Cabinet Mission Plan of 16 May dealt the first major blow to the Frontier Congress. It raised a ticklish question: how was the Frontier to group? With Sindh and neighbouring Panjab? Or, with Madras, Bombay, CP & Berar, Orissa and UP, with their vast Hindu majority? The subsequent failure of the Mission's Plan did not camouflage this stark, naked reality nor make it the less uncomfortable for the Frontier Congress leadership. Nehru's ill-timed October 1946 visit brought home ever more vividly the grim possibility that the Pathans may one day be ruled by a Hindu-dominated centre!

By end-1946, thanks to a rash of communal disorders all over the country which broke out in the wake of the League's Direct Action Day, the Frontier Muslim League made rapid organisational strides. Its loud, if dubious medical aid missions to riot-torn Bihar brought back blood-stained clothing and even the skulls of alleged Muslim victims. The fact that some Pathans among the large numbers resident in Bombay, were caught in the communal cross-fire there in September 1946 was grist to the League propaganda mill. Equally, it made the position of Muslim Congressmen increasingly untenable.

Communal troubles elsewhere in India apart, the League's fortunes brightened with growing religious fanaticism in the Frontier itself. In December 1946, trans-border tribesmen began raiding in Hazara district leading to large-scale Hindu and Sikh exodus to the neighbouring Rawalpindi district of the Panjab.

Early in 1947, the Frontier Muslim League launched its Civil Disobedience campaign *in tandem* with a similar movement by the party against the Unionist government in the Panjab. The objective was to demonstrate the League's command over the loyalty of Muslims at a time when the partition was becoming a grim possibility. In the Frontier, it was a generally popular movement involving not only local officials and party functionaries but ordinary people as well. Women and the youth were in the forefront and helped disrupt day-to-day administration in the towns and countryside leaving isolated clusters of Hindu and Sikh communities at the mercy of fanatical, angry Muslim mobs.

March 1947 was witness to mounting civil disorder and communal violence in Hazara and Peshawar; in April, the contagion spread to D I Khan where loss of life apart, damage to Hindu and Sikh property was unprecedented. For all the contempt with which Khan Sahib's government treated it, the fact was that the Muslim League was at long last taking a grip of itself. Its appeal to Islamic susceptibilities was constantly reinforced by the energetic influence of the Pir of Manki who travelled tirelessly with his message in the tribal areas as well as the settled districts. To no one's surprise, the League's blatant use of communal violence to achieve political ends reaped a rich harvest when Mountbatten conceded its demand for a fresh popular verdict on the province's future.

All the while, the mounting deterioration in the communal situation throughout India had led to an almost daily exodus of large numbers from the ranks of the Frontier Congress. The renegades swelled League ranks, lent it prestige, pockets of popular support and much-needed organisational skills. All this was enough to convince the provincial governor that the continuation of the Congress ministry posed a major threat to peace in the province.

The Pakhtunistan demand of the Frontier Congress surfaced so late in the day that the Muslim League succeeded in dismissing it as a mere bargaining counter. A clever if devious way of demanding accession to India. The Red Shirt plea that it was in a real sense the logical conclusion to their earlier championing of Pathan interests, as well as their distinct culture, and contained within it the powerful sentiment of the Pathan fear of Panjabi domination in the name of religion, did not register. No wonder while some Congress leaders in the province held that they might win a plebiscite on the issue of Pakhtunistan, others thought it unlikely, given the communal polarisation all over the country by the summer of 1947. By then the League's organisation in the Frontier was ready to embark on what had been called 'a positive Direct Action' policy so as to make its efforts at non-cooperation with the Congress government increasingly effective.

With the referendum, the Muslim League triumph was complete for while Khan Sahib still remained in office the League was now the real master in the province. All the same, its rapid rise during 1946-7 'established a dangerous illusion of permanence'. As a matter of fact, once the crisis had blown over, the League returned to its factional squabbles and particularisms. Within a year, the rift was there for all to see for with the emergence of Abdul Qaiyum and Pir of Manki factions, the League's influence 'declined as rapidly as it had grown'.

Jansson, who claims to have gone into party organisational questions 'in some detail', has expressed the view that during this entire period the Frontier Muslim League 'remained in disarray'. The ultimate victory of Pakistan in the NWFP 'was due to other factors than the work of the provincial Muslim League'. Rittenberg who is equally conversant with the organisational background endorses this line of reasoning affirming that 'even at the peak' during these years (1946-7) when the Muslim League 'seemingly unified town and country' against Hindus and the Congress, its position in the Pakhtun areas remained 'tenuous'. With 'disunity and disarray' its historical norms, the League's triumph in 1947 would appear to have 'occurred in spite of its organisational structure rather than because of it'. From all this one should not hasten to deduce that its internal jealousies and *parajamba* invalidated the League's general position. All the same, once a semblance of normalcy returned, the League melted away and true to 'traditional patterns', its ascendancy proved to be a nine day wonder—ephemeral, short-lived.

Syed Waqar Ali Shah's *Muslim League in NWFP* does not add much to what has broadly been spelt out in the text. To start with, it suggests that Aurangzeb Khan's performance as Premier (1943-5) gave a bad name to the Muslim League—'so much so that they (the people) hate the very name of such organisation' because of him. The ministers 'manipulated administrative appointments, selectively distributed licenses and permits, discriminated in allocating government funds, interfered in policy investigations and tried to tamper with the judicial process'. Again, the mutual bickerings among the League Premier's ministerial colleagues and party MLAs was such that 'the most prominent Leaguer' (Saad Ullah Khan) voted in favour of the no confidence motion brought against the Muslim League ministry! The Governor, Sir George Cunningham, noted that 'there is no question' that the average League minister had 'far less sense of duty then [*sic*] their Congress predecessors had' (pp. 68-70).

The Quaid, it would appear, had given his approval to the anti-Nehru demonstrations during the latter's visit in October 1946. Thus writing to Jinnah, the Pir of Manki informed him that 'while preparing the grounds to stage hostile receptions' against Nehru, he (the Pir) feared the Quaid's 'wrath' but 'when he heard about his (Jinnah's) approval, he was satisfied' (p. 116).

Nehru's visit gave the League 'an opportunity for effective publicity'. And Abdul Qaiyum informed Jinnah that 'what we could not hope to achieve in several years was in fact achieved within about a week' (p. 121).

All the hostile receptions during Nehru's visit were 'reported to have had the support' of the Governor 'who was a friend of the League'. By the end of 1946, Caroe had fallen foul of the Provincial Congress as well as the Congress High Command. He had 'developed an anti-Congress attitude because as he was [*sic*] a loyal British civilian' (p. 151).

Jinnah's invitation to George Cunningham to take over as Governor in August 1947 'was disliked' by some Frontier Leaguers. One of them, Arbab Abdul Ghafar viewed him (Cunningham) 'as the most unsuited person' whose return 'would result in the downfall of the Muslim League' in the NWFP (p. 152).

APPENDIX 2

Sir Olaf Caroe and the Frontier Government

VIDYA DHAR MAHAJAN

THE AGITATION of the Muslim League was started in the Frontier Province with the sole object of overthrowing the Congress ministry in that province. It has been reportedly stated that the top-ranking officials of the Frontier Government have a hand in the agitation. Khan Abdul Ghaffar Khan has openly declared that Sir Olaf Caroe had a hand in the conspiracy which has been hatched for the overthrow of the Congress ministry and the establishment of a Muslim League ministry in that region. According to him the object of the British officials in the Frontier Province is to create a buffer state between India and Russia and that can only be done if the League can be put into office in the Frontier and a major portion of the Punjab and the Frontier Province are included in the Pakistan zone. Mr Jinnah has already declared that the Pakistan State will remain a part of the British Commonwealth of Nations. Under these circumstances, he can count upon the assistance of the British bureaucracy in India who will try to maintain as much of British influence and control directly or indirectly, in India as possible. The state of Pakistan will be most handy.

Sir Olaf Caroe joined the Indian Civil Service in 1919, and was sent to the Frontier in 1923 as an officer of the Political Department of the Government of India. With that department he has maintained the most intimate contact for the last 24 years. As an officer of the Political Department, he served as the Deputy Commissioner of different Frontier districts, including Peshawar, up to 1932. He acted as Chief Secretary to the Frontier Government in 1933-4. In 1934 he was summoned to the headquarters and appointed as the Deputy Secretary, Foreign and Political Department of the Government of India. He officiated for some time as the Political Resident in the Persian Gulf. The Political Department again sent him as Agent to Governor-General in Baluchistan. During 1937-8,

* The *Tribune*, 2 June 1947.

Sir Olaf Caroe acted as Resident in Waziristan. He worked as the Revenue Commissioner in 1938-9 in Baluchistan. In appreciation of his meritorious services, Sir Olaf Caroe was appointed as Secretary in the Indian Political Department in 1939, and he carried on in that capacity till he was made the Governor and Agent to the Governor-General in the Frontier Province.

Man of Political Department

It is clear from the above that Sir Olaf Caroe is out-and-out a man of the Indian Political Department and as such can have no sympathy with the political aspirations of the Indians. He belongs to the school of the diehards of the type of Churchill. Churchill, Wavel and Amery are no doubt gone but the old spirit of hostility towards the Indian nationalist movement persists among some British Officers. Being anxious to safeguard the interests of his country, Sir Olaf Caroe must try to create all those circumstances which will help to perpetuate the influence of the British in the Pakistan zone. He can be credited with a lot of knowledge of strategy. His mental make-up is congenial for his mission.

Can fresh elections be ordered?

But the question is whether Sir Olaf can order fresh elections in the Frontier Province. The answer is 'No'. If Englishmen have still left in them any regard for constitutional propriety, the Frontier Governor cannot hold new elections under the present circumstances. The Frontier Ministry enjoys the confidence of 32 members out of 50 of the Frontier Assembly. So long as the Congress Ministry does not resign of its own accord, the Frontier Governor can do nothing in this matter. If he does that, he must accept the charge that has been levelled against him that he is backing the Muslim League agitation and like a British diehard, is doing all that he can to defeat the nationalist forces in the province. It is the duty of Congressmen not only in the Frontier Province but all over India to protest against unwarranted and uncalled for interference of Sir Olaf Caroe in the affairs of a Congress Ministry. Pandit Nehru and his colleagues must take up this matter with Lord Mountbatten. It is true that Sir Olaf is Agent to the Viceroy and as such, Lord Mountbatten is bound to back his subordi-nates, but that should not discourage Congressmen. The Congress members of the Interim Government must take up this matter with Mr Attlee.

Constitutional crisis may be created

If there is any truth in the statement that Lord Wavell was recalled by His Majesty's Government on account of his anti-Congress attitude and if the British Government is anxious to continue friendly relations with the Union of India, it can be safely stated that Sir Olaf Caroe can be either made to give up his present attitude of hostility or transferred to some other post. The urgency of the moment demands a strong attitude. The policy of submission on every front will not pay. Let Sir Olaf realise that the Frontier Ministry has the strong backing of the whole of the Congress organisation. A constitutional crisis of all-India importance cannot only be threatened but also created. If that involves dangers those must be faced. The Congress is used to these trials. If it could win victories in the past, it can do the same against this official of the Political Department who dares to challenge the Congress. This is no occasion for generosity or submission or pocketing the insult. The NWF Province can rightly act as the sword-arm of the Union of India. No sacrifice is too great to keep it. Let the Congress High Command make Dr Khan Sahib and Badshah Khan realise that they have their full support and the Congress will do all that lies in its power to bring the Frontier Governor to the straight path.

Section 93

It is being rumoured that the Governor will promulgate Section 93 and order fresh elections in the province. But this the Governor cannot do unless the English have cast away all regard for constitutional usage and law. In 1945, new elections were ordered in England while the government of Churchill was in power. It resigned because it failed to secure a majority in the new House but during the course of elections, Churchill's Government was in power. The same thing has happened on many occasions in England. In 1946, the Muslim League ministry was in office in Sind when the elections were ordered under the Cabinet Mission Scheme. The Governor of Sind did not promulgate Section 93 in the Province and then conduct the elections. Even, second time, the elections were conducted in Sind with the League ministry in office. The same was the case with the Punjab where the Unionist Ministry was in power when elections were held last year. The Unionist Ministry was not dismissed in spite of the protests of the Muslim League. If that is the constitutional law on the subject, the Frontier Governor can be plainly told that he cannot order new elections after the promulgation of Section 93 in the Province.

The Viceroy and the British Prime Minister can be approached to force the Governor to desist form what is manifestly illegal and unconstitutional.

Who can ask for elections?

Moreover it is the right of the ministry in power to ask for new elections and not that of the Opposition. This is the practice in all those countries where a system of parliamentary government operates. In 1945, new elections were held in England on the advice of Mr Churchill. In Sind also elections were ordered for the second time on the initiative of the ministry in power. It is well-known how the views of the opposition were ignored in the case of Sind. There is no justification for departing from the general practice not only in India, but also in England and the Dominions. It is not for the Muslim League to demand fresh elections but that is the right of the ministry of Dr Khan Sahib and that also whenever they please. The Frontier Governor must desist from usurping the legitimate right of the ministry regarding the ordering of new elections.

Let us not ignore the dangers of new elections when Section 93 is in force. Sir Olaf has a lot of personal influence throughout the Frontier Province because he was the Deputy Commissioner of many districts in the Province. He also acted as the Chief Secretary of the Province. As the Agent to the Governor-General he has control over the Political Agencies. A strange thing about the Frontier Province is that 'in political questions, there is no intermediary between the Governor and the local officer—an arrangement designed to secure both prompt disposal of references and the utilization of the expert knowledge of frontier conditions for which the head of the administration is selected' (p. 130, *The Indian Year Book*, 1945-6). In the Frontier Province, the cadre post of the Chief Secretary, Revenue and Divisional Commissioner, Secretary of Development Departments, the Home Secretary, the Deputy Commissioners, the Political Agents, Assistant Commissioners and the Assistant Political Agents are still reserved for the Indian Political Service. With all this paraphernalia under his control, with the determination of the Governor to bring the Muslim League to power, the results of fresh elections cannot truly reflect the opinion of the electorate.

APPENDIX 3

Letter from Lord Ismay, Delhi, 12 June 1947

My dear Olaf,

I cannot tell you how sad I am at the turn of events, or how deeply I feel for you and Kitty in the terrible wrench which confronts you. You have loved the Frontier Province and its people, always, and you have given your whole heart and soul to their service. If personal considerations were the only guide, no one has a greater claim than you to be allowed to see the thing through—for the two months that remain to us. But as it is, I am convinced that you take comfort in the thought that none of this matters at all as compared with the cause. I am also convinced that both you and Kitty take comfort in the thought that your consciences are clear, that you have both made the greatest sacrifices for the common weal, and that all your friends—and even many of your detractors—recognise the sterling work that you have done. I do not know of any decision which the Viceroy has had to make out here that has given him more grief than this. All of us in this small team are profoundly unhappy about it.

I do hope I shall see you both before you leave India. Meanwhile my love and prayers are with you.

Yours ever,
Pug

* Caroe Mss. In an epilogue to his unpublished manuscript 'A Price for Freedom', there are 19 documents; for most part, letters written to Sir Olaf Caroe from his many friends and well-wishers. The above letter is placed at number 9; another from the same writer, 'Pug' (Ismay), dated 2 April 1956 and addressed to Sir Olaf's wife Kitty, is placed at number 17.

APPENDIX 4

Sir Olaf's Resignation: Caroe to Mountbatten, 23 June 1947

In two days' time I expect to have handed over, but we have been too closely in touch for it to be necessary for me to attempt to tie up many loose ends in this letter. There is, however, one matter, and that is the position of the North-West Frontier tribes. Circumstances have been such that Your Excellency has been compelled to devote the greater part of your attention to political and ministerial matters within the province as they affect the parties in India, but you found time to speak to the tribes. What I wish to say now is that the most important part of the Governor's work up here is keeping the tribes steady. The tribal situation and the situation within the province of course react to one another continually, but by proper management a great deal can be done to maintain tribal steadiness. The fact that on the whole we have been successful in doing this during the last few years, including the last momentous year, is not the result of chance. It is in the first place a tribute to our system of tribal management over many years, while recent success owes a tremendous lot to the influence of Cunningham and the way in which he left the tribes for me to take over. During the last sixteen months, I have given a great deal of my mind and energy to this matter, have seen innumerable *jirgas*, and talked to tribesmen and to the ruling Chiefs in the north continually. I have made a great point of keeping the right men, as far as I could judge them, in the right places, and this includes not only the Resident and the Political Agents, but the Assistant Political Officers who belong to the Provincial Service. My Ministry have continually tried to interfere with postings and to bring unfair charges against officers in the tribal areas, mainly Indian, based on prejudice or false report. I shall tell

* Caroe Mss. Numbered 32, this is the last of the exchanges between Caroe and Governor-Generals Wavell and Mountbatten which forms the bulk of his unpublished Mss entitled, 'A Price for Freedom'. Datelined 23 June, the letter was written from Nathiagali, the summer resort of the Frontier government in the Muree hills.

Lockhart that it will be necessary for him during the next two months to keep an eye on this.

I have already written separately to you about the all-important question of fitting the tribes into the new Constitution and finding the money to run them during the interim period, and I have particularly emphasised the value of employment as the real method by which we maintain a steady frontier. This employment must be kept going. Mudie, to whom we lent a number of Frontier Constabulary platoons to deal with the Hurs, will tell you what splendid men they are, and the same applies to the Militias and Scouts in Waziristan, the Khyber and elsewhere. The *Khassadari* system, too, must be kept alive and improved, and it is worth remembering that we spend about eight times as much on *Khassadars* as we do on *Maliki* allowances.

Lastly, in my view the new Constitution should not aim at placing the tribes under the Provincial Government, which can never pay for them and too often must clash with them. The Agent who deals locally with the tribes must derive his own authority from a Centre, whether that Centre be of Hindustan or Pakistan. And in the long run I believe H.M.G. will not be able to divorce themselves entirely from interest in the maintenance of this most delicate and difficult land frontier.

2. It was inevitable that the Afghans would bring their weight to bear in this matter and raise the cry of Afghanistan irredenta, but it is interesting that they should have timed it and brought it into line with the Congress theme of Pathanistan. I do not myself think that this Afghan interference is going to be very dangerous, if (and this is the important point) the successor authority makes it quite clear that the tribesmen are going to get the benefits that they enjoy at present from this side. Tribal *Jirgas* are already asking the Political Agents if there is any objection to their going off to see the Afghans in Kabul, and the answer the Political Agents should be able to give is that the tribes receive benefits from this side and we are going to do our best to see that any successor authority, whoever it is, can be got to endorse this, so much the better. The pity is that it is impossible to get any line on matters of this kind out of the External Affairs Department at this moment.

3. This brings me to one reflection which I think I ought to make, namely that most of our troubles were started when Nehru took tribal affairs under his wing and followed this up with his ill-starred visit. Before that time the Province was going along very nicely all things considered, but it was an impossible thing to do to bring these tribes under a Pandit. Practically

all our frictions and tensions date from that time. And here I must put in a final word about Mahbub Ali's case. I told Khan Sahib that we should have to show Mahbub Ali a copy of Clark's finding, and he did not demur. It is very unjust to leave an officer who has been exonerated after suspension and a departmental inquiry without an opportunity of seeing the finding exonerating him. I could have given him the copy which I have here, but I did not think it right to do so without Nehru's authority. I must ask that, whether Nehru agrees or not, Mahbub Ali should be shown this document. It can be made clear to him that it is for his personal information only.*

4. Probably more is known in Delhi of what is in the Congress mind as regards the Referendum than we yet know, and it would be idle to indulge in speculation for nothing has come out since Abdul Ghaffar Khan's return. A state of dangerous tension exists in Peshawar and Bannu cities, where the Red Shirts started showing off by carrying large quantities of arms and letting them off in the air in the streets. This has led to the Leaguers doing exactly the same. Mark that once more it is Congress that led the way. I must of course leave it to Lockhart whether or not he asks for the promulgation of the two Ordinances which I sent up to be kept ready in case they are wanted to enable the Civil Forces, backed by toops, to deal with armed demonstrations during the Referendum. The proposed Ordinance to extend the penal provisions for election offences is a separate matter, and has been dealt with separately. Booth has settled down very well and seems to have already got a close grasp of the problems before him, and to be working steadily and with determination. He will need every support and encouragement that can be given.

5. As soon as I have handed over I shall be going to stay with Messervy for a day or two in Pindi, until my wife can get a little further with packing up our more private belongings, and we shall then go off to Kashmir. I don't want to go too far away from her during these days, as she will have much to do. Perhaps later I might take advantage of your very kind invitation, and she too if her health is good enough to stand up to the heat.

My gratitude for all your help and understanding.

* It would be of interest to note that when Mountbatten told Nehru about Caroe asking that Mahbub Ali be shown a copy of Justice Clarke's finding: 'Nehru was very generous about it and said that he had already given personal publicity to this finding and was only too glad that Mahbub should have it.' Mountbatten's Note on interview with Nehru, *Selected Works*, III, item 12, pp. 292-3. The interview took place on 8 July 1947.

APPENDIX 5

Letter from Norval Mitchell to Caroe, 23 September 1968

Dear Sir Olaf,

I AM EXTREMELY grateful to you for your letter of 21st September 1968 and for the enormous amount of trouble which you have taken in writing notes on my book. I appreciate this very much, and will pay the closest attention to all that you have said. Meanwhile I hope you will forgive me for dictating my answer. It is the only way in which I can handle the matter by return of post: and incidentally, the lady who is taking the dictation has had a big hand in the production of the manuscript.

I am particularly concerned to give you an answer on the point which you make about your own tenure of office. The first point I would make is that, in writing a Memoir within strict limitations, I have tried to avoid as far as possible anything that might injure feelings and possibly defeat the object of the book by introducing controversial matter about individuals. I did not in fact know how badly you had been treated in 1947 until I read Sir George's diaries. I do not have them any longer, but I distinctly remember a mention of the fact that Mountbatten's conduct in this respect was unpardonable. In all the circumstances, however, I thought it better to say nothing at all. At the same time I fully appreciate the point which you make, namely that silence might be interpreted as some sort of adverse criticism of yourself. I shall, therefore, now put the whole of that period under the microscope again and try to make it quite clear (and I am most sincere in this) with what fortitude and distinction you bore the burden of those almost intolerable years.

Your detailed criticisms will of course be of extreme value; and I am very pleased that in general you have found the book enjoyable and faithful.

Yours Sincerely,
(Sd.) Norval

* The letter, in original, was appended to Sir Olaf Caroe's copy of Norval Mitchell's *Sir George Cunningham: A Memoir*, Edinburgh, 1968, which he was gracious enough to pass on to the author.

APPENDIX 6

Letter from Iskander Mirza to Caroe, 26 September 1968

My dear Sir Olaf,

I got your letter an hour ago and am writing immediately.

In the first place I wish to express my grief and concern at the serious illness of Kitty. I had no knowledge else I would have written earlier. I hope she will be in prefect health very soon. Please give her my high regards and love. Nahich has gone to Paris because of her sister-in-law's illness. I expect her back soon. Taj was with me for two months but he is leaving for Karachi on the 28th.

The unhappy and dishonourable circumstances in 1946 and early 1947 in connection with your tenure as Governor of NWFP bring back some very unhappy memories. There was no doubt in my mind that Lord Mountbatten was no friend of yours and he was guided more by Nehru than by anybody else, and Nehru firmly believed that all those incidents in Malakand, Razmak and Khyber during his visit as Minister of External Affairs were created by officers of the Political Service and you were Governor at that time. I tried through the late Sir Girja Shankar Bajpai that Nehru should avoid going to tribal areas as passions were inflamed because of communal riots in Bengal, Bihar and Bombay. But Nehru listened to the Khan brothers and when incidents did take place, the poor political service was blamed and even I was suspect because I gave that advice to Sir Girja Shankar in all good faith.

* Caroe Mss. The letter was written, Caroe noted, 'in answer to an inquiry by the writer (who was reading Norval Mitchell's biography of George Cunningham) on the point why Jinnah, who did not know Cunningham, had asked for his return to the Province in August 1947. Iskander Mirza was in Delhi at the time and in touch with affairs.'

Iskander Mirza, quondam President of Pakistan, had fled to London (from where the letter was written) after Ayub took over in a major *coup d'état* (1958).

Lord Mountbatten wanted to keep Nehru happy and even before you went to Kashmir stories were going round that you had a nervous breakdown and required rest. I told the late Nawabzada Liaquat Ali Khan of your great qualities and after the referendum urged that you should go back as Governor and that Muslim League was honour bound to insist on this. But believe me there was no honour then or later. No other reason but health was given to sabotage you and I was quite helpless. Lord Mountbatten must have told Lord Ismay that you won't go back.

Sir George Cunningham's return was a great surprise. I learnt later that he was not at all willing to come back as Governor and pressure was put on him by no less a person than His Majesty King George VI. In 1945 I did tell Mr Jinnah that Sir George was a wonderful man and during the War kept the Frontier quiet. But I don't think this would make Mr. Jinnah ask for him.

But what did the politicians do to Sri George. Behind his back they pushed Tribesmen into Kashmir. Sir George was about to resign in late 1947 and I had to beg of him not to do so. They got rid of a good friend like Mudie and installed that fanatic Nishtar as Governor. I don't think you should feel sorry. Knowing as I do you could not have stuck all those dishonourable intrigues so very rampant since the very inception of Pakistan. *Everybody is here enamoured of Ayub but what about the terrible corruption rampant in the country and the example set by Ayub and his family?*

*I am attempting to write my memoirs and when they take some shape I will ask your advice. My trouble is all my papers perished and I have to go by memory which is not good now specially for dates. I think when you have some time we can have lunch somewhere and have a long talk. You ask questions and I will answer. Perhaps you might get some satisfactory material.**

Yours ever,
(Sd.) Iskander Mirza

* Paragraphs in italics have been omitted in *CM*.

Bibliographic Note

A BRIEF BIBLIOGRAPHIC note may not be out of place here. To start with, among the *unpublished* sources, of the greatest interest are the papers of Sir Olaf Caroe, housed in the former *India Office Library and Records* (now India Office Records, of the Oriental and India Office Collections, of the British Library in London) listed, Mss Eur C 273 (Caroe Papers). This writer has in his possession some private papers of Sir Olaf including his correspondence with Lady Caroe, Iskander Mirza and Norval Mitchell. As well as the entire corpus of Caroe's fortnightly reports to Governor-Generals Wavell and Mountbatten along with the telegraphic exchanges with the latter leading to his resignation. There is also an account of his years in retirement, 'From 1947 On', in a typed manuscript.

Sir George Cunningham's papers as well as his Diary (which draws to a close in August 1948) are now part of the India Office Records, Mss Eur D 670 (Cunningham Papers). The Diary is extremely revealing both of its author as well as his candid impressions of men and events.

A first-hand, eye-witness account of these years is to be found in the hitherto unpublished Memoirs of Sir Fraser Noble. A member of the Indian Civil Service who had earlier served at Miranshah (Waziristan), Sir Fraser arrived in Peshawar in July 1944—and was to leave exactly three years later. He held a number of the most sensitive posts in the administration: Assistant Director of Civil Supplies; Controller of Rationing; Home Secretary; Joint Deputy Commissioner, Peshawar. And finally, as 'Civil Aide' to the Referendum Commissioner. Through Sir Fraser's courtesy this writer had an opportunity to read the relevant chapters (viz. nine to fifteen) of his singularly well-composed and by and large objective assessment of all that he saw and heard. More important, Sir Fraser took time out to scrutinise at length an earlier draft of the Typescript and made a number of useful comments and suggestions. As the reader would doubtless observe, both the Memoirs and the Comments have been liberally drawn upon.

Another first-hand account of an intimate eye-witness is furnished by the Memoirs of A N Mitchell (Mss Eur D 944, in IOL & R). A member of the ICS who had joined the service way back in 1930, Mitchell had returned to the Frontier early in April 1946 after a six-year stint in the princely states of eastern as well as western India. He was briefly Home Secretary and Development Secretary by turns (April-June 1946) and then took over as Finance Secretary. When de la Fargue proceeded on home leave, early in April (1947), Mitchell took over as Chief Secretary and continued to occupy that post until the former's return, four months later. He handed over charge on 31 July, thereby not only relinquishing his post 'but also a life's vocation'. The last chapter, chapter XIII, entitled 'A Time to pluck up that which is planted' (Ecclesiastes III. 2) of his extremely candid account of life in the final days of the Raj, affords a graphic picture of how an insider, who was both an eye-witness as well as a top functionary in the provincial administration, reacted to men and events. While researching for his study, *The McMahon Line & After* (Macmillan, 1974), the writer met Mitchell in England (1969) and sought his views on his relations with, and assessment of, Sir Olaf Caroe. Especially in that the latter had been charged, unfairly it would appear, with some sharp practice in dealing with documentary evidence relating to the Line.

In India, the release of *Cabinet Papers, 1941-62,* available at the National Archives of India (NAI), offers a useful tool. *Inter alia*, there is a file on the NWFP with a report by Brigadier Booth, the Referendum Commissioner, giving details of the July 1947 referendum with sketches of 'an ideal polling booth' and 'instructions to a voter casting votes'. Booth notes that 'fortysix individuals were arrested for either taking papers out of polling stations with the intent to sell them, or for impersonation'. For a corrective, the reader may check on Wali Khan's *Facts Are Facts* and Jansson's *India, Pakistan or Pakhtunistan,* both listed later in this note.

For official documentation there is no fuller coverage than in the late Professor Nicholas Mansergh's (Editor-in-chief) *Constitutional Relations Between Britain and India: the Transfer of Power, 1942-47,* HMSO, 12 vols, VIII-XII, 1979-83; the respective dates being VIII (1979), IX (1980), X (1981), XI (1982) and XII (1983). Mountbatten's *Report on the Last Viceroyalty, 22nd March to 15th August 1947,* cited above as *Mountbatten Report*, serves to supplement the massive documentation in the *Transfer of Power* volumes X-XII. While submitting it, Mountbatten noted: '17 Viceroy's Personal Reports, in all, were written and dispatched. They form a full week by week record of events during my Viceroyalty and show fully on what ground the various decisions which had to be made, almost inevitably with great speed, were based.

'In order that there should be, apart from these weekly record of events, a more connected account of the last Viceroyalty, the attached report has been prepared.'

The Report is in six Parts: Part A, 22 March-15 April; Part-B, 15 April-6 May; Part C, 6 May-4 June; Part D, 4 June-5 July; Part E, 5 July-25 July; Part F, 25 July-15 August. The writer had access to the Report through the good offices of Lord Mountbatten (1968). It is part of an excellent archives which he had an opportunity to rummage through.

For supplementing this minehouse of information the reader may consult the *Selected Works of Jawaharlal Nehru,* second series, Vols 1-3, (New Delhi, 1984-5). The 'second series', which covers the period from 2 September 1946 onwards is still continuing. Vol. 16, part 2 which brings the coverage up to 31 October 1951 has just been published; the series is to cover the period up to May 1964 when Nehru died. The 'first series' of the *Selected Works* which covers the period 25 February 1903 to 2 September 1946 runs into 15 volumes and was published between 1972 and 1985.

Indian archival and non-official sources relating to the period promised in the long-awaited 'Towards Freedom' series (and designed to supplement the 'Transfer of Power' volumes listed in a preceding paragraph) have not yet been published barring a solitary volume: P N Chopra (ed) *Towards Freedom 1937-47*: Vol. I, *Experiment with Provincial Autonomy, 1 January-31 December 1937*, Indian Council of Historical Research, New Delhi, 1985. Inter alia, references here are to the formation of a Congress ministry in the NWFP and of Pandit Nehru's visit to the province. All in all, they do not add much to what is already known on the subject.

The importance of the Muslim League in general, and of Mohammad Ali Jinnah in particular, to any re-construction of the story of the transfer of power cannot be gainsaid. Even though quite late in the day, two volumes of *Jinnah Papers* have been published to date.* The first, entitled 'Prelude to Pakistan', covers the period, 20 February 1946 to 2 June 1947. It is in two parts. Part I has a total of 718 documents including enclosures annexes and annexures; Part II, of 14 Appendices on issues raised or relating to Part I. The second volume, entitled 'Pakistan in the Making',

* Z H Zaidi (ed.) *Quaid-i-Azam Mohammad Ali Jinnah Papers,* Vol. I, Parts 1 and 2, and Vol. II, Oxford University Press, Karachi, 1993, 1994.

covers a period of four weeks, from 3 June to 30 June 1947. Besides its ten appendices, it contains 353 documents.

It may be of interest to note that a very small percentage of documents in these papers emanated from the Quaid himself. In volume I, a bare 70; in volume II, a meager 55 written by Jinnah himself. In the event, one has to draw not so much on the Quaid, as his correspondents, to get a clearer understanding of some of the issues involved.

In our limited context relating to the NWF, two facts emerge quite clearly. One, the Quaid's direct involvement in the Frontier Muslim League's stance *vis-a-vis* the Congress leadership in the province. Thus he established a 4-member committee which was not only to oversee the provincial League but also the impending referendum in the province. More, Jinnah indicated that he would meet Abdul Ghaffar Khan *only* if the provincial League leadership was so inclined. Again, the tone and tenor of the League propaganda among the tribal areas comes out vividly in the communications of some of the tribal leaders. Thus one of the Mahsud Maliks boasted that he it was who had heckled Nehru during his October 1946 visit; another serving officer in the Khyber Agency, was not averse to highlighting his contribution in keeping the Afridis away from any constructive dialogue with New Delhi.

League functionaries in the tribal areas as also in the settled districts kept the Quaid informed both of what they were doing or planning to. Sahibzada Khurshid, a member of the Political Service, was in contact with Jinnah advising him about tribal affairs and of his assessment of men and things in the Frontier. Both Firoz Khan Noon whom evidently the Quaid did not quite trust as well as Abdur Rab Nishtar whom he did, were profuse in their advice furnishing *inter alia* draft statements for Jinnah's approval. One of the Quaid's not infrequent correspondents, a Mrs K L Rallia Ram from Lahore, was so rabidly anti-Hindu and her assessment of Dr Khan Sahib and his younger brother, the Frontier Gandhi, so blatantly partisan that one wonders if Jinnah took her at her face value.

Among secondary works, Wali Khan's *Facts Are Facts* (New Delhi, 1987) is important though repetitious and, at places, contradictory. A son of the late Badshah Khan, Wali Khan was close to the principal actors and professes to offer 'an honest account' of his father's struggle as well as that of the Red Shirts. He mercilessly lampoons the Muslim League outfit in the NWFP for its 'heinous act' of supporting the 'infidel British while hiding behind the veil of Islam'. His observations as a contemporary witness have a measure of relevance, and yet a modicum of caution is necessary in accepting them as the honest truth. Another major disadvantage is the multiple translation: the author's original in Pushtu was rendered into Urdu and then translated into English! How much of the esence, and nuances, of the original are reflected in the end-product is debatable. Besides, it is to be borne in mind that AGK was prevented from offering the Pathans a third choice—that of Pathanistan.

Norval Mitchell's slim biography, *Sir George Cunningham* (Edinburgh, 1968) rests squarely on his subject's papers and diaries apart from newspaper clippings and other peoples' memoirs and has been written with great empathy and understanding. Incidentally Caroe's papers reveal that Cunningham had the distinct impression that Mountbatten's conduct, in relation to Caroe, was 'unpardonable'. It is also clear that Caroe had scrutinised Mitchell's manuscript before it went to the printers.

Three excellent works on the subject which cover a great deal of common ground and rest on meticulous research are Erland Jansson, *India, Pakistan or Pakhtunistan: the Nationalist Movements in the North West Frontier Province, 1937-47* (Uppsala, 1981), Stephen Alan Rittenberg, *The Independence Movements in India's North West Frontier Province* (Durham, 1988) and Amit Kumar Gupta, *North West Frontier Province Legislature and Freedom Struggle 1932-47* (New Delhi, 1976). While comparisons may be odious, Jansson has an edge over the other two especially in the detailed study he offers for the years with which this presentation is principally concerned. His analysis of the growth of the Khudai Khidmatgars and the change that came over the political landscape during 1946-7 makes for useful reading.

Even though on the face of it, Rittenberg's may appear to be more recent, in actual fact his 1977 thesis long remained in manuscript and was not published until over a decade later; Jansson, has in fact, made critical use of it. Compared to him, Rittenberg's canvass is larger for he takes into his beat almost half a century of the Frontier's history, from the very inception of the province (1901) to the transfer of power in 1947. Gupta's great strength lies in his careful use of archival sources available nearer home as well as private papers, periodical literature and newspaper holdings. His focus on the provincial legislature—the work is part of a series on the role of the central and state legislatures in India's freedom movement—makes it inevitable that legislative debates and parliamentary proceedings are heavily drawn upon.

Ian Talbot's slender volume on *Provincial Politics and the Pakistan Movement* (London, 1988) surveys the growth of the Muslim League in the north-western as well as the north-eastern parts of British India in the crucial decade preceding Pakistan's birth. His solitary chapter on 'The

Troublesome Frontier' underscores the point that 'without the Frontier, Pakistan would have led a tenuous existence even without the Kashmir dispute' and that the outcome of the Referendum 'justified the local (Muslim League) leadership's resort to direct action despite the communal disorders it had brought'.

The scope of Ainslie T Embree's (ed.) *Pakistan's Western Borderlands* (New Delhi, 1977) goes far beyond our limited purview both in the area it surveys as also its timescale. The editor's introductory pages (xi-xviii) as well as his more detailed 'Pakistan's Imperial Legacy' (pp. 24-40) are useful in the broader context of viewing post-1947 years: for 'political arrangements for an unadministered frontier, while suited to the limited social aims of the imperial power . . . were dysfunctional for a national state basing its legitimacy on an identity of territorial integrity and nationality'. Rittenberg's piece on 'Continuities on Borderland Politics' (pp. 67-84) draws heavily on his thesis referred to above while Leon B Poullada's 'Pushtunistan: Afghan Domestic Politics and relations with Pakistan' (pp. 126-52) is useful for an understanding of why Muslim League leadership so grossly misunderstood Badshah Khan's advocacy of the Pakhtun cause. Poullada heavily underlines the fact that the Raj 'never succeeded in completely pacifying or winning over the loyalty of the Pushtun tribes' and that British influence in Afghanistan remained largely 'tenuous and perilous'. Again, that while Pakistan felt 'concerned' over the centrifugal tendencies inherent in any full-fledged independence movement among its own Pushtuns, for Afghanistan, Pushtunistan 'is a symbol of a glorious past, a pragmatic formula for the political present and a harbinger of a more powerful future'.

Of peripheral interest is Charles Chenevix Trench's *Viceroy's Agent* (London, 1987). A member of the Political Service, Trench's book is largely concerned with those of his colleagues who served the Raj during the thirty odd years (1919-47) preceding the transfer of power. In a brief reference, he offers a colourful, if not altogether reliable, account of Nehru's October 1946 visit to the Frontier based on the impressions of the Political Agents posted there at the time. His conclusions: Nehru had 'behaved foolishly, sometimes hysterically, but with considerable courage'. At the same time, Nehru's visit 'must have fortified his hatred and distrust' of the Indian Political Service even though a judicial inquiry later 'found no evidence' to support his allegations that the politicals had ' instigated' the demonstrations against him.

D G Tendulkar's impressive biography of Badshah Khan, *Abdul Ghaffar Khan: Faith Is a Battle* (New Delhi, 1967) though not directly relevant to this essay affords a good understanding of the thinking and politics of Khan Abdul Ghaffar Khan and offers an authentic picture of the background against which the transfer of power drama unfolded both in New Delhi as well as the NWFP

In a recent study, M S Korejo, *The Frontier Gandhi: His Place in History* (Karachi, 1994), an incumbent of the Pakistan Foreign Service turned scholar; makes two major points regarding Badshah Khan. One, in that so far as he held Congress responsible for 'throwing him to the wolves' and 'not intimidating' (Korejo's words) Pakistan over the issue of Pathanistan, Badshah Khan lacked 'enough courage to stand up' to Gandhi and Nehru and of 'suppressing his conscience' when he should have been 'outspoken'. And of becoming 'eloquent' when it was too late. Two, that his 'bona fides' were suspect in so far as he did not 'publicly' denounce the secret contacts which Congress had allegedly established with the Afghan government to lend support to the cause of Pakhtunistan. And while these contacts became 'more intimate and sinister', the Khan kept his counsel. Sadly, Korejo's charges are not sustained by his sources of which he has at best, it would appear, made a selective and a little less than honest use.

Another study, Yunas Samad, *A Nation in Turmoil: Nationalism and Ethnicity in Pakistan, 1937-58* (New Delhi, 1995) makes a pointed reference to developments in the NWFP during the years 1945-7. Its third chapter, 'A brief moment of political unity: mass nationalism and communal riots 1945-47', makes for fascinating reading and is especially relevant to all that was happening in and around the Frontier. Its trenchant assessment deserves notice especially in that events outside the province 'polarised' the Sarhad where hitherto communal issues 'had been subordinate' to regional concerns. Again, the Congress fear that India was becoming 'ungovernable' led to its acceptance of the principle of partition which in turn sounded the 'death knell' especially for its supporters in the Frontier province. Left 'rudderless', the Khudai Khidmatgars raised the Pakhtunistan issue as a bargaining chip; none the less, it 'could not prevent' the eclipse of Pathan ethnicity by Muslim nationalism.

Baren Ray's 'Pakhtunistan National Movement and Transfer of Power in India' in Amit Kumar Gupta (ed.) *Myth and Reality* (New Delhi, 1984) underscores the point that US policy towards Pakistan in the post-1947 years represented 'a neocolonialist hold superimposed upon the colonial institutions established by the British' and that responsibility for much of this mischief lay squarely with Olaf Caroe and men of his ilk. The paper draws upon an impressive array of secondary sources to buttress Ray's thesis on the Raj's alleged manoeuvres and machinations preceding independence especially as these related to the Frontier.

Syed Waqar Ali Shah, *The Muslim League in the NWFP* (Karachi, 1992) is the work of a young Pakistani scholar which confines itself to the 'rise' of the Muslim League in the province in the late 1930s. And surveys events leading to the holding of the referendum followed by the installation of Abdul Qaiyum as the 'new Chief Minister' in place of Dr Khan Sahib a bare week after the transfer of power. What holds the author's attention is 'the Frontier Contingent' at the Lahore (1940) session of the Muslim League (Chapter 2), the formation of Sardar Aurangzeb's ministry (1943), Abdul Qaiyum's 'entry' into the Muslim League (1945) and the Quaid's two visits to the Frontier (1936, 1945). The 'Last Phase' (Chapters 4 and 5) is in two parts, concerned largely with events during 1945-6 and 1946-7. Resting broadly on well-known secondary source material, there is nothing very revealing either about the author's new finds or even his conclusions. Reading between the lines one could easily make out how irrelevant the League was in the larger political map of the Frontier until Sardar Aurangzeb's swearing in as head of a ramshackle coalition. And how a largely violent, and unprincipled, campaign of its so-called civil disobedience movement enabled the Muslim League to wrest political initiative, and power, from a popularly elected government in the last few months preceding the birth of Pakistan. In the event, it was now the turn of Dr Khan Sahib, and the Khudai Khidmatgars, to look as helpless spectators whom events passed by. And now reduced to a state of political oblivion, if also irrelevance.

In British India, the *Tribune* (Lahore) occupied an important place in the political, and intellectual, life of the Panjab. As well as the NWFP and Sind. Its pro-nationalist leanings were well-known as also its newsworthiness and relatively high standards of journalism. Its impact on the English-knowing elitist groups—and not them alone—was widely felt. And indeed a subject of comment. It would have been ideal to scan the paper for the entire period covered in this study. Short of it, the span of less than a year from October 1946 for which the Lahore daily has been broadly drawn upon, appeared particularly relevant.

Inasmuch as the Muslim, or more appropriately the Muslim League viewpoint, as reflected in the *Civil & Military Gazette* (Lahore) and the *Dawn* (Delhi) as well as a number of other newspapers is well-orchestrated in the *Jinnah Papers*, the *Tribune* may to an extent help balance the tilt.

Index

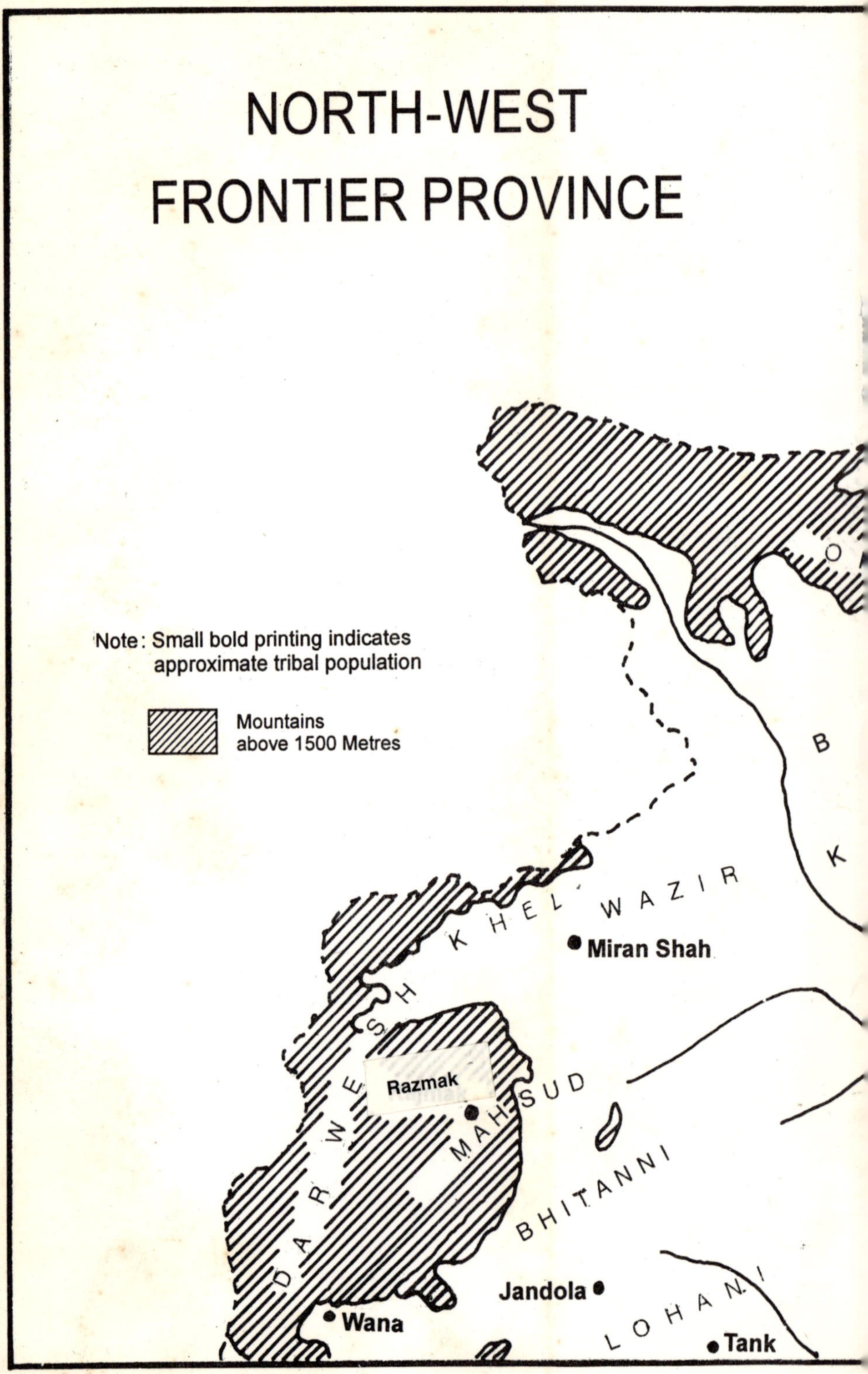
NORTH-WEST
FRONTIER PROVINCE
Note: Small bold printing indicates
approximate tribal population
Mountains
above 1500 Metres
O
B
K
KHEL WAZIR
Miran Shah
DARWESH
Razmak
MAHSUD
BHITANNI
Jandola
LOHANI
Wana
Tank